The Object of the Atlantic

FLASHPOINTS

The FlashPoints series is devoted to books that consider literature beyond strictly national and disciplinary frameworks and that are distinguished both by their historical grounding and by their theoretical and conceptual strength. Our books engage theory without losing touch with history and work historically without falling into uncritical positivism. FlashPoints aims for a broad audience within the humanities and the social sciences concerned with moments of cultural emergence and transformation. In a Benjaminian mode, FlashPoints is interested in how literature contributes to forming new constellations of culture and history and in how such formations function critically and politically in the present. Series titles are available online at http://escholarship.org/uc/flashpoints.

A list of titles in the series begins on p. 273.

The Object of the Atlantic

Concrete Aesthetics in Cuba, Brazil, and Spain, 1868–1968

Rachel Price

NORTHWESTERN UNIVERSITY PRESS | EVANSTON, ILLINOIS

the modern language initiative

THIS BOOK IS MADE POSSIBLE BY A COLLABORATIVE GRANT FROM THE ANDREW W. MELLON FOUNDATION.

Northwestern University Press
www.nupress.northwestern.edu

Digital Printing

Library of Congress Cataloging-in-Publication Data

Price, Rachel, 1975– author.
The object of the Atlantic : concrete aesthetics in Cuba, Brazil, and Spain, 1868–1968 / Rachel Price.
pages cm. — (FlashPoints)
Includes bibliographical references and index.
ISBN 978-0-8101-3013-5 (pbk. : alk. paper)
1. Atlantic Ocean Region—Literatures—21st century. 2. Literature and history—Atlantic Ocean Region. I. Title. II. Series: FlashPoints (Evanston, Ill.)
PN849.A85P75 2014
809.89163—dc23

2014004907

Contents

Illustrations

Acknowledgments

The research and writing of this book took place over several years and in multiple contexts. I wish to thank especially Ranjana Khanna, Alberto Moreiras, Sibylle Fischer, Fredric Jameson, Michael Hardt, and Matt Cohen. Indispensable debates took place at Duke University with too many friends and colleagues to name, but I wish to thank particularly Beatriz Balanta, Nico Baumbach, Brian Carr, Amy Carroll, Marta Hernández, Jorge Marturano, Jennifer Rhee, and Shilyh Warren.

In Brazil, I benefited from research at the Casa das Rosas Espaço Haroldo de Campos de Poesia e Literatura and from discussions with Helba Carvalho, Augusto de Campos, Neide Dias de Sá, Wlademir Dias-Pino, Jorge Luiz, Marcos Siscar, and Luciana and Glaucia Villas-Bôas; I especially thank Fabio Durão for many collaborations over the years. In Cuba, thanks to the staff of the Biblioteca Nacional José Martí, the Archivo Nacional de Cuba, and to Ana María Andreu, Arturo Arango, Kevin Beovides, Víctor Fowler, Eneida Marín, Eduardo Marín, Urbano Martínez Carmenate, and Lizabel Mónica Villares.

Paul Firbas, Daniela Flesler, Gabriela Polit-Dueñas, and Katie Vernon all made helpful suggestions while I was at Stonybrook University, as did Susan Martin-Márquez, who kindly read and commented upon a chapter. I am grateful to a Mellon Postdoctoral Fellowship that enabled a stimulating year of exchanges at the Cogut Humanities Center and the Hispanic Studies Department of Brown University. In Providence

I was happy to rekindle a friendship and intellectual exchange with Jacques Khalip, a great sounding board from a neighboring field. I particularly thank Adrián López-Denis, to whom I am indebted for pushing me to think more critically and for sharing his vast knowledge of Cuban history and culture.

At Princeton University I have had the good fortune to work in an extremely supportive environment. Thanks to Silvana Bishop, Karen González, Beth Heisler, and Nikki Woolard for their administrative support, and to my colleagues in the Department of Spanish and Portuguese Languages and Cultures, particularly those who read or discussed portions of the manuscript: Bruno Carvalho, Rubén Gallo, Javier Guerrero, Germán Labrador, and especially Pedro Meira and Gabriela Nouzeilles for extensive and important last-minute comments. A special debt is owed to Arcadio Díaz-Quiñones for his generous reading. I would also like to thank undergraduate and graduate students, some now colleagues, who have helped me think through some of these ideas: Sergio Delgado, Duanel Díaz, Ashley Evelyn, and Nathaniel Wolfson. I have also benefited from a research group on empires sponsored by the Princeton Institute for International and Regional Studies (PIIRS). Thanks to the members of this group, especially Jeremy Adelman, for his interest in the questions behind this book and for his shrewd comments. I learned from exchanges formal and informal with colleagues outside of my department, including Eduardo Cadava, Susana Draper, Rachel Galvin, Matheus Gato de Jesús, Sarah Porciau, Sonya Posmentier, Irene Small (who was very helpful during final revisions), and Alexandra Vazquez. My thanks go as well to Fernando Acosta for his gifted work as a librarian for Latin American and Iberian studies. Several trips to archives were generously supported by Princeton's University Committee on Humanities and Social Science and its Program in Latin American Studies, whose staff, including Rosalia Rivera and Jillian Halbe, I much appreciate.

Many friends and colleagues from beyond these institutions have also been helpful: James Brittingham, Odette Casamayor, Lisa Cerami, Michelle Chase, Sarah Doty, Joshua Dubler, Kenneth Goldsmith, Shambhavi Kaul, Jacqueline Loss, Dylon Robbins, Sam Steinberg, and Anya Zilberstein. My research was helped by the holdings at the New York Public Library and by assistance from Lauren Ziarko, archivist at Manhattanville College Archives. I am grateful to Cathleen Skeen for her editorial help and to Michelle Clayton, who went far beyond the call of duty to improve the book's ideas and language with her dedicated and inspired editing. Thanks also to the anonymous readers' helpful suggestions.

Finally, I wish to thank my family members for their support and for their contributions to this and other projects. I like to think that these contributions began with a grandmother I never met: Dorothy Lee (née Demetracopolou) grew up in Constantinople in the final decades of the Ottoman Empire; one legacy of empires is multilingual environments that, in her case, may have inspired her studies in linguistic anthropology. While researching Brazilian concrete poetry's engagement with cybernetics, I was surprised to find my grandmother listed as a guest at the seminal Macy Conferences where cybernetics was first developed; I later learned that she published alongside Marshall McLuhan and others of the Toronto School of Communications. Thanks to Sabra Lee, to Hermelinda Zegarra, to Michael, Seth, and Lucero Price, to Bettina Funcke, and to Lou Funcke Price, for reminding me of childhood's sensuous world of subjects and objects.

I wish to acknowledge permission to reprint material that previously appeared elsewhere. A rather different version of Chapter 5 was published as "The Spirit of Martí in the Land of Coaybay" in *Hispanic Review* 77, no. 2 (Spring 2009): 245–66, and a small portion of Chapter 6 was published as "Object, Non-object, Trans-object, Relational Object: From Concrete Poetry to *A Nova Objetividade*" in *Revista de Letras da UNESP* 47, no. 1 (2007).

The Object of the Atlantic

Introduction

In the early 1890s the Cuban poet, journalist, and revolutionary José Martí was living and writing in exile in New York City. When he wasn't lecturing on Cuban independence, documenting immigrant life, or appraising the city from the heights of an elevated train, Martí wrote hundreds of columns for Latin American and U.S. newspapers from his office near Wall Street. It was there, too, that he composed some of the most innovative poetry of his day. His prose and poetry addressed these various facets of his life: political organizing, late nineteenth-century New York City, and the technological and financial changes that facilitated speculation on commodities at the nearby stock exchange. In one notebook from around this time he scribbled "Todo el arte de escribir es concretar" [All the art of writing is making concrete].[1] With this statement, Martí hints at what ties together much of his writing—his notes, his chronicles, his poems—and hazards a new poetics.

We catch a glimpse of what this new poetics might look like in his outline for a "book of landscape poetry," which seems to propose not nature but New York's Fulton Market as its urban setting:

> Un libro de poesía de paisaje: El libro del Trabajo.—Fulton.—Mañanita de Otoño—Látigo—Carnes—Gente Apresurada—Atmósfera—Abren las tiendas sus bocas avarientas y al pasajero ansioso sus maravillas tientan. (*Obras completas* 22:313)

> [A book of landscape poetry: The Book of Work.—Fulton.—Autumn Morning—Whip—Meats—Harried People—Atmosphere—The stores open their greedy mouths and their marvels tempt the anxious passerby.]

In this sketch of the market, what leaps out as "concrete" is both the scene captured and the means by which Martí rendered it. The notes' language reduces the buzzing sensations of the harried morning to discrete, crystallized items. The wares are also concrete, thingly: meats and marvels peek out from the voracious mouths of stores, seducing the passerby. The arrangement of Martí's writing concretizes this reality on the page, too. The chain of things set apart by dashes constitutes the very "atmosphere" of the market that it sets out to record, visually reproducing the mix of people, meats, and products laid cheek by jowl. Of course, these are notes, which partially accounts for their concise, skeletal form. But in Martí's published chronicles, poems, and speeches, a similar approach emerges. This concrete poetics responds to a particular moment of geopolitical change: one in which a concentration of capital moved from Europe to a rapidly industrializing United States and one in which debates about sovereignty addressed economic as well as territorial spheres.

This geopolitical frame at first might not seem apparent: the scene evokes a lyrical, Baudelairean snapshot of an urban market on a crisp autumn morning. But the greedy shops point to other concerns that would drive Martí to found the Cuban Revolutionary Party in 1892. Products are central to Martí's writing in these years, and not only to his poetry. He writes tracts against the Spanish empire that critique its limits on Cuban trade. Products are also at the heart of his articles about a rising United States, which, he predicts in 1889, will shore itself up economically by unleashing upon Latin America and the Caribbean a flood of useless, excess goods. Martí's poetics of the concrete thus responds to a moment in which Spain's territorial empire foundered before growing U.S. economic influence in the region. In representations of this shift, products were emblematic.

Seventy years later, in São Paulo, Brazil, a group of poets published a manifesto for a new poetry titled the "pilot-plan for concrete poetry" (1958), modeled on architect Lúcio Costa's "Pilot Plan for Brasília," the new capital. "The concrete poem," Augusto de Campos, Haroldo de Campos, and Décio Pignatari famously declare in the pilot-plan, "is an object in and for itself, not an interpreter of exterior objects and/

or sensations more or less subjective" [*é um objeto em e por si mesmo, não um intérprete de objetos exteriores e/ou sensações mais ou menos subjetivas*].[2] "Concrete poetry" of the 1950s, then, proposes a poem as an object: something material, visual or sonic, tangible and architectural. By heralding a poem that is a nonmimetic, nonexpressive object, the group iterates the historical avant-garde's desire to create, not imitate, updated in an optimistic era of postwar development in Brazil.

Two years prior, one of the authors of the pilot-plan, Haroldo de Campos, had published a poem entitled "no â mago do ô mega" [in the m arrow of o mega] (1956) that similarly advances poetic thingliness in both its form and theme (See Figure 1.) Lines from the visual poem read "a coisa / da coisa / da coisa" [the thing of the thing of the thing], suggesting the promise, deferred satisfaction, and sheer repetition of industrial commodities. What is striking, however, is that the poem focuses on the essence within the letter "O," or the sign o (zero): in other words, it centers around a void, conceptually and visually. The poem's emphasis on nothingness, on that "ex nihilo" that enables creation, confirms what an easily overlooked phrase in the pilot-plan would announce: concrete poetry was also interested in an "OBJETO virtual," an object influenced by cybernetics and information theory.[3] Midcentury Brazilian concrete poetry, then, featured poems as objects, poems about products, and poems concerned with the increasingly virtual nature of communication.

Separated by seven decades and a continent, Martí and de Campos both, in the course of extensive poetic and critical oeuvres, propose "concrete" poetics that bring together writing technologies, philosophical meditations, consumption, and historicity. Although their contexts are radically different, I see these two poets as marking the outer boundaries of a century-long arc, beginning in 1868 and ending in 1968, comprehending a thing-oriented aesthetics in the Iberian Atlantic. *The Object of the Atlantic* analyzes examples from this body of literature, art, and philosophy, which is attentive to objects and things, and which often is interested in using language's own materiality (typography, diacritics, sound, taste) to comment on much broader shifts in thinking about time and subjectivity. Language becomes thing-like in a period during which vast shifts in sovereignty and capitalism were frequently *emblematized* in things and commodities.

In chapters dedicated to Martí, to Brazilian literature from the 1870s to the 1880s, to the post-1898 writing of Spanish author Ramiro de Maeztu, to Cuban literature from the first republican

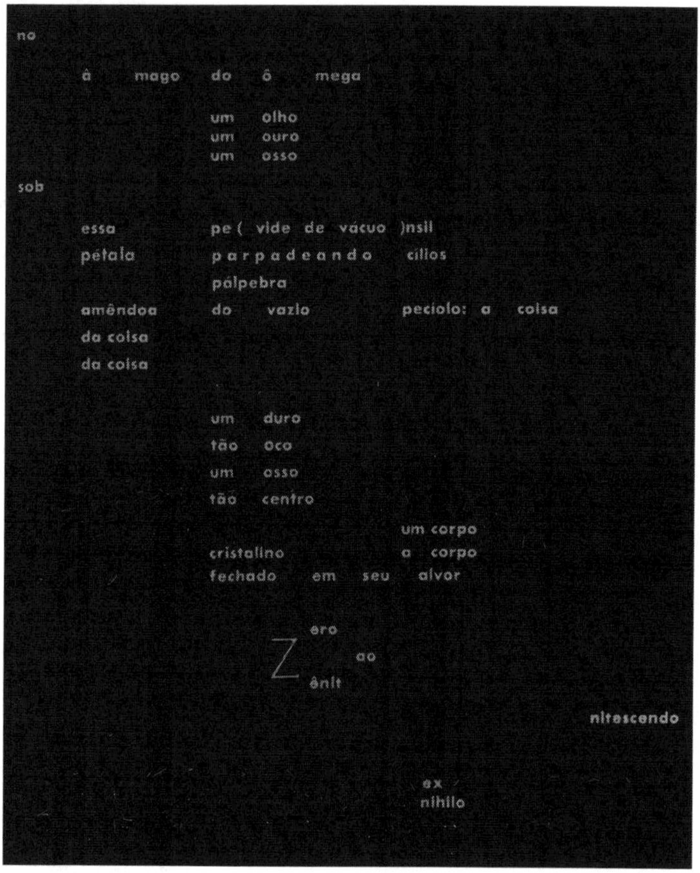

Figure 1. Haroldo de Campos, "no â mago do ô mega" (1956). Courtesy of Ivan Persio de Arruda Campos.

period (1902–33), to Brazilian concrete and neoconcrete poetry and art from the 1960s, and to theories of the concrete more broadly, I trace how this aesthetic emerged, evolved, and dissolved into a post-concrete era. The century bounded by Martí and de Campos could also be understood as one in which struggles over states' sovereignty ceded to a dawning rule of the market. By highlighting how the mid-twentieth-century works discussed in the second half of the book draw on themes, writers, and thinkers from the late nineteenth century, *The Object of the Atlantic* also proposes that the earlier period remains a charged repository of ideas for futures alternative to those that came to pass in the twentieth century.

OBJECTS IN THE ATLANTIC

Objects and material culture are today of renewed interest across a number of fields. Scholars of literature and art history have explored, for example, things and property in Victorian England; "a sense of things" in U.S. modernism; the "socialist objects" of Russian Constructivism; the legacy of surrealist objects in Latin American literature; and "thing theory" in general. Scholars in the fields of philosophy and the history of science have reconsidered objectivity and have rejected the integrity of either objects or subjects; indeed the binary itself. The recent philosophical movement of speculative realism, also known as "object-oriented ontology," claims to be interested in the ontology of objects themselves, beyond human agency. Recent ecocriticism, on the other hand, insists on the incoherence of either subjects or objects, given the teeming, messy porousness of both "humans" (seen now not as singular entities but as massive containers of microbes and other beings) and "things"—in Jane Bennett's coinage, "vibrant matter."[4]

As these examples of "object-oriented" scholarship suggest, reading material culture can have multiple and widely varying ends. It may trace the circulation of commodities, question the categories of subject and object, understand how objects "mean" through local anthropologies, or speculate on the ecological future of the planet. Objects clearly take on different meanings in different contexts. What, then, were the specific pressures that shaped a turn to objects in the Iberian Atlantic? And what connects an interest in material culture with an *aesthetics* of objects and objectivity?

The Object of the Atlantic examines the emergence of a specific body of concrete aesthetics in the late nineteenth century and its dissolution a century later. I begin in the 1860s, when antislavery mobilizations were common to Brazil, Cuba, Spain, and the United States. These political movements motivated by what Fred Moten calls "the resistance of the object," an object that speaks—a subject—accompanied the last decades of formal empire in the Americas in Cuba, Spain, and Brazil.[5] Then, in the 1890s, the Atlantic world witnessed a transition from older, territorial empire to less territorial forms of economic hegemony and a more fully global capitalism. Such a transition, I claim, is the background for a concrete poetics, as we glimpsed earlier in Martí. As mass production and markets become increasingly important in the early twentieth century, literature thematizes things. By the late 1960s, however, the global economic context changes again.

Production, labor, and finance grow more virtual. Concrete aesthetics turns toward process and immateriality.

This broad periodization deserves a bit more detail. In the final decades of the nineteenth century, new technologies multiplied global connections and pulled far-flung economies into an increasingly global market. A boom in Latin American exports for industrializing North Atlantic markets followed, as old staples such as sugar and coffee fetched new manufactured commodities.[6] While most Latin American economies were led by exports of commodities (sugar, coffee, minerals), incipient industrialization also began in the region.[7]

As markets became more global, some longstanding empires dissolved and ceded to new states. In these decades Cuba repeatedly fought for and eventually gained independence from the Spanish empire. Spain, in turn, lost Cuba, Puerto Rico, and the Philippines, lamenting its postimperial diminishment (it retained African possessions). In these years, too, the Brazilian Empire (1822–89) became a republic. These changes in sovereignty, furthermore, took place as the United States emerged as a new hegemonic actor in the Atlantic.

But pressures from a new economic power were not the only obstacles facing the new republics. Abolition had come late to Cuba (1886) and Brazil (1888), and racialized slavery's prolongation had fostered correspondingly radical and abiding desires for what a postimperial future might look like. A war for abolition and national independence that dragged on in Cuba between 1868 and 1878, for instance, helped forge the conviction among Cubans of many classes and colors, fighting alongside one another, that independence ought to mean more than nominal sovereignty: it should ring in a truly egalitarian society. The following 1895 Cuban revolution was led by a majority nonwhite army.

In Bahia, Brazil, a poor, religious community of many thousands grew up around a millenarian leader between 1893 and 1897. Canudos, as the community came to be known, in many ways provided for groups of people for whom the state did not. Far from hailing the new republic, the people of Canudos, which included recently emancipated persons, were wary of what the new republic might enact, including a return to slavery. Indeed, African-descended people throughout Brazil feared the oligarchic republic for the same reasons. Canudos was right to be suspicious: it was annihilated by the national army in 1897 after a series of increasingly desperate sieges.

In both Cuba and Brazil, in others words, the late nineteenth century saw radical hopes for sovereignty and liberation cede to hierarchical, discriminatory republics. As these republics began to enjoy economic growth in the early twentieth century, an emergent consumer culture of new objects was simultaneously celebrated and at the same time came to seem a poor substitute for the states' failure to provide equally for citizens. The late nineteenth-century transition from messianic and emancipatory struggles in the Iberian Atlantic to republics of consumption foreshadowed the extent to which the market would become transcendental in the late twentieth and early twenty-first centuries. But the alternative futures and temporalities of the interregnum between empire and nation in the late nineteenth-century Iberian Atlantic, which were recuperated by writers and artists in the mid-twentieth century, also remain sites today for thinking about politics in a more postnational moment.

Cuba's and Brazil's prolonged histories of slavery and empire shaped not only their subsequent republics but Spain as well, where, in an immediately postcolonial, postslavery moment, a language of things was advanced to contrast with a now ridiculed language of sovereignty. For instance, the Spanish journalist Ramiro de Maeztu, son of a Cuban-born sugar mill owner, moved from Spain to Havana in 1891 in an unsuccessful attempt to rescue his family's failing mill. His three years working in Havana informed a subsequent series of essays that anchor a lofty rejection of aesthetic and philosophical romanticism in the more particular repudiation of Cuban, Puerto Rican, North African, and Philippine anticolonial struggles. Maeztu's position was summed up in his 1915–16 series of articles titled "On the Primacy of Things," published alongside T. E. Hulme and Ezra Pound in the London-based journal *The New Age*. Maeztu's positions were typical of his formerly Fabianist, conservative Anglophone peers. But in a quibble with Bertrand Russell over liberalism, Maeztu's antiromantic critiques of sovereignty, subjectivity, and personality turned not on a generic Hegelian bondsman but on a "black, Cuban slave" from the Maeztu family's former sugar mill. His thing-based philosophy must be read within the context of this Atlantic history of empire and slavery, and in light of the fact that the ex-colony Cuba prospered at the dawn of the twentieth century while Spain struggled.

Cuba's—and Brazil's—early twentieth-century prosperity owed in large part to expanding markets for commodities in the industrializing North Atlantic. When this moment of expansion crashed, they, like other Latin American nations, turned away from importing industrial products from abroad to strengthen internal markets. Between

1930 and 1970, Latin American nations moved away from export-led economies and began import-substitution industrialization programs, replacing imports with national products and seeking to build national markets. While the provenance of the new consumer products changed, their importance did not—far from it. With what desires and occult philosophies were these new things invested? In what ways were the debates over sovereignty in the late nineteenth century packaged in the new commodities?

Maeztu's screed against sovereignty and subjectivity indicates one afterlife of nineteenth-century struggles in a twentieth-century discourse of objects. Cuba's postindependence literature offers another. Between 1902 and 1958, many authors alternately celebrated and lamented a tide of new products that came to represent both modernization and economic dependency, a kind of blood money for the sidelined dreams of a more equitable society. Following the 1959 revolution, as consumption was nationalized, the libidinal (and political) charge of products was amplified in the very efforts to move beyond dependence.

In Brazil, steady economic growth from the 1930s through the 1960s underwrote an expanding industrial society and, with it, new artistic and poetic movements informed by the constructivism of the postwar culture. In these years, the messianism of the late nineteenth century, epitomized in multiple religiously inflected movements in Brazil, emptied into things. Werner Hamacher has called this funneling of messianic conceptions of history into things the "messianism of commodity language": language in which religious promises of redemption are lodged in commodities that then carry a "general . . . transhistorical value."[8] The corpus of concrete writing I examine in *The Object of the Atlantic* frequently lodges in commodities and in everyday objects the transhistorical values that in the late nineteenth century had been invested in theological—literally messianic—movements or in political projects of emancipation. Thus while the following chapters focus on literature's engagement with objects and "objective" writing, they also underscore how this engagement is often ultimately about time and historicity, about the different futures imagined either in concert with or against, variously, dependent, monocultural economies; financial speculation; developmentalism; and an incipient networked globalization.

By the late 1960s the messianic historicity of things was exhausted, at least in the view of cultural producers. The promises of consumer culture, which had done little to paper over the disappointments of the early twentieth-century republics, rang increasingly hollow even as the global market began its unprecedented expansion, to be redoubled after 1989. Art began to embrace processes, rejecting objects as mere commodities in a global art market. Cybernetics, the study of self-organizing systems that deeply interested Brazilian concrete poets in the 1950s, led to the first massive computer networks; in Chile, Salvador Allende's government even created a cybernetic economic system (Cybersyn/Proyecto Synco) between 1971 and 1973. Art and literature were transformed by mass media. Language's materiality now increasingly meant electric images, algorithmic results, vibrations.

A general arc from materiality to dematerialization, then, transpires in the century covered here. And yet, I argue, a subtler tension between the material and the immaterial, between commodities and speculation, and between objects and their networks was part of concrete writing all along. In fact, such a tension between thingliness and virtuality was noted in the late 1970s by the Cuban author and critic Severo Sarduy in a series of seminal but rather cryptic essays.

MAPPING CONCRETUDE

In "Hacia la concretud" (1979) Sarduy coined the word "concretude," or "concreteness," to describe the style of select Cuban and Brazilian authors and to indicate a more broadly applicable concept.[9] Sarduy described "concretude" as an aesthetics that, like earlier baroque poetics, yoked opposing tendencies: word-images that could be frozen things but that were also a flux of letters transmogrifying into one another like words morphing on an electronic billboard in an airport.[10] Concretude, Sarduy wrote, is "a thing like a drawing, a diagram, a figure that expresses quickly and well not only the objects, but also their relationships, the invisible structures that link them" (*Antología*, 240). In other words, concretude is a visual literature that describes both objects and the networks into which they are inserted. Sarduy's aesthetic concretude here recalls a Marxian notion of the concrete as an understanding of totality "as universal interrelationship," now rendered visible—a drawing or diagram of things and their relations.[11]

The Object of the Atlantic takes up Sarduy's broad notion of concretude as literature (and art) interested in objects and the networks in which they circulate, the totality in which subjects and objects exist. But it extends its scope beyond midcentury Brazilian poetry and beyond Sarduy's thought. Indeed, the book began not as an exploration of Sarduy's theories but as an attempt to better understand Martí's poetics, which, as the notes on Fulton Market suggest, engage with a moment of intense change in sovereignty and capitalism. As I mulled over the striking similarities between Martí's poetics and the later, Brazilian poetics, the question remained: did anything link 1890s Cuba (and New York) and 1960s Brazil? Why was "the concrete" a compelling goal for writers and artists in both moments? And what might these connections tell us about the literature written between these two moments, the same period to which the historian Emily Rosenberg ascribes "political modernity," when many nation-states emerged from empires and embarked on developmentalist modernization, a modernization that reached its grotesque extreme in state repressions around 1968?

As I pursued this question, I perceived additional connections between Martí and later concretisms. While Martí labored away in his Front Street office in lower Manhattan, just blocks from Wall Street, the Brazilian poet and journalist Joaquim de Sousândrade, an ardent republican in the last years of the Brazilian Empire, was uptown drafting what today is his best-known canto, "Wall Street Inferno," detailing the same geopolitical and economic changes of concern to Martí. Sousândrade culled lines for his canto from scores of newspapers. He thus highlighted poetry's engagement with journalism's circulation of information, as well as with typesetting. Both of these Latin American poets would be rediscovered in twentieth-century moments in which their writing on speculative capital and industrialization, new media technologies, and Atlantic political imaginaries again seemed urgent: Martí by authors from the Cuban republic (Martí's collected writings were published progressively from 1900 through the 1940s), Sousândrade by the Brazilian concrete poets, who republished selections of his poetry in 1964, the year of a right-wing authoritarian coup.

Of course, an interest in writing's materiality was not unique to Martí or Sousândrade but was common in the first decades of the twentieth century. The media critic Friedrich Kittler has identified 1900 as the inaugural date for a kind of European literature that no longer sought to express romantic interiority but instead imagined itself as a record of the objective data of the external world, a form of recording like the era's new media technologies such as typewriters, films, and gramophones.[12] Similarly, a turn to the thingliness of everyday experience replaced expressionist art in the 1920s German movement of "new objectivity" [*Neue Sachlichkeit*], which rediscovered "the charm of the object."[13] And in 1930 the Dutch artist Theo van Doesburg penned a "Manifesto of Concrete Art."

Closer to home, Latin American *modernismo*—which Martí is credited with inaugurating, even as he is often excepted from its frequent charges of escapism—also has been read as a "cult of the object."[14] Yet *modernismo* was object-oriented typically in its interest in precious luxury items or through its attempt to approximate advertising's *strategies*, while disavowing everyday material culture through flights to a world of princesses and swans. In Noé Jitrik's reading, for instance, *modernismo* assumed the *logic* of products and machines but did so by avoiding either their form or content. It was *like* the mass-produced objects it otherwise excluded from its pages: clichéd, serial (in its rhymes), accumulative (in its examples of erudition), interested in value (of adjectives), aping industrial production but not engaging with its things.[15]

Even studies that focus more specifically on the links between objects named in modernist literature and their larger historical context have often insisted on an ultimate divorce between the two. Roberto González Echevarría, for instance, explicitly situated *modernismo* within a context of imported products but saw poets' relationship to things as one of disavowal rather than mimesis—or, as he put it, a "critical disconnection" with the world of things. For González Echevarría, *modernista* literature is "product, not process," unlike the literature of objects that I read, which tends to highlight *both* their discrete objecthood *and* the networks—whether commodity chains or communications technology, imperial networks or intersubjective exchanges—into which they are inserted.[16]

Ericka Beckman's recent analysis of what she coins a "modernist import catalogue," by contrast, takes up *modernista* texts' engagement with historical commodities. She elucidates the connections between, for instance, the poetics of the Colombian *modernista* José Asunción Silva and his day job writing ad copy for his family department store. Beckman echoes González Echevarría, however—from a decidedly more Marxist position, to be sure—in seeing *modernista* luxury objects, whose "phantasmagoric" nature owes to the "suppression of their origins in a social process," as separated from their context (they are, in short, commodity fetishes) and therefore available for resignification by poets.[17] Writing about modernism in a more global context, Nicholas Brown has likewise claimed that attention to "the thing" is an index of "the impossibility of representing the field of productive forces from within the field of commodities."[18] For all these readings, modernist or *modernista* objects betray an absent totality paradoxically through their resolutely miniature things.

This study zooms out from the fetishes of *modernismo* to register a much broader interest in objects and in postromantic writing that both precedes and follows the movement. In contrast to the ways that some critics have read objects in *modernismo*, I find objects' links to larger forces not disavowed but placed front and center, where they serve as vehicles for registering historicity. In the 1890s Martí, for instance, claimed that "la cosa más pequeña, insignificante en sí, adquiere valor sumo, como símbolo del tiempo" [the smallest thing, insignificant in itself, acquires the utmost value as a symbol of the times] (*Obras completas* 19:297). Things are symbols of the times. And the relations between things and humans indicate larger geopolitical forces.

For instance, in a poem (1914) and a short story (1931) both titled "Los muebles" [The furniture] by Cuban authors Bonifacio Byrne and Alfonso Hernández Catá, respectively, furniture becomes uncanny and murderous: in a postindependence Cuba repeatedly described by period authors as "dematerialized" by foreign capital, political and economic control is virtual and works its way into intimate spaces, turning the most familiar, stolid things uncanny. In Maeztu's proto-fascist writings from the 1910s and 1920s, goods are equated with the "good" that the former Spanish empire wrought as a global, Catholic, transcendental institution. In late 1950s Brazil, by contrast, concrete poetry instantiates the radically immanent against the expansively expressive and shrinks history and time itself into blocks of synchronic language as if to suggest that developmentalism's infinite teleology were simultaneously a kind of end of history. A visual poem by Augusto de Campos, for instance, anagramizes the word "terremoto" [earthquake], revealing the word's partial contents (e.g., "temor," "morte"; fear, death) to suggest that all the future fallouts from the tremor were already present in its very roots. Historicity and unfolding in time and space are shrunk, halted in the synchronic flash of a single word.

In these examples we see how concretude is used to discuss and render large questions of history, economics, and dreams about the future. Again, the messianic discourse associated with nineteenth-century emancipatory movements is diverted in the twentieth century into mundane objects and commodity language: Cuban campaigns for abolition and national liberation haunt the new furniture that dresses a disappointing postindependence, postoccupation world; Catholic global empire—celebrated by the Spanish right in the face of colonial losses—returns in a notion of money as religiously inflected; Brazilian messianic futures inhere in closed forms. In multiple examples of "concrete" writing, what is at stake is not only a use of material culture to think historicity but attempts to register both existing and alternative temporalities on the page.

1898: THE CONTROL REVOLUTION

A 1926 Cuban novel by José Antonio Ramos thematizes the transition from a world defined by struggles over sovereignty to a globalized world of things and media. "Wake up, *mon vieux*," a son implores his father in the fictitious Latin American nation of Coaybay:

> que el mundo se transforma a nuestros ojos. Ya no es posible aquella exaltada independencia de nuestras patrias delirantes . . . El ferrocarril, el telégrafo, el cable submarino, el gran trasatlántico . . . el linotipo, la telegrafía y la telefonía sin hilos, quién sabe si la aviación, al fin, antes de pocos años, tienen que admitirse también como elementos históricos de incontrastable valor espiritual. ¿Qué importa que estemos perdiendo día a día un poco de los viejos valores: aquella absoluta e invulnerable independencia, por ejemplo?[19]
>
> [for the world is transforming before our eyes. That exalted independence of our delirious patrias . . . is no longer possible. The railroad, the telegraph, the underwater cable, the great transatlantic . . . the linotype, wireless telegraphy and telephony, perhaps even aviation, before too long, will also be seen as historic elements of incomparable spiritual value. What does it matter that we are losing day by day a little of the old values: that absolute and invulnerable independence, for example?]

The older generation addressed here—*mon vieux*—traded in a romantic rhetoric of independence. But for a younger generation in the 1920s such language does not describe the new historical moment. Now media are the carriers of historical, even "spiritual" values. Networks effectively *dissolve* states' independence from one another, as all are inserted into a global capitalist market—a transition often dated to the 1970s or 1980s but visible here as defining the late nineteenth and early twentieth centuries as well.

What had happened between these two generations? Precipitating the transition from "delirious patrias" to an investment in objects and media in Ramos's novel *Coaybay* was the portentous moment termed "1898," named after the year in which the United States entered Cuba's 1895 war with Spain.[20] In fact, however, the 1890s saw not just one war but a string of conflicts in which empires were challenged throughout Asia, Latin America, and Africa. At the same time, global capital was increasingly concentrated in the United States.[21]

The moment was repeatedly described as a global *translatio imperii*, or transfer of empire, in which the United States was seen as an economic power overtaking older territorial empires. The dawning century may have been new, but the discourse of *translatio imperii* was not: it had defined the Atlantic even before the first Europeans crossed the ocean. Europe had long construed the Americas as the end time and place of history, the final destination in empire's movement. The old theological discourse was preserved in new analyses of the emergent century.

The political theorist Carl Schmitt argued that 1898 marked the arrival of "modern" forms of control that eschewed territorial annexation in favor of military and economic pressure.[22] Schmitt claimed that this putative change from formal territorial rule to more military and economic control was both facilitated and accompanied by a sea change in how information shaped industries. The historian of science James Beniger identifies a different but related "control revolution" in his book, which chronicles the rise of information industries from the nineteenth century through the 1980s. Beniger argues that in the twentieth century information came to surpass all other commodities, taking the place of industry "as the sector best reflecting the extent of a nation's development."[23] In other words, information became the commodity most indicative of a nation's "development." The 1890s Atlantic, then, was seen as witnessing a "control revolution" both in Schmitt's sense and in Beniger's: with the decline of Iberian imperial power and the rise of U.S. hegemony in the region, sovereignty came increasingly to be understood not in territorial but in economic terms, and new media technologies, among all products, were seen to index the "futurity" of nations. Subsequent decades saw in Latin America what John Kraniauskas has called the "total apparatus of development conceived as the imperial time of capital."[24]

Economic, political, and technological changes of this scale can be difficult to grasp. Literature, with its richness of detail and speculative reach, often perceives and registers such change more readily—sometimes even before it takes place. Spanish author Nilo Fabra's uncannily clairvoyant short story from 1897, for instance, titled "La Guerra de España con los Estados Unidos: Páginas de la historia de lo por venir" [The war of Spain and the United States: Pages from a history of the future], imagines an imminent war between Spain, Cuba, and the United States—one year before the United States actually entered the Spanish-Cuban conflict.[25] "La Guerra" opens in 1890s Wall Street, "secret government [*gobierno oculto*] of the great Republic" (13). Rumblings about a plan to establish colonies of African Americans in the Antilles have led to an outright war, spurred by a Spanish attack on a purportedly U.S.-owned "pirate" ship *The Lone Star*, which prompts the United States—"with obvious bad faith and shameless cynicism"—to call for restitution (46, 79, 38). (One year later the USS *Maine* would be sunk under mysterious conditions in the port of Havana, prompting—or permitting—U.S. entry into the ongoing war between Cuba and Spain.)

In Fabra's tale, Cuba's Captain General retaliates by severing the circum-Atlantic network of communication technologies that is mapped onto old slave routes:

> [D]e orden del Capitán General de Cuba se cortaban las comunicaciones telegráficas directas de la isla con el país enemigo, que existían por medio de tres cables submarinos paralelos entre la Habana, Cayo Hueso y Cabo Romano. Quedaba, sin embargo, una comunicación segura entre España y la grande Antilla, pasando por territorios neutrales, como era la vía Batabanó, Santiago de Cuba, Jamaica, Puerto Rico, Cayena (prescindiendo de otras estaciones intermedias), Pernambuco, el Senegal, Canarias y Cádiz. (46)
>
> [On order from the Captain General of Cuba, the island's direct telegraph communication with the enemy country was cut off, which existed via three parallel submarine cables between Havana, Key West, and Cayo Romano. A

> secure communication remained, however, between Spain and Cuba, passing through neutral territories, such as the path between Batabanó, Santiago de Cuba, Jamaica, Puerto Rico, Cayenne (lacking other intermediary stations), Pernambuco, Senegal, Canary Islands, and Cádiz.]

It is significant that in this speculative fable a struggle for Atlantic hegemony involves the cutting of telegraph lines that overlie early modern Atlantic trade routes. (After the explosion of the USS *Maine* in 1898, the United States cut Cuba's coastal cables.)[26] For the story's palimpsestic networks highlight the transition, however incipient, from the region's reliance on the older sugar and slave industries (indicated by the names of infamous slave ports such Havana, Cádiz, Pernambuco, the ports of Senegal) to the increasing influence of finance capital, undergirding and undergirded by a future information society. In many ways the two phases—the first dependent on transatlantic commodities trade, the second on transatlantic telecommunications—represent not so much radically different economic phases as a continuum. They do, however, resonate with Beniger's idea that information replaced merchant goods and territory as a privileged commodity in the twentieth century.

DEMATERIALIZATION

The splitting of products and economies into both physical and speculative sides—a consistent dualism, on a more aesthetic plane, in the examples of "concrete" writing explored in this study—began to haunt analyses of capitalism at the beginning of the twentieth century. Vladimir Lenin's pamphlet about the post-1898 world, *Imperialism, the Highest Stage of Capitalism* (1916), commented on the split between the all-but-invisible role of speculative capital and its material manifestations. Capitalism, Lenin wrote, had "arrived at a stage when, although commodity production still 'reigns' and continues to be regarded as the basis of economic life, it has in reality been undermined and the big profits go to the 'geniuses' of financial manipulation," enabled by new technologies.[27] Similar positions were taken later by thinkers such as Ernest Mandel, for whom "late capitalism" is characterized by *both* finance capital and industrialization, or Gilles Deleuze, who perceived in the post-1945 period centuries of societies structured by sovereignty transitioning to societies of control again thanks to media, especially computers.[28] Deleuze wrote that nineteenth-century capitalism "of concentration, for production and for property," contrasted with a twentieth-century capitalism "no longer . . . for production but for the product, which is to say, for being sold or marketed" ("Postscript" 5). Thus Deleuze sees a transition to a capitalism at once more virtual—"in societies of control . . . what is important is a code"—and more intensively about things (5).

In this regard, the 1890s anticipate forms of globalization often associated with the more recent past, since by the late nineteenth century transnational commodity chains were already fully global, enabled by credit and finance.[29] Manuel Moreno Fraginals, for example, describes the late nineteenth-century sugar industry in Cuba as at the forefront of a change from a world of "commercial, physical, tangible" elements to a world that has been "dislocado" [dislocated] toward more virtual realms, once the laying of a submarine cable in 1867 permitted electronic trading.[30] The economic historian of tables and figures then unexpectedly likens this shift to a coeval aesthetic transformation: "Sugar too had undergone the transition from the realism of Courbet to the fantastic world of Cezanne, revealing a new dimension of things" (*El ingenio* 14–15).

Moreno Fraginals's description of concrete goods (sacks of sugar) being "dislocated" by virtual encryptions of information about the goods—trading in futures, or what the sugar will fetch at a future time—establishes an antecedent for an aesthetic "concretude" that Sarduy defined in "Rumo à concretude" (which appeared in English translation as "Toward Concreteness"). For Sarduy, a similar dislocation marks a move we might alternately gloss as one from modernism to postmodernism, or from an analog to a digital era, a "new dimension of things." In "Rumo à concretude" Sarduy defines concretude as an opposition between "image/fixity" and mobility, which owes to a "metaphorical dislocation" in which "a hard edge or formal limit" morphs into "letters that surge up" on an electronic board [*a* hard edge *ou claustra formal . . . letras que surgem . . . como no quadro negro eletrônico de um aeroporto*].[31]

The simultaneously material and immaterial nature of commodity culture was evident to artists writing long before the "dematerialization" of the art object in the 1960s. As Maria Gough has shown, Russian Productivist artists in the 1920s were ostensibly concerned with objects but produced them in a context of increasing information exchange.[32] The Russian vanguard artist El Lissitzky wrote in a 1923 article that "[t]he idea which moves the masses to-day is called materialism, but what precisely characterizes the present time is dematerialization."[33] This insight would be recuperated and repeated in 1968 by both Argentine critic Oscar Masotta to characterize 1960s Argentine art ("Después del Pop: Nosotros desmaterializamos") and U.S. artist Lucy Lippard to describe U.S. conceptual art (*Six Years: The Dematerialization of the Art Object*).[34]

The century-long period between 1868 and 1968, then, witnessed a transition out of Iberian empire and racialized slavery and into an era of nominal republicanism, which in turn saw more intense globalization and, with it, the eventual erosion of nation-states in the face of an absolute reign of the market. This periodization roughly coincides with what Charles Maier calls the "long century of modern statehood," when prior forms of sovereignty such as empires were replaced in many parts of the globe with nation-states.[35] Reified during this period were not only the object but also the nation-state, and particularly the conjunction of the two: in Latin America, the developmentalist national-popular state.

In the Iberian Atlantic, October 10, 1868 more specifically marks a military uprising in Spain that led to the abdication of Queen Isabel II and eventually to Spain's first, short-lived republic in 1873. It also marks the related inauguration of Cuba's wars for independence and abolition, which followed a Spanish-Moroccan war in Tetuán in 1859–60, led by the former captain general of Cuba, Leopoldo O'Donnell, a war that itself followed O'Donnell's violent repression of an antislavery conspiracy in 1840s Cuba.[36] The year 1868, then, inaugurates a second era of republicanism in the Iberian Atlantic, well after Latin American independence in the early nineteenth century and amid much anticolonial and antislavery mobilization in both North Africa and the Caribbean.

The 1968 that ends this study, on the other hand, saw the intensification of authoritarian states throughout Latin America that partially responded to new expressions of creativity and knowledge, the emergence of new political subjects, and, simultaneously, a transition in the arts away from the integrity of objects. In hindsight, the period can be seen as marking the rise of forces that Saskia Sassen has argued "denationalize what had been constructed as national—whether policies, capital, political subjectivities, urban spaces, temporal frames" (1). It marks a disillusion with and dissolution of the nation-state but also a growing state repression.

The era saw anticommunist national security doctrines established throughout the region and, in 1968, Mexico's massacre of protestors at Tlatelolco square; the Brazilian dictatorship's Fifth Institutional Act, which closed the National Congress and authorized censorship of art, music, and print, in addition to suspending habeas corpus for crimes deemed political; and praise for, then censure of, the Cuban poet Heberto Padilla's book *Fuera del juego*, which led to Padilla's show trial and "autocrítica" in 1971.

At the same time, the simultaneous *dissolution* of hardened forms of politics, thought, and art also associated with "1968" coincided with the emergence of a more networked, more virtual, and more extensive capitalism. If, as Gonzalo Aguilar has argued, Brazil's concrete poetry movement ended in 1968, so too did "concretude" more broadly understood as a modern era in which the developmentalist nation-state was a hegemonic form.[37] The ambiguous nature of the watershed resists neat conclusion.[38]

In the same year the first networked computer system was designed in the U.S. Department of Defense. ARPANET (later DARPANET) built on decades of research in cybernetics, information theory, computation, and Cold War military strategy, much of which was followed by the Brazilian concrete poets: in 1968, concrete poet Augusto de Campos published his essay "Informação e redundância na música popular," which applies Information Theory to pop music.[39] In 1968, too, Chilean scientist Humberto Maturana, a pioneer of cybernetics, came upon some of his ideas about "autopoeisis" through the experience of "trying to say something new" during the student takeover of the University of Chile.[40] That year the concrete artist Waldemar Cordeiro, in conjunction with physicist Giorgio Moscati, created *Beabá*, an algorithmic, computer-generated artificial language (and performance/poem) based on Portuguese phonemes, the first of his pioneering computer art. Cordeiro explicitly understood his computer art to be a continuation of concretism: Brazilian concrete art alone, he wrote, utilized "digital methods of creation . . . [and] furnished algorithms of ongoing use."[41] As these examples suggest, the 1960s' dematerialization of the art object emerges from, even as it also represents a break from, prior emphases on the object.

OVERVIEW OF CHAPTERS

The following chapters trace a history of concretude that is by no means exhaustive. They do not tell a history of Latin American concrete art movements, for instance. Other genealogies might, similarly, pay greater heed to literature's uptake of *musique concrète* and its legacy in Brazil, in Cuba—where in 1953 Alejo Carpentier, just back from France, gave Juan Blanco a copy of Pierre Schaeffer's *À la recherche d'une musique concrète* (1952)—and elsewhere. A case could easily be made for a wholly "Southern Cone" concretude capped by 1970s and 1980s *neobarroso* writers Néstor Perlongher and Roberto Echavarren; such a history might emphasize the Argentine Grupo Madí in the 1940s and critics and artists such as Masotta, Roberto Jacoby, Marta Minujin, Rubén Santantonín, and Leandro Katz. Along the same lines, a more strictly neobaroque literary history could also be told (and has been).[42] What I highlight, instead, is the relevance of an Atlantic frame for concrete aesthetics. The "object" in the book's title, then, refers not only to the things, commodities, visual literature, and new media of the early twentieth-century Iberian Atlantic but also to the way that longstanding Atlantic philosophies of history continued to shape literature, art, and politics in the twentieth century: the conversion of the eschatological horizons that shaped the Atlantic world into a "messianism of commodity language."

Chapter 1 lays out the historical and aesthetic underpinnings of the idea of concretude explored in subsequent chapters. It highlights how the medieval discourse of *translatio imperii* was used to suggest a twentieth-century transition to economic hegemony out of formal empire and explores in what ways this discourse is a problematic and particularly Atlantic legacy. In the chapter's second half, I turn to Severo Sarduy's series of essays on concretude, which themselves, in conjunction with Sarduy's own poetry, inscribe the phenomenon within an Atlantic frame. These essays identify central features of "concretude" such as innovative language, a dialogue with black Atlantic history and aesthetics, and an attention to things as well as the virtual—features that recur in subsequent chapters.

The chronological delineation of concrete aesthetics begins in earnest in Chapter 2. Exiled from Cuba in New York City, Martí became increasingly interested in the materiality of language. He devised new grammars to change the way we read. He investigated language's similarity to architecture. He was fascinated by new media technologies, like the long-forgotten glossograph, which transcribed the tongue's vibrations into a script. But beyond this response to the city and its modern culture, his poetics respond to the changing nature of Cuban independence struggles and modernity: while his romantic poetry is peopled with the corpses of the

1868 independence wars, later work replaces these relics with more industrial fragments.

From New York City Martí campaigned against the Spanish empire and took a keen interest in the popular culture and evolving politics of the United States, while warning against U.S. economic hegemony and imperial designs. Although singularly eloquent and well placed, he was not, however, alone in these observations. Overlapping with Martí in Manhattan, Joaquim de Sousândrade similarly wrote for newspapers in Brazil and the United States, militated for a republic (against Dom Pedro II's empire), and wrote a delirious canto set in Wall Street for his epic *O Guesa errante. O Guesa errante* describes an odyssey throughout the Atlantic world undertaken by a mythical figure (borrowed from indigenous mythology) named the Guesa, who travels from the Andes through Brazil, Senegal, the Caribbean, Central America, and New York. But Sousândrade was not well-known in his day, as was Martí. The poem's fame today owes to its reissue in 1964 by the concrete poets Haroldo de Campos and Augusto de Campos, who hailed the epic as a forerunner of a "poetics of concretude." Chapter 3 reveals how the circa 1900 transition from interiority to exteriority that Kittler perceives in German literature also may apply, with different implications to be sure, both to *O Guesa* and to literature about the 1890s war of Canudos. In particular, the chapter highlights repeated uses of the biblical scene describing disembodied "writing on the wall" as a metaphor that announces, often through new media, the rise of Wall Street, the imperiled "walls" of Dom Pedro II's empire, and the destroyed walls of the city of Canudos.

Across the Atlantic the clashes of the 1890s yielded rather different spoils. For the diminished Spanish empire, the recent wars, coupled with a newly powerful United States, provoked a national crisis in Spain. The authors and critics that emerged from this moment came to be known, however problematically, as the Generación del '98. Chapter 4 argues that in Maeztu's writings the enduring reverberations of the 1890s echo in a twentieth-century theory of things, as well as in developmentalist fascism, North African colonization, and postromantic literary ideals. Maeztu, who lived in Havana between 1891 and 1894—the eve of the 1895 Cuban Revolution—forever attributed to these years his enduring obsessions with the relations between Spain, its American and African colonies, and the Anglophone world, as well as with the evils of "subjectivity." Today few histories of modernism discuss Maeztu's London exchanges with T. E. Hulme and Ezra Pound, but the latter's Imagist antisubjectivism would, in turn, be a crucial reference for the very Brazilian concrete poets who republished Sousândrade. Thus Maeztu's poetics, which I trace to a reaction against Atlantic emancipatory movements, may inform seemingly unrelated objectivisms.

Chapter 5 turns back to Cuba to examine post-1902 republican literature. I examine a number of novels, plays, poems, and magazine advertisements that depict a republic as much haunted by unmet promises from the 1860s and 1890s generations as it is defined by the goods of a new era of consumption: "the primacy of things" indeed. The chapter considers the vanguard magazine *Revista de avance*, images from the journals *Carteles* and *Social*, as well as plays, poems, and novels by Bonifacio Byrne, José Antonio Ramos, and Alfonso Hernández Catá, among others, to explain why materiality and immateriality become keywords and recurrent themes in postwar literature. Early works are haunted by the spirit of Martí, whose spectral nature allegorizes what period authors saw as the nation's "dematerialization" by foreign banks and landowners. But later works by these same authors locate crucial affects and historical imagination in things, technologies, and unhomely interiors—an uncanny materialism.

Brazilian literature and art of the 1950s perfected the language of objects, which had been approached more obliquely by prior concretisms. Concrete poetry, the signature poetic movement of midcentury Brazil, aimed to produce poems that would be "useful objects," an "ultimate realism" in which poems no longer represented things but were things in their own right. Though the poetry was seen by some as a mere *expression* of developmentalism, Chapter 6 argues that concrete poetry and art were, from the beginning, concerned with immateriality, information, nonlinear temporality, and plastic form as much as with products and teleology. The chapter highlights this continuity by focusing on debates between concrete poets, "process/poets," and neoconcrete artists over "the object" and the "non-object." The book closes with a consideration of the dematerialization of the art object in the work of the Brazilian artist Lygia Clark and in the work of Sarduy. Both were interested in objects but rejected the messianisms and rigid ideologies invested in them in the first half of the twentieth century. Though such an interest in immateriality and immanence was present in concretude from the beginning, something does end with what Clark calls "the end of everything." Sarduy and Clark close the era of concretude and embrace process.

CHAPTER 1

Espiral Negra

Concretude in the Atlantic

As the nineteenth century turned into the twentieth, Iberian and British transatlantic empires were on the wane. The United States was emerging as a regional economic hegemon, eclipsing Britain both globally and more particularly in Latin America.[1] In the Cuban War of Independence (1895–98), in the Brazilian civil war of Canudos (1896–97), and in the South African War (1899–1902), imperial or recently imperial actors faced challenges to sovereignty as well as to accelerating capitalism. Harkening back to early modern discourse, writers throughout the Atlantic described this change as an instance of empire's persistence and movement.

The classical notion of the movement of empire (*translatio imperii*) had been adapted by medieval Christian historians such that "world history" came to mean the movement of power westward and the transfer of learning from Egypt to Spain.[2] More, this geographic movement from East to West portended the end of time. Hugh of Saint Victor, a German theologian from the twelfth century, believed that Divine Providence had willed that "universal government" would move westward to warn of the end of the world, "for the course of events ha[d] already reached the edge of the universe."[3] As Djelal Kadir and Nicolás Wey Gómez have shown, these ideas laid the foundation for Europe's notion of the Americas as the end time and place of history: having arrived in Spain, history's imagined course was extended across the Atlantic.[4]

This determinism lingered on at the dawn of the twentieth century. In 1900 the U.S. intellectual Brooks Adams asserted that for some thousand years "the tendency of the economic center of the world has been to move westward, and the Spanish war [of 1898] has only been the shock caused by its passing the Atlantic," prophesizing that "Probably, within two generations, the United States will have faced about, and its great interests will cover the Pacific."[5] Cuba's independence war was for Adams but one link in a chain of events that would constitute a "revolution" in which "civilizations pass from an old to a new condition of equilibrium" (1–2). At stake in the Cuban and South African wars was nothing less than "the seat of empire" (12). In these assertions Adams conjured with broad brushstrokes a geographical, temporal, and civilizational juggernaut. The shift he imagined from European territorial empires to U.S. economic hegemony was rendered in the religious language of inevitable imperial inheritance. This, too, had earlier roots: as Sophus Reinert has recently explored, *translatio imperii* was also translated in the early modern period into a *financial* theory according to which "different states, at different times and with varying degrees of constancy, have managed to claim hegemony."[6]

Adams was hardly alone in his assessments. Such quasi-theological discourse was common in Latin America after the Uruguayan writer Enrique José Rodó published his essay *Ariel* (1900). *Ariel* famously pitted spiritual and *belletristic* Latin America against a crude and materialist United States. If Rodó was mistaken in his diagnosis—there is, of course, nothing essentially or culturally spiritual and intellectual about "Latin Americans," as there is nothing essentially brutish, imperial, and avaricious about "North Americans"—the desire to move beyond Rodó's curiously stubborn myth has perhaps blinded us to the ways in which his analysis was a kind of misrecognition of real changes in capitalism and geopolitics; Beckman has suggested, for instance, that we read his aestheticism not as a culturalist move but as the product of "a subject shaped by bankruptcy" (152). Indeed, while different forms of his argument appeared throughout the region, not all presented a post-1898 U.S. hegemony in cultural terms, and some thinkers, like Pedro Henríquez Ureña, were critical of Rodó's schematism.[7]

For the Brazilian military engineer and reporter Euclides da Cunha, author of the canonical account of the Brazilian army's campaign against Canudos titled *Os Sertões* (1901) [*Rebellion in the Backlands*], the United States was different from former empires in that it was not principally territorial but economic and technological.[8] Da Cunha differs from Rodó, however, in presenting industrialization not as an *opposition* to spirit but as itself on "a higher plane": "The recent imperialism dominant in North American politics is not a material fact of territorial conquest, or geographical expansion at the expense of winnowing weak nations—but rather, on a higher level, the triumph of activities, the irresistible course of an incomparable industrial movement" [*numa esfera superior, o triunfo das atividades, o curso irresistível de um movimento industrial incomparável*].[9] Da Cunha, like Rodó, translates industrial and economic growth into transcendental and geographic terms. And for da Cunha, as for Brooks, the Atlantic crossing will find its millennial end point in the Pacific.[10]

Authors such as da Cunha, Martí, and Sousândrade were keenly engaged with this discourse, even when their more poetic literature was not, or was not explicitly. Similarly, reflecting back on this moment in the early 1920s, the avant-garde Chilean poet Vicente Huidobro, best known as the founder of the antimimetic poetics of "creacionismo" and as the author of the visually arresting poem-book *Altazor*, penned a satirical anti-imperial pamphlet. *Finis Britannia* (1923) echoed the language of *translatio imperii* and warned prophetically of the hapless end awaiting (a conflation of) Anglo-American empires:

> You have protested with indignation against Spain for having established concentration camps in Cuba, but you have established the same, or worse, a few years later in the Transvaal. . . . The United States, which protested with the same indignation against Cuban reconcentration camps, has just implanted a regime with the most hateful manner in the island of Saint-Domingue, an independent Republic that they want to annex. "Beware, American people, not to create hate and not to weave the cord with which you will be hanged!" . . . *Finis Britannia* is already written on one page of our century. And if the Englishman didn't have such avarice before his eyes, he would see engraved on the flank of his island the Mané, Thecel, Pharès of Babylon.[11]

The last line is a reference to the "writing on the wall" in the Book of Daniel, writing that announces a change of empire. In Chapter 3 I will explore in greater depth allusions to this biblical scene that served as a common referent for other poets of the period later associated with a "concrete" poetry tradition, such as Martí and Sousândrade. What I wish to call attention to here are the ways in which the wars in Cuba, the Transvaal, and the Brazilian hinterlands were interpreted—often together—in a mythopoetic language of imperial change.

Clearly, "1898" implied more than a Cuban-Spanish-U.S. conflict. Indeed, in 1963 the Spanish historian Jesús Pabón proposed the concept of a global 1898 in which leading European and Asian imperial powers faced nascent anti-imperial movements and weakening economic might.[12] Not only were Cuba, Spain, and the United States involved in what was shorthanded as "1898," he argued, but so too were Portugal (with respect to the British Ultimatum of 1890), Japan and China (who in 1895 signed the treaty of Shimonoseki/Maguan concerning the fate of Korea), the Transvaal and Britain (which also withdrew from Venezuela in 1896 under U.S. pressure), France (which struggled to control the Sudanese town of Fashoda in 1898), Italy and Ethiopia (1896), and Angola and Mozambique, whose borders were delineated in a secret meeting between Britain and Germany. To Pabón's imperial history I would add the Pan-African Congress, convened in 1900 precisely to contest the European partition of Africa.

For Schmitt, too, as we have seen, 1898 was a crucial moment for geopolitical rearrangements. In *The Nomos of the Earth* (1950)—a treatise on Eurocentric "world order"—he identifies 1898 as a moment of redistribution of the *nomoi*, or divisions, of the globe.[13] Although here "1898," reminiscent of a Spenglerian theory of civilizational cycles, is again identified with the inauguration of a U.S. twentieth century, Schmitt's theory gestures toward a more strictly economic (nongeographical) shift. According to Schmitt, the "War of 1898" marked a global beginning of sovereignty's control via resources rather than territory. The "external, emptied space of the controlled state's territorial sovereignty remains inviolate," Schmitt wrote, referring to Caribbean nations under the influence of the United States, yet "the material content of this sovereignty is changed by the guarantees of the controlling power's economic *Grossraum*" (252). After the war, Schmitt contends, "territorial sovereignty" becomes "an empty space for socio-economic processes" (252).[14]

Schmitt's diagnosis is totalizing and ignores much that does not fit into his purported division of before and after. Territorial sovereignty remained a goal for twentieth-century decolonization movements, as territorial empire persisted well into the twentieth century, and in the Caribbean the promise (or "specter") of "another Haiti"—a revolution from below for control over a territory—was repeatedly invoked during the Spanish-Cuban-American war both in support of, and against, the Cuban cause. Indeed, as Gareth Williams has noted in a critique of Schmitt, it is the Haitian Revolution, and not the 1823 Monroe Doctrine, that inaugurates a notion of the "Western Hemisphere."[15] If empire and anti-imperial struggles remained concerned with territory well into the twentieth century, the perception of economic influence substituting for military or territorial control in the Americas had *pre*-1898 precedents: not only in Britain's "informal empire" in Latin America in the nineteenth century but in late nineteenth-century European financial policies more extensively.[16]

Yet this notion of the 1890s Atlantic as a fulcrum in the shift from territorial to economic empire has been echoed, from a far different place on the political spectrum, by Giovanni Arrighi in his history of modern capitalism, *The Long Twentieth Century: Money, Power and the Origins of Our Times* (1994). According to Arrighi, the fifty years between 1870 and 1920 were a period in which the seat of capital—particularly finance capital—moved from England to the United States. For Arrighi, as for Schmitt, global powers tend to operate by logics of "territorialism," "capitalism," or some combination of the two (33). Territorialists associate power with the extent of their domains. Capitalists associate power with "command over scarce resources," the acquisition of territory being a mere by-product. For the former, money is a means to acquire more territory. For the latter, territory is a means to acquire further monies.[17]

In Arrighi's view the different approaches imply different strategies for growth. Territorialists increase power by expanding their container. Capitalists accumulate wealth within small containers (33). And the two strategies can coexist. For instance, the early Spanish empire was seen as territorialist, but capitalist accumulation drove its transatlantic colonization. The British Empire, in some senses more explicitly capitalist from the outset, was deeply concerned with territorial expansion. Indeed, historians such as John Elliott and Jorge Cañizares-Esguerra have emphasized similarities between the two empires' strategies in the New World,[18] while Lauren Benton has studied the coexistence of empires' "impulse" to territorial rule and to juridical arrangements that "transcended or splintered territory."[19]

Whatever their strategies, by the late nineteenth century both Iberian and British empires saw the United States as a rival. It was, to use Arrighi's divisions, something of an "expansionist container"—was not 1898 the clearest manifestation of this trend? Yet it was one for whom a main strategy for accruing power was the accumulation of wealth through industrial production. And rather than end European quasi-religious teleologies of empire, the United States continued to cast territorial expansion in religious terms.

As Schmitt observed, emergent media networks facilitated the acquisition and maintenance of nonannexing power, since such control could now more easily be exercised from afar.[20] Since these technologies extended what had been earlier empires' ambitions to connect far-flung locales, they were imbued with abiding imperial philosophies of history. Bernard Stiegler, for instance, sees late nineteenth-century communication technologies as extending a logic that characterized Europe's first American conquests. The first transatlantic cable thus becomes for Stiegler Europe's tool for a modern day "'discover[y]' of a new continent—and its stock market"; even "the beginning of the decline of the 'Old World,'" whose eclipsed preeminence turns out to have depended on "a significant delay in transmission."[21] "Old World" empires built the space of the Atlantic via ships that circulated between Africa, Europe, and the Americas ferrying bullion, slaves, and sugar. With the laying of transatlantic cables, virtual capital blossomed, emblematized in stock market profits that depend upon taking advantage of differences (delays) across space and time.

For Stiegler and Schmitt, then, the early modern transatlantic imperial move is echoed in late nineteenth-century expansions of media that enable speculative trade. They suggest capitalism's evolution takes place both within and through the constitution of an Atlantic space. Indeed, the Atlantic has often been thought of as isomorphic with the rise of modern capitalism. C.L.R. James, Paul Gilroy, Antonio Benítez Rojo, Stephan Palmié, Ian Baucom, and Édouard Glissant have all written important books that place the *modernity* of the Atlantic, or sometimes, more specifically, the Caribbean, at their center of their studies, a modernity that is dependent on a savage capitalism.[22]

James sees sugar plantations as anticipating the modern industrial proletariat (86), while Benítez Rojo writes, "the history of the Caribbean is one of the main strands in the history of capitalism, and vice versa" (5). Palmié suggests that "the Caribbean might well be regarded as one of the first truly modern localities" (41). Baucom uses Arrighi's economic history to propose a specifically "Atlantic" mode of accumulation and temporality in which modern finance capital was underwritten by slavery insurance, producing a "long twentieth century." (Jorge Cañizares-Esguerra, for his part, has offered caveats *against* Atlantic historiographic paradigms.)[23]

These scholars of the Atlantic revise the idea that modernity originates in narrowly European traditions, whether philosophical, political, literary, anthropological, or economic. They move beyond national paradigms toward a supra-, infra- or extranational approach that emphasizes the problematic exclusion of slavery from celebratory narratives of enlightenment philosophy. And they intervene in necessary ways to alter a stubbornly resilient discourse in which "Latin America" and the "Caribbean," among many other regions, continue to be cast as underdeveloped and peripheral. Modernity in such revisionary accounts, then, emanates from rather than arrives at the region. Likewise, Alejandro Mejías-López has recently inverted transatlantic literary history to underscore *modernismo*'s origins in Latin America and its "conquest" of Spanish literary tradition. He thus revises what is essentially a narrative of *translatio studii*, a transfer of learning from Europe to the Americas, and keenly contests an abiding Arielism in Latin American studies according to which Latin America has never been more than a colonial then neocolonial victim, derivative and dependent upon greater powers.

But there are problems with narrating the history of capitalism as Atlantic, and it is time, I believe, to move beyond proving the modernity, however revised, of the Atlantic world. For one, economic histories that make the Atlantic isomorphic with the emergence of modern capitalism have come under scrutiny in the past decade. More important, little is gained by establishing that the history of modernity is a more truly Atlantic phenomenon than narrowly Eurocentric histories once proposed. For as the history of *translatio imperii*—mapping power's progress geographically—suggests, the very concept of modernity itself is, at least partially, a nefarious legacy of the Atlantic. In Mejías-López's reversal of *modernismo*'s innovation and influence, for instance, what remains at stake is still principally who can claim modernity.[24] If one sets out to prove how modern the Atlantic world really is, one risks ignoring the fetishized status of "the modern" itself, a product of the same teleological mind-set that construed "the Atlantic" as a discrete space and end time.

There remains, however, a utility to an Atlantic paradigm, in part because Atlanticist discourses—from theories of *translatio imperii* to dreams of modernity—are no less real in their effects for being constructions. Arrighi's own late scholarship, precisely when it leaves the Atlantic behind, suggests a useful approach for considering both how the Atlantic is singular and how it is part of a global history.

As Baucom has explored, in *The Long Twentieth Century* Arrighi brings the Atlantic into focus as a map within which capitalism repeats a cycle of accumulations. First, capital concentrates in a given territory's banking system as merchant capital. It is then converted into speculative capital, after which it exhausts its home and relocates. The series of temporary shells in which capital made its home are constellated around the Atlantic: Spain and Genoa in the fifteenth and sixteenth centuries, Holland and Britain in the seventeenth and eighteenth to nineteenth centuries, and the United States between roughly 1870 and 1970—at which point capital begins to decamp to Asia and the Pacific. Glossed by Baucom as a return of the same (system of finance capital) and a specifically Atlantic form of accumulation, Arrighi's cycles seem to reinscribe an Atlantic-centric *translatio imperii*, in which it is now capital, not celestial empire, that moves its seat eastward from the Mediterranean to the United States.

The reemergence of strong Asian economies in recent decades, however, compelled Arrighi and others to reject the idea that "our times" are the teleological end point of a mutating path of Atlantic finance capital.[25] Focused on contemporary China, Arrighi's last book, *Adam Smith in Beijing* (2007), agreed in large part with the late work of the economic sociologist Andre Gunder Frank.[26] Although Gunder Frank is best known as a cofounder of 1970s Latin American dependency theory, by the time he wrote *ReOrient: Global Economy in the Asian Age* (1998), about the centrality of Asia to the global economy, he had disowned his own prior notions of core and periphery within a global capitalism.[27] Indeed Gunder Frank questioned the very notion of "capitalism" as a discrete historical entity. He criticized narratives in which "the Atlantic" is *the* paradigmatic birthplace of modernity and called the Atlantic phase of capital accumulation but a blip—albeit a significant one—in a history in which Asia was and will be again the center of the global economy.

Gunder Frank argued that Europe only ever emerged as an economically powerful region by using Latin American money to take advantage of Asian markets (5). The spectacular wealth of the Atlantic world was, then, but one half of an exchange between Latin American mines and the specie they produced, and Asian economies in need of silver but in possession of goods.[28] This hypothesis was echoed by Kenneth Pomeranz, who sought to explain China's industrial and economic divergence from Europe in the eighteenth century and discredited the notion that eighteenth-century Europe uniquely enjoyed a "capitalist mode of production" or a "consumer society."[29]

Yet Pomeranz conceded that the Americas were important for subsequent Western economic might and consumer culture in the nineteenth and twentieth centuries. Like Gunder Frank, Pomeranz links the growth of Atlantic trade and consumption to Chinese monetary policies. But he is also careful to point out that mercantilism and the transatlantic slave trade played key roles in establishing a modern division in labor between producers of primary materials and manufactured products (24–25). Furthermore, while dismissive of a false division between a materialist West and a belated "rest," Pomeranz nonetheless grants a special place to consumption and luxury goods in the history of Atlantic capitalism, which he attributes to an "economic conjuncture," not a singular "materialism" (128–30, 161). Because sixteenth-century China, at almost 40 percent of the world's economy, was remonetarizing to silver, there was little reason for Latin American ships to send to China anything but the precious metal (160). The ships that returned with Chinese "prestige" goods such as porcelain and tea became key actors shaping a modern world economy (161). Suddenly *modernismo*'s investment in "oriental" luxury goods looks rather different: instead of an escapist interior, the chinoiserie and precious baubles that *modernismo* foregrounds seem a return of the repressed, a half-unwitting testimony to the historical link between Chinese and Latin American economies during another moment of massive insertion into a global market.[30] Modern capitalism is not particularly or solely an Atlantic invention, then. But these studies do point to a notably Iberian Atlantic role in the global market, one that links the slave trade and the exchange of mined metals for prestige goods.

Literary, philosophical, and artistic concretisms of the modern era, I argue, often channel or comment upon this history, in part because the philosophies attendant upon the earlier moment resurface in the imperial 1890s and live on in a messianism of commodities. Indeed, the very elements that Pomeranz flags as central to Atlantic economies—mercantilist investment in metals and an African diaspora coerced into forced labor (a situation out of which new languages emerged)—stud Severo Sarduy's multiple, allusive, but opaque essays on "concretude," to which we now turn.

MARIANO BRULL'S DAUGHTERS, ALFONSO REYES'S *JITANJÁFORAS*, HAROLDO DE CAMPOS'S *GALAXIAS*, SEVERO SARDUY'S *CENTRO NEGRO*

Severo Sarduy's essay "Hacia la concretud" was a touchstone in his oeuvre of literary criticism. He reworked or reproduced fragments of it in subsequent writings, and versions exist, each slightly different, in Portuguese, French, and English.[31] Experimental and poetic in its form, "Hacia la concretud" is loosely devoted to Haroldo de Campos's poem *Galaxias*, but it more generally articulates Sarduy's theory of "concretude." The essay describes characteristic uses of metaphor, image, movement, and vowel vibrations in Latin American poetry in which sound, vision, and form predominate over narrative. Its Portuguese version, "Rumo à concretude" (written in 1978; published in 1979), was appended to de Campos's book of critical essays *Signantia quasi coelum = Signância quase céu* (1979) and quickly became a classic commentary on Brazilian concrete poetry.

Yet something that has been overlooked regarding the multiple versions of Sarduy's seminal essay is that they all begin with a scene of Cubans gathered in a genteel drawing room in Paris, where a Cuban poet entertains a group that represents a Latin American intellectual and diplomatic elite, implying a connection between the concretude of the midcentury Brazilian poets and an earlier Cuban poetics. The English version (1986) begins:

> A living room, Paris, in the thirties—or maybe the late twenties. Bourgeois furnishings, curtains before the trees along an avenue in the XVIth arrondissement. Possibly a little rain outside.
>
> In the diplomatic world of that time, solace for those nostalgic for Cuba would be provided by readings given in the melancholic pause after dinner. The reading would begin with Doctor Baralt reciting stale Romantic verses, prolonging his repertoire on especially dreary evenings to the arduous rhymers of the Restoration.
>
> It was in this scene of plush, benevolent exile—the insular distance alleviated perhaps by the persistent scent of imported fruit and mahogany furniture, and a few *guarachas* on the phonograph—where it occurred to Mariano Brull, a poet from Camagüey born at the end of the century

> and a connoisseur of angels "to renovate the well-worn genres." ("Towards Concreteness" 62)

No sooner has Sarduy's essay on a vanguard poetics begun than its bourgeois gathering of expatriates points us toward a regression of allusions that multiply like a baroque hall of mirrors. For the comfortable setting with which Sarduy's essay opens is lifted from "Las jitanjáforas," a 1942 essay by the Mexican writer and critic Alfonso Reyes that was itself comprised of two of Reyes's earlier essays, including "Alcance a las jitanjáforas," published in the avant-garde Cuban magazine *Revista de avance* (1930).[32]

Jitanjáforas, Reyes explained, were poems that play with nonsense sounds and with onomatopoeia, a poetic sensibility that ostensibly inaugurated Cuban vanguard poetry. Reyes's essays, in turn, place us some time between 1924 and 1927, "los días de París," when the Mexican author was a diplomat in France ("Las jitanjáforas" 27). He found himself at a gathering of Cubans, described here only as a "sala de familia" that included Brull and his two daughters. One of the daughters surprised the circle by performing one of her father's more experimental poems, eventually published in Brull's book *Poemas en menguante* (1928):

> Filiflama alabe cundre
>
> ala olalúnea alífera
> alveolea jitanjáfora
> liris salumba salífera
>
> Olivia oleo olorife
> alalai cánfora sandra
> milingítara girófara
> zumbra ulalindre calandra.

Upon hearing the poem Reyes baptizes the verses "jitanjáforas," then expands the term to denote sound poetry that, like its rhyming figure of speech "metáfora," can be used variously. According to Reyes's definition, *jitanjáforas* are pure excess, nonutilitarian, and playful, like the girls who deliver them: "Las palabras no buscan aquí un fin útil. Juegan solas, casi" [Here words don't seek a useful end. They play alone, almost] (*La experiencia* 191).

Reyes had first ventured his concept in a piece published in the Argentine magazine *Libra* (1929). There Reyes writes of the *jitanjáfora* as artifice and absolute creation, crystallized as objects, a theory reminiscent of Huidobro's *creacionismo*, with its emphasis on creation, not imitation. The 1929 essay was remarked upon by the Cuban press. It was a period in Cuban history in which, as Chapter 5 discusses, objects received particular scrutiny amid a consumer boom but which also saw the beginning of worldwide economic depression. A Havana newspaper reviewed Reyes's 1929 essay, zeroing in on this claim: "The word was given to us first . . . in order to possess objects [*para apoderarnos de los objetos*]. But with it we made other, new objects. This is called 'creation' [*creación*]; that is—in Greek—'*poesis*.'"[33] The Cuban critic Francisco Ichaso followed with an additional commentary on *jitanjáforas* that reasserted the import of poems as "concreción lírica" [lyric concretion].[34]

Reyes's interpretation of Brull's *jitanjáforas* took the term outside its original Atlantic context and made it available to Latin American vanguards everywhere. Brull, for his part, owed his interest in sound poetry to Mallarméan symbolism.[35] But Brull's coining of the phrase also coincided with the rise of "afrocubanista" poetry; so-called *poesía negra* or *poesía mulata*. Early commentaries on the movement used the concept of *jitanjáfora* verse to cite, mimic, or parody African vocabularies in Cuban oral culture.

Fernando Ortiz, for instance, argued that the *jitanjáfora* was a kind of weak translation of African codes calcified in liturgy and sound, for which the original meaning was lost.[36] But he mainly used the term to describe the strategies of poets such as Nicolás Guillén and the Puerto Rican Luis Palés Matos, whose poetry, Ortiz observed, describe "a visionary people, between exotic geography and jitanjaphoric resonances of the Puerto Rican multitude"; he cites Palés Matos: "Musumba, Tombuctú, Faranfangana— / Caserío irreal de paz y sueño . . . / Alguien disuelve perezosamente / Un canto monorrítmico en el viento, / Pululado de úes que se aquietan / En balsas de diptongos soñolientos, / Y de guturaciones alargadas / Que dan un don de lejanía al verso" [Musumba, Tombuctú, Faranfangana— / Unreal village of peace and dreams . . . / Someone dissolves lazily / A monorhythmic song in the wind / Teeming with u's that grow still / In the base of sleepy dipthongs / And elongated gutterations / That give a touch of distance to the verse].[37] Ortiz observes about this passage: "There we have almost all the Afro-Antillean themes and what is typical of their style: laziness, sleepiness, guttural sounds, nasalisms, labialisms (a neologist would say *bembismos*), rhythms, songs, dance, plasticity, sex, dark dipthongs in prolonged cadences of *o* and *u*" (26). Avant-garde "negrista" innovation is, in this reading, a series of tics: explosive guttural, labial nonsense, onomatopoeism, dynamic sensuality—in short, what Sianne Ngai has called "animatedness," the inhuman grimaces and movements attributed to racialized subjects for whom the "ostensibly positive qualities of liveliness, effusiveness, spontaneity, and zeal become affects harnessed to a disturbing racial epistemology, such that these emotional qualities . . . are made to function as bodily, hence self-evident, signs of the raced subject's naturalness or authenticity."[38]

The racism behind one connotation of *jitanjáfora*, however, occludes a possibly real parallel influence of Kongo visual script practice, preserved in Abakuá and Palo religious societies, traditions important to Sarduy's novels and poetry.[39] In the U.S. context, Harryette Mullen has called attention to Afro-diasporic oral arts from bebop to scatting that employ nonsense sounds to produce what she describes as a liberatory "unshackling" from meaning and from "the pragmatic function of language as a conveyer of cognitive information." Drawing on Robert Ferris Thompson's work on African diasporic aesthetics, Mullen suggests that this oral jitanjaphorism (she does not use the term) may have a corollary in *written* texts "unshackled from any phonetic representation of human speech or graphic representation of language," writing systems such as *anaforuana*, the emblems used in the West African–derived religious practices of Abakuá. (See Figure 2.) Mullen draws on Thompson's documentation of Kongo traditions found in both Cuba and Brazil of "'writing in the spirit,' sometimes referred to as 'visual glossolalia' . . . writing as if copied from 'a billboard in the sky,'" and a practice of "reading" objects (*nsibidi*) and ideographs (Mullen 680).[40] Of course, one must be wary of readings, even if celebratory, that champion Afro-diasporic aesthetics as sublimely beyond discursive representation. Moreover, here *anaforuana* and other Abakuá signs are graphically representational: they signify to an initiated elite.

Abakuá liturgy and codes entered Cuban popular culture in the 1920s with the explosion of *son* music and were picked up by avant-garde writers. Alejo Carpentier's novel *Écue-yamba-ó* (written in 1927; published in 1933), later disavowed by the author as a failed attempt at endogenously rendering African-derived societies in Havana, for instance, includes photographs of Abakuá objects and a glossary of two dozen words from the *ñáñigo* lexicon, indicating to the uninitiated

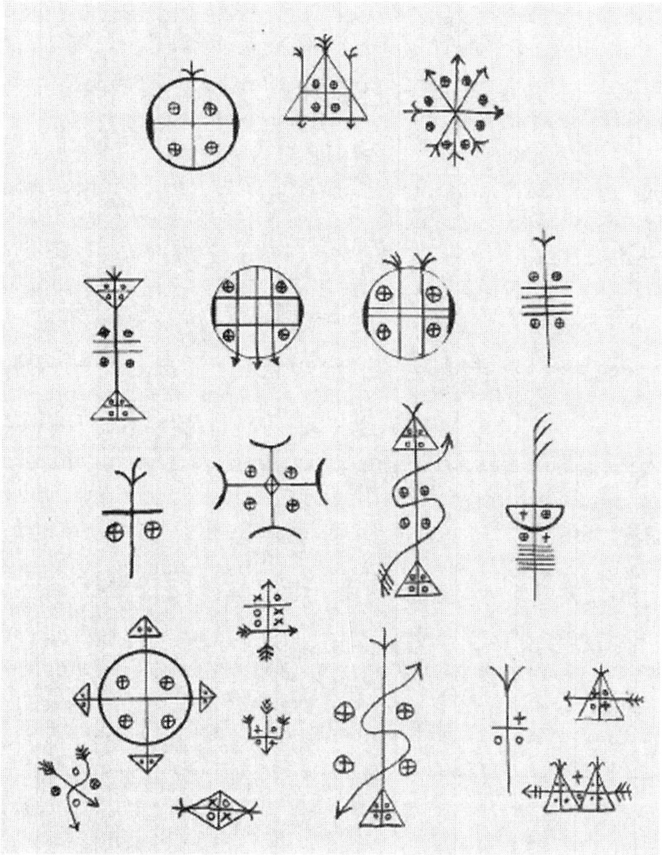

Figure 2. Lydia Cabrera, *Anaforuana: Ritual y símbolos de la iniciación en la sociedad secreta Abakuá* (Miami: Ediciones R, 1975), 295. Courtesy of the Estate of Lydia Cabrera.

reader that what might look like nonsense "jitanjáforas" were meaningful words with histories and translations—however resistant to being decoded: "*Enagüiero* (form of salute, in *ñáñigo* dialect); *Munifambá* (*náñiga* dignitary); *Senseribó* (or *Cece-ribó*) (a kind of chalice, adorned with feathers and shells)."[41] If *Écue-yamba-ó* offers a troubling, "animating" depiction of its main character (described as a "doctor in gestures and cadences. The sense of rhythm beat in his blood" [31]), it simultaneously suggests that nontransparent sounds, symbols, and vocabulary are a hieroglyphic writing, a kind of concretude that Sarduy would later recuperate.[42]

To return to Sarduy, then, we can say that "Hacia la concretud" opens with the borrowed episode about Brull and his daughters as recollected by Reyes in "Las jitanjáforas," with an encrypted history of *jitanjáforas*, as applied to discussions of *poesía negra*, trailing in its wake. But Sarduy also changes something. He adds the small detail that in this comfortable Parisian scene an "insular distance" is mitigated by the "persistent scent of imported fruit" and some "phonographs of *guarachas*."[43] The insertion of these signature Cuban elements—fruits, *guarachas*, insular distance—is important; they are elements of a primal scene of concretude that will reappear in at least two other publications by Sarduy.

In Sarduy's undated essay "Barroco americano," under the subheading "Dos lenguas inventadas en América" [Two languages invented in America], the bourgeois salon returns as the ur-scene of American avant-garde language. Sarduy again places us in the sedate living room, though he has now moved it to Brussels (Brull served as a diplomat in both Paris and Brussels).

> Allá por los años veinte, comisionado en Bruselas, y no sabiendo qué hacer para animar una languideciente velada intelectual, a la que refrescaban grandes abanicos de plumas y copetines de anís, Mariano Brull, poeta y embajador de Cuba, hombre extremadamente elegante y gran amigo de Paul Valéry, no encontró mayor recurso que vestir con crinolinas y polizones a sus tres niñas, las cuales, con la cara bien empolvada y flores de papel en el pelo, entraron al gran salón para recitar algunos versos de su papá. No sabían, pues las palabras estrictamente no significan nada, que estaban a punto de inventar una lengua, la *jitanjáfora*, que, por hallarse entre los invitados un famoso crítico, iba a hacer fortuna en las vanguardias literarias sudamericanas de aquella época. (*Antología* 176–77)

> [Some time in the 1920s, stationed in Brussels, and not knowing how to animate a languorous evening gathering, freshened by great feather fans and glasses of anise *aperitivos*, Mariano Brull, poet and Cuban ambassador, an extremely elegant man and good friend of Paul Valéry, could think of nothing better than to dress his three daughters is crinolines and bustles, who, with well-powdered faces and paper flowers

> in their hair, entered the great room to recite some of their father's verses. They didn't know, for the words didn't mean anything exactly, that they were on the verge of inventing a new language, the *jitanjáfora*, which, thanks to the presence among the guests of a famous critic, was to find great success among South American vanguards of the era.]

The girls, their artifice heightened by tulle, face paint, and paper flowers in their hair, are now "on the verge of inventing a language" and about to enter literary history, thanks to the famous critic in the audience. In "Dos lenguas" Sarduy thus emphasizes the link between sound poetry, experimental poetics, and a celebrated but also parodied American originality: they are languages invented in America but staged and authenticated in Europe.

The scene appears again in Sarduy's book *La simulación* [Simulation] (1982) under the subheading "Anamorphosis."[44] The essay is inspired by Jacques Lacan's reflections on the use of anamorphosis in baroque painting in his famous Seminar XI, *The Four Fundamental Concepts of Psychoanalysis.* (Sarduy's lifelong partner, François Wahl, Lacan's editor at Editions Seuil, introduced the two; Wahl believes Sarduy attended this seminar).[45] Anamorphosis describes apparently distorted, illegible images that, when viewed from the proper angle, suddenly resolve themselves into a clear picture. The example that both Sarduy and Lacan use is Holbein's painting *The Ambassadors*, whose foreground image of a strange milky smudge, when viewed from the side, turns out to be a skull, a caution against the *vanitas* of mastery and knowledge. For Sarduy the idea of anamorphosis was important insofar as it signaled the fact that in analysis, as in literature, meaning is not disclosed immediately but must be approached obliquely.

This notion that literature's meaning is not always encountered head-on but is sometimes observed elliptically, or by circling around a center that may not immediately reveal itself, will be important to Sarduy's interest in voids (explored in the epilogue to this book). It also underscores how concretude, despite its brutalist connotations, actually describes a play between fixity and movement, thingliness and absence. What is more, these accruing iterations of the same scene, refracted and re-presented, themselves begin to form an anamorphic image of Sarduy's notion of concretude. Hidden behind the hackneyed Cuban signifiers (tropical fruit, *guarachas*, Cuban poets) are the bare bones of what concrete writing might be. But we must move obliquely to the side to perceive the outlines of this aesthetic.

In the version of the bourgeois salon that appears in *La simulación*, anamorphosis transposes the diplomats' austere, revolutionary discourse of Cuba's New Man to the more uninhibited context of gay prostitution. The diplomatic mission of Cubans in Paris has been updated to the post-1959 revolutionary period; the rain—which had been vaguely sultry, requiring fans and cooling anise-flavored drinks—has become wintry; and the room is the setting for the discreet engagement of prostitutes: the "simulation" of the title is a conversation ostensibly about *café con leche* which, when decoded, concerns an assignation between Cuban communist diplomats and French male prostitutes. The opening setting should be familiar by now:

> Mitigaban las pausas de sobremesa, con insistentes añoranzas tropicales, el olor tenaz y dulzón de las frutas importadas, dispuestas con excesiva simetría en un compotero de loza, la caoba de los muebles, y hasta algunas guarachas fonográficas que dispersaba en la sala cerrada el desmesurado pabellón de una bocina.
>
> Nunca se abrían las cortinas opacas: evitaban las ortogonales negras de los árboles de invierno, idénticos a lo largo de la avenida, la llovizna puntual del mediodía, y sobre todo ese gris metálico y unido del cielo, que anunciaba en las islas lejanas tiempo de ciclón.
>
> Dos hermanas consulares, apropiadamente nostálgicas de ciertos sabores inefables . . . evocaban en premeditados monólogos la austeridad insomne de los días revolucionarios.[46]
>
> [After-dinner pauses, with insistent tropical longings, mitigated the strong and cloying scent of imported fruits, arrayed with excessive symmetry in a ceramic bowl, the mahogany furniture, and even some phonographic *guarachas* that scattered the horn's blasts in the shuttered living room.
>
> The opaque curtains were never opened: they kept out the black orthogonals of trees in winter, identical all along the avenue, the prompt midday drizzle, and above all that uniform, metallic gray sky that in the distant islands announced hurricane weather.
>
> Two consular sisters, appropriately nostalgic for certain ineffable flavors . . . evoked in premeditated monologues the sleepless austerity of the revolutionary days.]

The "strong and cloying scent of imported fruits" fills the silences of the dessert table, while the "phonographic *guarachas*" feature brassy horns. *Cubanidad* intrudes—anamorphically, from offstage—through the orifices in these French scenes. The fragrance of tropical fruit overwhelms the nose, that sense organ most attuned to memory. (Such heady insular fruit will itself be the topic of Sarduy's neobaroque series of *décimas*, "Corona de las frutas" in *Un testigo perenne y delatado*, poems written in a traditional Cuban meter about mangos, pineapples, papayas, guanábanas, etc.) (*Obra completa* 1:226–29). As the room fills with the cloying bouquet, Cuban music displaces the sounds of the French city.

An additional set of representations is introduced into this scene, in which concretude is staged in Paris and Cuba is remembered (an anamorphic sidestepping). A conversation about "café," "azucar," and "leche" is decoded: "'Sweet,' in that simple hermeneutic—the whites 'milk,' the blacks 'coffee,' etc.—signaled the docile tendencies of those who, at the rear of the delegation, feigned resigned submission . . . the 'strong,' as might be expected, meant quite the opposite" (*Obra completa* 2:1274). The *café con leche* are assignations to be undertaken by otherwise homophobic and ascetic revolutionary diplomats.

More important than the insular distance and tropical fruits are the insistent *guarachas*. The *guaracha* dates at least to the nineteenth century, when it became popular as a *costumbrista* version of Afro-Cuban rhythm, associated with *teatro bufo*, a genre whose staple skits included blackface performances. (The *guarachas* played in Brull's salon in the 1920s and 1930s would likely have been something more like the music of the Trio Matamoros.) Sarduy's small addition of the *guaracha* connects the *jitanjáfora* beyond Brull to both a historical Afro-Cuban musical tradition and a tradition of caricatured *costumbrismo*.

The phonographic *guarachas* have, moreover, passed through their own anamorphosis. The regional musical form recorded in Cuba has been reproduced via the new media of the 1920s. The artificiality of the recorded voice points to another aspect of concretude important both to Sarduy and to the larger tradition that this study's subsequent chapters engage. For concretude emphasizes not just the materiality of language but the new media that transform language into other forms: waves, bytes, inscriptions on a gramophone; Sarduy himself experimented with radio plays. Insular distance is punctuated here by the imported fruit and by means of the gramophone, both bearing multiple meanings. Fruit serves as a vehicle for exilic nostalgia but also symbolizes a romantic and kitschy Cuban nature and perhaps Latin American export economies. The gramophone, a recording technology that exteriorizes the voice, also circulates sound and bridges time (the time elapsed since the original recordings) and distance (from the recordings' original sites).

Reyes's essay had dwelled on the nonsense aspect of Brull's poem and on acoustic and graphic elements of poetry. Sarduy introduces details from a more pointedly Atlantic history: imported fruit; a *jitanjáfora* that, as we have seen, was tied to Ortiz's work on "poesía mulata"; and the introduction of *guaracha*-playing phonographs. Sarduy links this literary and sonic history to a constructivist history of Brazilian aesthetics to which the second half of his essay is dedicated. By connecting a tradition that is oral, Cuban, and more broadly Antillean, as employed by Guillén in the poems of *Sóngoro Cosongo* (1931) and in the onomatopoeic "Sensemayá" from *West-Indies, Ltd.* (1934) to Brazil's pioneering concrete poets, Sarduy links the Brazilian poetry he characterizes by its visual and "syntactic geometry, like a precise and programmed crinkle of white orthogonals" to an improvisational, aural, and oral tradition, a tradition, to be sure, also alive in Brazil. In this, I believe, Sarduy is emphasizing Afro-Antillean and improvisational components of "concretude" rarely associated with the Brazilian movement known for its lettered and hermetic aesthetic and public.[47]

Sarduy's essays on concretude thus amalgamate a writing that is visual as well as mathematical and algorithmic, with approaches that are more sonic or improvisational—or both, as in the case of jazz. This union of a programmatic tradition of writing (Sarduy's last talk, given in 1991 at the Universidad Internacional Menéndez Pelayo in the Canary Islandos, was titled "Poesía bajo programa" [Programmed poetry]) with a historically Atlantic musical, rhythmic, and oral tradition highlights key attributes of Sarduy's concept of concretude.

Sarduy comments on and participates in this tradition in his own series of poems titled "Mood Indigo," visual poems about the history of Afrodiasporic music, a music whose precise permutations had, as Sarduy notes, inspired the "syntactic geometry" of Piet Mondrian's *Broadway Boogie-Woogie* (1942–43) (paintings cited in the Brazilian poets' pilot-plan).[48] "Espiral negra" (1970) spirals inward like a hurricane passing over the key sites in the history of black Atlantic music: New York, Paris, the Antilles, New Orleans, Havana, Nigeria, the Congo, Rio, Recife, and back through Virginia to end at a black center, a *centro negro*.[49] (See Figure 3.)

This "black spiral" of notes in a (sea) blue mood is an iteration of what Benítez Rojo famously called the "repeating island." "What is it that repeats?" he asked rhetorically in the introduction to his classic text on Caribbean culture. "Let's say the unforeseen relation between

ESPIRAL NEGRA

a Piet Mondian bailando
al woogie-boogie
al boogie-woogie
al Haig
con elegguas a la Cigale
cajas huesos botellas en los tobillos al Cotton Club
bambú de las Antillas con campanillas al Chori otra vez
frascos llenos de piedras a Nueva Orleans en las muñecas al Tin Angel
quijadas de caballo a La Habana de la Costa de Oro al Riverside
tríangulo banjo cueros a Congo Square del Congo a Virginia al Saint Germain
con cajas de tabaco de Nigeria a Río del centro negro al Tabou
al Eddie Condon de Río a Recife del Río al Caméléon
al Central Plaza los reyes sometidos con cascabeles al Half note
al Stuyvesant Casino las mejillas tatuadas con castillos de plumas al Chori
al Jimmy Ryan's inmóvil como un río con pulseras de oro al Cafe Bohemia
al Ember's wasn't dat a wide ribber spiritual/spiral al Nick's
al Voyager's room flechas rojas, minúsculas al Society
al Composers al Cafe Metropole
al Savoy ballroom al Birdland
al Apollo Theater al Carnegie Hall
al Ecole Julliard

Figure 3. Severo Sarduy, "Espiral negra" (1970). Courtesy of the Herederos de Severo Sarduy.

a dance movement and the baroque spiral of a colonial railing" (4). Or of an *espiral negra.* A swirling and evolving Atlantic that engulfs the syncopated rhythms of Mondrian (visual, abstract geometric painting) and bebop (sonic, nonrepresentational improvisation).

We see a canon of concretude emerging that draws on circum-Atlantic archives, underwritten by the histories of slavery and emancipation that shape many of the aesthetic positions developed. Still, it is not a solely black Atlantic, and the object that emerges and dissolves in the arc of Sarduy's study, and in this book, only sometimes coincides with what Moten describes as a black radical tradition of vanguard poetics that emerges from a speech whose "elevating disruptions of the verbal," like those Mullen observes, "take the rich content of the object's/commodity's aurality outside the confines of meaning . . . by way of this material trace" (6). Instead, "Hacia la concretud" progresses like the storm of "Espiral negra," circling elliptically about concretude, throwing out with centrifugal force the elements that make up the aesthetic: Mondrian's fusion with jazz; pure sound and pure image; the signifier decoupled from the signified; and an outside to exchange value. Concretude is baroque excess, artificiality. It is communications technology and Cuban clichés. It is *Galaxias* and tropical fruit and geometric order. Pairs, often opposites, accrue: Lezamian fixity and flux; Cuban and Brazilian literature; order and nonsense.[50]

The poem's image of a circling system—that hurricane so often thematized in Caribbean literature—also nods to the 1950s movement of cybernetics, concerned with self-generating systems and an important influence on both Brazilian concrete poets and some of the French intellectual currents around Sarduy. Sarduy was a member of the French structuralist group Tel Quel, for instance, a context for his interest in how concrete poetics interrupted the equivalences established between a word and the thing it represented, or paper and gold ("Towards Concreteness" 62), and for objects' importance to a new kind of novel, the *nouveau roman.* An interest in the larger systems into which subjects are inserted likewise informs Sarduy's notion of concretude as "post-subjective": as "a production of meaning before, or outside of, the subject" ("Towards Concreteness" 64).[51]

Theorizing postsubjectivity was widespread in his adopted France in these years. The philosopher of science Gilbert Simondon, a significant influence on Deleuze and Bernard Stiegler and a figure who has recently been rediscovered by the field of new media studies, proposed a theory of *concrétisation* in 1958.[52] Simondon—better known for his theory of a relational process of individuation—proposed that *technics* or technology tends toward *concrétisation* as it moves from abstract principles to increasingly self-sufficient systems. *Concrétisation* represented for Simondon a new, machinic ontology whose import he curiously tied to Atlantic history: Simondon argued rather scandalously that Western philosophy must adapt to technical objects in the same way that, in the face of Atlantic slavery, philosophy had had to theorize abolition and affirm "the value of the human person" (9). Whereas romanticism had to defend subjects and personality against the objectification of racialized slavery, twentieth-century philosophy had to affirm a posthuman, postsubjective exteriority. A becoming-individual, beyond the categories of subjects and objects, that Simondon sees in both humans and machines in the twentieth century (later picked up by Deleuze) was the extension of a process of subjectivization in the face of objectivizing slavery during the romantic period.[53] In these years, too, Marshall McLuhan—translated into Portuguese by concrete poet and semiotician Décio Pignatari—was busy perceiving, in inventions such as the telegraph, humankind's "outering or extension of consciousness," as nerves moved outside of the body.[54]

In summary, these were some of the immediate contexts for Sarduy's concretude: the cybernetics of the postwar period, French structuralism and poststructuralism, with which Sarduy was intimately acquainted and to which he contributed, and above all Sarduy's own research into and writing on Latin American baroque poetics, including Brazilian concrete poetry and Cuban popular culture. The question remains, however, how the earlier vanguards, cited in these essays, and Martí's, Sousândrade's, and Maeztu's "concreteness" might connect to Sarduy's mid- and late twentieth-century aesthetics.

In "Towards Concreteness" Sarduy argued that Brull's "orthophonic" daughters belonged to a discontinuous textual history marked by "constant vacillations and reverses, by leaps and useless repetitions, by parodies and plagiarisms, a history almost without dates: synchronic vision of what has been, is being and will be written—like a single web that expands across all time and all languages" (62). He admits that in tracing the history of Brazilian concrete poetry, it would have made more literary historical sense to examine Brull's peers in Brazil—Oswald de Andrade, João Cabral de Melo Neto—than Brull himself. But he passes over these more sensible options in favor of the "orthophonic girls" and a stubbornly nonlinear history ("Rumo à concretude," 118–19). If Sarduy suggests a dense map, he does not spell it out. The following chapters offer one possible constellation.

CHAPTER 2

José Martí's Material Traces

Martí's claim that writing's art lay in "making concrete" has been seen by some as a kind of symbolist poetics, by others as an attempt to freeze contingency.[1] Few would disagree that the aesthetic is connected to Martí's work as a New York–based journalist charged with rendering colorful, terrible, and transient scenes for readers in Latin America; Julio Ramos reads it as part of Martí's assumption of an ideology of work and efficiency (*Desencuentros* 174). But here I wish to call attention to how it functions, too, as a description of his pioneering formal and grammatical innovations—innovations that gave shape to new temporal and geopolitical rearrangements, pieces that he assembled from a catastrophic history. As Martí wrote elsewhere, "A vida a retazos, poesía de retazos" [for a shattered life, a poetry of shards], shards of an Atlantic history as scattered and as interconnected as the Cuban archipelago (*Obras completas* 22:309).[2]

This chapter examines the emergence of Martí's poetics of the concrete during a career that spanned romantic and postromantic styles. Martí's poetics map onto broader literary trends: he is, of course, considered an inaugurator of *modernismo*. But his poetics also responds to specific political pressures. It shifts its target from *political* to *economic* sovereignty, following changing structures of power in the Atlantic (the end of a formal Spanish empire; increasing U.S. economic power in the region).

When targeting Spanish empire, Martí's rhetoric addresses questions of legal sovereignty, independence, and republicanism. Here

Martí's engagement with the categories of subject and object enact a trend that Juan Marinello saw as common among American romanticisms: all sport a "messianic zeal" that abandons subjectivism to materialize in great, transindividual movements of liberation.[3] Later, when Martí writes against the rise of U.S. economic hegemony in the region, his language both mirrors and critiques what he sees as a specter of surplus commodities—objects—waiting to be unleashed on Latin America (*Obras completas* 6:46). To be sure, these shifts are neither absolute nor pure. Subject and object remain fluid categories in Martí. He once proposed a "filosofía de relación" [philosophy of relation] as his own version of Krausianism (a German organicism) in which reification and subjectivity would both be overcome. But the shifts are worth examining more closely to understand the connections between the historical moment and his poetics.

When Martí wrote as a teenager against Spanish rule, he did so in the context of debates about abolition and republicanism engaged during the ongoing "Ten Years War." By 1889 new fears were stirred by the Pan-American Monetary Conference, held in Washington, D.C. In his chronicles about the conference, which he attended as a delegate, Martí describes the regional threat posed by the United States in terms of products and speculation. At the same time, however, his own language grew increasingly attentive to objects and products. His unique style of "making concrete," already visible in early chronicles from the 1870s, takes on a new urgency and becomes particularly useful in the 1890s as a means for rendering a new moment in global capitalism. The critic Fina García Marruz once contrasted a baroque, frozen quality in Martí's chronicles about Spain with a proto-cinematic, fleeting temporality in his U.S. chronicles ("El tiempo" 386). While her suggestion that a comparison between Martí's chronicles from Spain and those from the United States might be revealing of his *aesthetics*—not simply his politics—inspires my reading here, I argue that Martí's chronicles and poetry do not so much place the thingly and the temporal in opposition but insist upon their fusion.

Martí's move from messianic subjects to objects imbued with multiple temporalities still smacks of a romantic idea of things, not a leaving-behind but a translation of earlier ideals. Jacques Rancière has described aesthetic romanticism as the idea that art contains many temporalities—the outmoded, the contemporary, the futuristic. In this commingling art and life "exchange their properties."[4] The overlap in temporalities, Rancière argues, allows "common objects" to become art: now "each object can be withdrawn from its condition of common use and viewed as a poetic body wearing the traces of its history" ("The Aesthetic Revolution" 143–45). Even Marx's concept of the commodity is, for Rancière, an instance of this aesthetic theory, indebted to the world of Balzac's shops ("The Politics of Literature" 21). Rancière's analysis holds for Martí's discussions of subjects and objects as well: the transition from what Ramos called the poet's "reino interior" to what we might contrast as an *objeto exterior* marks not a wholesale aesthetic or philosophical change but a continuity of reading practices—one in which, nevertheless, objects take on increasing importance.

Keeping these continuities in mind, this chapter examines how Martí's poetics themselves reflect both anticolonial politics against Spanish empire and an ambivalent embrace and critique of U.S. material culture, which he equated with both the promise of prosperity and the threat of undue economic power. In describing a future, independent Cuba situated between the two powers, Martí has recourse both to familiar romantic tropes and to postromantic, "objectivist" poetics. Sometimes, for instance, he turns to romantic prophecy and to images of animated skeletons to embody his vision of Cuba's past, present, and future. Yet to render a future time, which he sometimes figures as a millenarian, ecstatic hiatus that, like the Atlantic Ocean itself, would insulate Cuba from both powers, Martí moves from the subjective to the objective. He invents innovative diacritics to mark pauses. He recognizes that new media—from the phonograph to the now forgotten glossograph—are means to exteriorize interiority and to turn subjective unfolding into art. Martí's interest in materiality channels, but revises, an earlier messianism.

THE CRUCIAL ANTILLES

Time and space in Martí's work are inseparable. The Antilles are *crucial* in his work, as García Marruz has written, for they lie at the geographical *crux* between Africa, Europe, and the Americas.[5] Temporally, they connect the religious teleologies that drove the first transatlantic empires with the teleologies of the 1890s, which were shaped by speculative capital and ideologies of manifest destiny. The early twentieth-century capitalism cited the late medieval past. For Peter Sloterdijk, futures trading is philosophically and historically indebted to the notion of a "new world" and to global expansion: "Since Columbus's time, globalization means the general futurization of state, private and epistemological commerce."[6] Against this move, Martí will seek to create alternative times.

Martí draws on Cuba's geographic and temporal centrality when he imagines it as a foil for both Spanish empire and U.S. economic hegemony. A new temporality would engage but rewrite the providentialism of the Spanish empire on the one hand and the speed characterizing the financial speculation that Martí witnessed in New York City on the other. He uses providentialist historiography against itself. When he writes of believing in "tierras anteriores" and "tierras venideras," "prior" and "future" lands, he renders metaphorical medieval geopolitics' coincidence of time, place, and government (*Obras completas* 21:246).[7] He uses the language of *translatio imperii* but reverses its trajectory.

Economic realities bolstered the reversal. Any notion of Spain as more "advanced" than its colony Cuba was belied by the island's comparative wealth. In an 1873 article commemorating the Spanish Republic, "La República Española ante la Revolución Cubana," Martí affirms a political "reversal" of the storied westward emanation of power: "The pit [*fosa*] that divided Spain and Cuba has filled, through Spain's doing, with corpses. . . . Cuba knows that the Republic doesn't come dressed for death, but it cannot forget so many days of gallows and pain. Spain has arrived too late; the law of time condemns it [*España ha llegado tarde; la ley del tiempo la condena*] (*Obras completas* 1:93). "The law of time" condemns Spain and maps onto the *space* of the Atlantic Ocean separating metropole and colony, a *fosa*, grave or abyss, filled with death.

Elsewhere Martí asks his Spanish readers why they do not rise up in solidarity with Cuba's independence war; whether, "given these many historical reasons [*razones de tiempos*]; given all these rights acquired by constancy and the years that Cuba wished to eclipse you [*adelantarse a vosotros*], it is worth possessing a Cuba against its will, through blood and force, through a new right to conquest which, if ever execrable, is doubly so in you?" (*Obras completas* 1:101). With phrases like "razones de tiempos" and "adelantarse a vosotros," Martí employs a language of temporal and spatial progress but one in which Cuba leads Europe.

By the late nineteenth century the island was economically closer to the United States than to Spain. While anticolonial Cubans focused on formal independence from Spain and (often, but not always) opposed annexation to the United States, the United States had become Cuba's largest trading partner. By the time of the 1895 war, roughly 90 percent of Cuban exports were bound for the United States.[8] Indeed, some historians have argued that Cuban independence was the result principally of the forces from an increasingly global economy of the 1890s, rather than political pressure.[9]

In a May 2, 1895 letter to the *New York Herald* soliciting favorable coverage of the Cuban War of Independence, Martí fuses economic, moral, geographical, and temporal registers:

> Los cubanos reconocen el deber urgente que les imponen para con el mundo su posición geográfica y la hora presente de la gestación universal. . . . A la boca de los canales oceánicos, en el lazo de los tres continentes, en el instante en que la humanidad va a tropezar a su paso activo con la colonia inútil española en Cuba, y a las puertas de un pueblo perturbado por la plétora de los productos de que en él se pudiera proveer, y hoy compra a sus tiranos, Cuba quiere ser libre, para que el hombre realice en ella su fin pleno, para que trabaje en ella el mundo, y para vender su riqueza escondida en los mercados naturales de América, donde el interés de su amo español le prohíbe hoy comprar. (*Obras completas* 4:153)
>
> [Cubans recognize the urgent duty their geographic position imposes upon them with respect to the world and the present hour of universal development. . . . At the mouth of the oceans' canals, at the intersections of the three continents, in the instant in which a restless humanity is going to stumble upon the useless Spanish colony in Cuba, and at the doors of a people perturbed by the plethora of products that there could be bought, and which today it buys from its tyrants, Cuba wishes to be free, so that man can realize in her his full destiny, so that the world may set to work within her, and to sell her hidden riches in the natural markets of America, where the interest of her Spanish owner today prohibits purchases.]

The letter, crafted to foster strategic support within the United States, appeals to economic interests rather than sentiment. It argues that the revolution is born not of "patriotismo fanático" (recalling Ramos's "patrias delirantes") but of a strategy to liberate Cubans from Spain, which Martí characterizes earlier in the letter as "inferior to Cuba in its aptitude for modern work and free government" (*Obras completas* 4:152). In short, Martí presents Cuba as better prepared for modern capitalism than Spain and yet ripe for a gendered near-plunder as well. This was typical at the time: Oscar Zanetti claims that Cubans generally considered themselves superior to Spaniards: "more open, more modern, more cosmopolitan."[10] But there is a rhetorical slippage in Martí's letter from the economic to the world historical. He describes an independent Cuba, "de espíritu universal y deberes especiales en América" [with a universal spirit and special duties to the Americas], as geographically and temporally duty-bound to fulfill both the Atlantic's commercial needs and humanity's *Bildung* [*su fin pleno*] (*Obras completas* 4:152).

Martí's reassessment of Cuba's crucial, Atlantic, and ultimately universal position culminates in the messianic proclamation that "an error in Cuba, is an error in America, is an error in modern humanity" (*Obras completas* 3:143). Cuba becomes synecdochal for liberation more generally. The independence of a nation Martí called "the balance of the Americas" was to guarantee Spanish American independence and northern honor (*Obras completas* 3:142). For this crucial "future land" a new time was needed.

MARKET TIME

In the 1895 letter Martí was critical of what he perceived to be Spain's "belated" and stymied republicanism and its "belatedness" in matters of industry ("trabajo moderno"). At the same time, however, he was wary of the temporality of the global market and speculation, which he witnessed in the United States. His writing offered an alternative: his signature genres, the chronicle and the poem, themselves mark time. Just as poems divide time into syllables, rhythms, and accents, Susan Stewart has observed, so chronicles divide continuous history into chunks and series.[11] But whereas chronicles register a transitory and aging present, poetry may appeal to "a prophetic language of transition."[12]

Martí alternates between describing the present and conjuring futures. He does this most palpably in his chronicles, which he wrote for a variety of newspapers over decades, among them Mexico's *Revista Universal*, Venezuela's *Revista Venezolana*, and, principally, Argentina's *La Nación,* but also in newspapers published in New York City: *The Sun*, *The Hour*, and *La América*. In what are known as his North American scenes, written for *La Nación*, he covered a vast number of themes, from daily life in immigrant neighborhoods to congressional politics to celebrations of Americana in the U.S. West (gleaned from other newspapers). The chronicles typically juggle distant geographies and carefully modulated paces, miming the global operation of capital yet accommodating alternative temporalities.

What will be a signature use of colons is visible as early as Martí's 1875 "Fiesta en Tultepec," written when he was just twenty-two years old and living in Mexico. Notice, for instance, how he conveys the rush of a party through a chain of descriptions: "La orquesta embellecía la función a cada instante con piezas hermosas ejecutadas de una manera sorprendente; dulcificaba los instrumentos de viento: el altar estaba lleno de incienso: el templo estaba lleno de camisas blancas y rebozos azules" [The orchestra enlivened the function at every turn with beautiful pieces executed surprisingly; it sweetened the wind instruments: the altar was filled with incense: the temple was full of white shirts and blue hats].[13] But the use of colons that visually string together far-flung places and times into a delicately connected whole—a concrete diagram—comes into its own in his New York chronicles.

For example, in "Cómo se caza ahora la zorra" [How they fox hunt today], Martí likens a Newport, Rhode Island, fox hunt to speculative pursuits on Wall Street. From there he moves to reflections on the relation between political economy and form. Martí begins with a sketch of an aristocratic idyll. Suddenly the dashing lead in the hunt gets word that he has lost money in stocks and must hurry back to New York:

> ¡Y qué mal que le sienta al moderno cabalgador en esta ansiosa batida la casaca rosada! Desvístesela: da a un caballerizo el corcel de la fiesta, monta en la locomotora, digno caballo de los hombres nuevos; apéase en la Bolsa, que parece presidio, toda llena de hombres de color cetrina, y miembros pobres, como de quien no saca sus dineros de las fuentes sanas y legítimas de la naturaleza, sino de sombríos y extraviados rincones: vende y compra: grita y le gritan: manotea, como gañán que riñe: va de este lado y aquel, empujado por salvaje ola humana: con carcelarios himnos

corean los negociantes frenéticos las grandes noticias de alza y baja; como traviesos gorrioncillos cuando comienza a caer la lluvia, agrúpanse en los corredores y dan voces cuando arrecia el ruido, los niños recaderos, pobres pájaros de nido podrido. Y en una vuelta de aquella Bolsa elíptica, acaso queda en miseria, porque el río Denver baja y el Pacífico del Norte sube, el galán de rapada cabeza y atildado mostacho que poco antes movía apetitos de bellas cazadoras y lucía hinchadas riquezas en la ciudad de los palacios a orillas de la mar que nutre y embalsama.

Y así se mezclan aquí,—porque no sin intención las pongo juntas, para que como son se vean,—las primerías feroces de la vida virgen, las parodias pueriles de la vida monárquica, las convulsiones aceleradas de la vida moderna. Así corren mezclados estos meses: con botas de exploradores de las selvas llaman todavía a las puertas de estos veloces edificios,—que por lo frágiles y mudables, parecen espuma parda o encarnada;—los esposos membrudos de las desentendidas hermosuras que en salones colgados de tapices de Aubusson y de Persia, reclinan, a la lumbre misteriosa de vénetas lámparas, en cojines de raros relieves sus espaldas sedosas. (*Obras completas* 9:457–58)

[And how the pink riding jacket chafes at the modern rider in this anxious upheaval! He takes it off: gives a gentleman his party steed, mounts the locomotive, that dignified horse of modern men; he alights at the Stock Exchange, which seems a prison, all filled with ashen men of lank limbs, as belong to someone who derives his riches not from nature's healthy sources, but from dark and hidden recesses: he sells and buys: he yells and is yelled at: like a brute looking to fight: he is pushed here and there by the savage human wave: the frantic businessmen cry in prison chants the news of risings and fallings; the message boys, like mischievous sparrows in the rain, cluster in the corridors and squawk when the noise worsens, sorry birds of a rotten nest. And one turn of that elliptical Exchange, because the Denver River has lowered and the North Pacific risen, almost leaves him ruined, that gentleman of short hair and twirled mustache who so recently stoked the appetites of beautiful huntresses

> and who sported abundant riches in the city of palaces, at the banks of the bountiful, fragrant sea.
>
> And so here are mixed—because it was not without intention that I put them together, that they be seen as they are—the ferocious victors of virgin life, the puerile parodies of monarchic life, the accelerated convulsions of modern life. Mixed in this manner, the months speed by: still sporting boots of forest explorers they knock on the doors of these speedy buildings,—so fragile and mutable as to seem darkened or solidified foam;—the handsome husbands and the ignorant beauties that rest their silky backs in salons hung with tapestries from Aubusson and Persia, against cushions boasting strange reliefs, under the mysterious glow of Venetian lamps.]

The series of phrases separated by colons graphically renders a dizzying simultaneity. Each segment sandwiched between colons is a fragment of a scene held up for our inspection. The network of colons conveys the synchronic nature of the global stock market, where the fates of distant rivers and railroads shudder instantly through the Exchange, as they do the paragraph. A single turn of the Exchange leaves the protagonist "almost . . . ruined" because the Denver River has fallen and the North Pacific risen. The "puerile" reenactments of monarchy dress uncomfortably the new hunt for riches in a medley of historical moments—primitive accumulation, feudalism, and late capitalist conspicuous consumption.

It is not just the content that is concerned with shifting fortunes. The punctuation quite deliberately—"no sin intención"—renders equivalent distant actors in a global economy of speculation. The form enacts the culture of the stock market: harried, pitching, linking far and near through the exchange of commodities—made equivalent, as the colons make chunks of language equivalent. The theoretical sums exchanged between distant markets find their fleshy equivalent in the pushing, shoving crowd on the floor, where the men and, moving back to the realm of representation, words, too, come into contact: "he sells and buys: he yells and is yelled at: like a brute looking to fight: he is pushed here and there by the savage human wave: the frantic businessmen cry in prison chants the news of risings and fallings; the message boys, like mischievous sparrows in the rain, cluster in the corridors."

Elsewhere in his chronicles, however, Martí *interrupts* the flows of capital and the "accelerated convulsions of modern life." In the following excerpt, for instance, the Knights of Labor shut down a headlong rush of speculation, shut down cities, and stem the prose:

> Acá apenas se tiene tiempo para vivir. El cráneo es circo, y los pensamientos son caballos azotados. . . .
>
> Nadie se duerme, nadie se despierta, nadie está sentado: todo es galope, escape, asalto, estrepitosa caída, eminente triunfo. Es una procesión de ojos sedientos, montados sobre piernas aladas,—las piernas de Mercurio. . . .
>
> La médula se retuerce, y encoge como un cuero húmedo puesto al sol: el alma se va del cuerpo como de un pomo roto las gotas de esencia. . . .
>
> Pero en lo social, ¡cómo va creciendo, a manera de conquistador, la asociación de los Caballeros del Trabajo, que manda ya en una suma enorme de los trabajadores de los Estados Unidos, y es representante, y es gobernador, y es ministro, y gana batallas a los monopolios, y puede, si lo decide su consejo supremo secreto, hacer cesar a una misma hora el trabajo en Estados enteros! (*Obras completas* 10:363–64)
>
> [Here there is hardly time to live. The brain is a circus, and thoughts are whipped horses. . . .
>
> No one sleeps, no one awakes, no one sits down: all is gallop, escape, assault, sudden fall, eminent triumph. It is a procession of thirsty eyes, mounted on flighty legs,—the legs of Mercury. . . .
>
> The marrow retracts, curling like wet leather in the sun: the soul flees the body like essence from a broken bottle. . . .
>
> But in the social field, how the Association of Knights of Labor grows, like a conqueror, which now commands an enormous number of workers in the United States, and is representative, and governor, and minister, and wins battles against the monopolies, and can, if its secret supreme council so decides, within an hour halt work in entire States!]

In this passage the Knights of Labor freeze work in entire states, restoring a time otherwise gone like the soul that escapes from a broken bottle. The time to think, to live, to sleep, to sit is only restituted when the Knights of Labor stand up to monopolies. Martí introduces the association within his rushed chronicle as a way to halt the flow of a certain time that his prose mimics, one that is too rapid to live: the same gallop, assault, fall, triumph of the *bolsa*.

In these chronicles, Martí explicitly seeks in his prose to render the way everyday life felt in Gilded Age New York City, shaped by speculation and monopoly capitalism. Often such writing is read in contrast to Martí's lyric poetry. But if we read his poetry bearing in mind the ongoing interest in rendering temporalities, as well as Martí's interest in how history condenses into things, we find possible connections between political economy and poetic form.

Just after he reported on the Pan-American Conference held in Washington, D.C., between 1889 and 1891 (and five years after the chronicle just mentioned), Martí wrote and published his *Versos sencillos*. The preface to the poems famously links the "simple," traditional rhyme schemes with the financial and political backdrop. "My friends know," he wrote, "how these verses emerged from the heart. It was that winter of anguish, in which out of ignorance, or fanatical faith, or fear, or courtesy, Latin American nations came together in Washington, under the fearful eagle" (*Obras completas* 16:63). The preface details a retreat to the mountains to write the poems, seemingly contrasting romantic, pastoral lyricism and a frightening, imperial finance system.

But the structure of the poems permits an alternative reading. The *Versos sencillos* set up broad, abstract first couplets, followed by more particular, often devastating second ones. The first two lines proffer something *seemingly* desirable, rich, universal, or complex; the second the *actually* dear, humble, and natural. The verses move from the abstract to the material, from the classical world to intimate locales, from formal niceties to dark twists:

(from I)

Todo es hermoso y constante,
Todo es música y razón,
Y todo, como el diamante,
Antes que luz es carbón. (*Obras completas* 16:65)

[All is beautiful and constant
All is music and reason

And all, like the diamond,
Before light is coal.]

Here we move from the abstract, "constant" (universal) classical or platonic spheres of reason, beauty, and music to the dirty, primal, and productive reality of coal. Again:

(from II)

Yo sé de Egipto y Nigricia
Y de Persia y Xenophonte;
Y prefiero la caricia
Del aire fresco del monte. (*Obras completas* 16:66)

[I know of Egypt and Nigritia
And of Persia and Xenophonte;
And I prefer the caress
Of the fresh mountain air.]

The ancient lands of the classical world prove arid and distant before the tactility of the mountain breeze. Or, finally:

(from XI)

Mi paje, hombre de respeto,
Al andar castañetea:
Hiela mi paje y chispea:
Mi paje es un esqueleto. (*Obras completas* 16:84)

[My page, an honorable man,
Clacks when he walks:
My page chills and sparks:
My page is a skeleton.]

The feudal values of honor and respect cannot cover up death. In all three cases the stanzas begin with an ideal (beauty, constancy, respect) or a panoramic view, in which history is comprehensible before us like a globe (Egypt, Persia), then narrow down to a particular. First declaring something apparently abstract, universal, and benign, then zeroing in on the personal, concrete, particular, or hidden side behind these ideals, the "simple" verses are less distant from the context of the Pan-American Conference than they might seem.

In his reports on the conference, Martí sought to debunk its discourse of manifest destiny, geographic determinism, and imperial overreach; his "versos sencillos" similarly particularize the apparently universal and reveal the superficially benign to be suspect. By "concretizing" these abstractions—as he would concretize, in coeval chronicles, debates over proposed economic policies and the conference's discussion of a single pan-American currency—Martí made more tangible to his readers the abstract workings of international economic policy.

A final symptomatic correspondence between the topics of the conference and the coeval poems is possible, if far from conclusive: the poems' logic also mirrors aspects of speculation, suggesting the dialectical mode by which Martí both reproduces and critiques economic logic. The *Versos* derive their power from creating a rhythm of expected difference. The reader comes to anticipate the contrast between a statement and its modification, first couplet and second. The strategy no doubt borrows from a long tradition of popular riddle poems, Andalusian *jarchas*, and early modern enigmas. But capitalizing on difference—that difference between an abstract system and concrete reality—also recapitulates the logic of financial speculation, which Martí critiqued at various points. For speculation depends upon difference: difference in space, in markets, and in time.

Stiegler claims that the idea of "information" emerges out of nineteenth-century electronic communications networks, beginning with the telegraph. (Cuba's first telegraph lines were laid in 1844 and its first telegraph installed in 1851; the island's telegraph system was connected to the U.S. system in 1867 via a submarine cable.)[14] Minor delays in networks were quickly exploited by financial markets to great profit. For Stiegler, a seminal moment in the history of telecommunications was thus the first use in 1836 by Parisian investors of telegraphic delays in order to enrich themselves through speculation at the Bordeaux stock exchange. Stiegler refers to this manipulation of time differentials by stock markets to argue that information *as such* is defined by the fact that not everyone possesses it, "that it can itself become a commercial object, and that its value correlates with the time and place of its diffusion" (Stiegler 2:102). Information renders time a good.

Moreno Fraginals's classic study of the Cuban sugar industry, *El ingenio* (1964), makes the same argument. It emphasizes the relation between a concrete good (sugar), and the importance for futures markets of possessing information about such goods (23). In the final decades of the nineteenth century the different exchanges were not regulated, so it was possible to speculate on London prices, with New York opening five hours behind (20–21). The telegraph, which linked markets and revolutionized business practices, now "demanded an acceleration in the methods for obtaining, processing, coding and decoding information, laying the foundation for what many decades later would be called 'informatics'" (25). These are the connections and media networks that "Cómo se caza ahora la zorra" makes visual and into which Martí liked to throw a wrench: as José Lezama Lima once observed, Martí's surprising syntax and connections reverse expected causality to propose new times.[15]

CUBA SUI GENERIS

Martí imagined new temporalities through a variety of strategies: by halting or reversing apparently inevitable flows; by inventing new diacritics, as we will see later in the chapter; and by modeling a Cuban national time on a notion of his own subjective exceptionalism. In Martí's work, sons remake fathers, spared of the need for mothers: "Nació en si mismo / hijo de si mismo"; "Yo nací de mi mismo"; "obras literarias son como los hijos: rehacen a sus padres" (*Obras completas* 21:162, 167, 164) [He was born of himself / son of himself; I was born of myself; Literary works are like children: they remake their parents (or fathers)]. Martí's revision of the linear, reproductive logic that undergirds the nation thus hinges upon a certain gynophobia.[16] Male authorship takes the place of female reproduction in producing the future.

In addition to male parthenogenesis, Martí turns to resurrection as another form of emergence without reproduction. Such imagery was common in romantic rhetoric. Ian Balfour has pointed out how Fichte's *Addresses to the German Nation of 1808* cite Ezekiel to liken the German state to a skeleton in need of revival: "“"I will lay sinews upon you, and will bring up flesh upon you, and cover you with skin, and put breath in you, and ye shall live; and ye shall know that I am the Lord . . . there was a noise, and behold a shaking, and the bones came together"”" (51). Martí does something similar. (Fichte may or may not have been an influence on Martí, whose notes do show that he knew Fichte's work.)

Martí's poems are littered with animated bones standing in for the nation. As we have seen, the *Versos sencillos* emphasize a clacking, sparking skeleton. The poem "Astro" features a corpse made of "warm bones" that under a "sol radiante / Resucitó gozoso, vivió un día, / Y se volvió a morir—" [radiant sun / Is resuscitated with great joy, lived a day / And died again—].[17] In "Crin Hirsuta" it will be the poet's verse that rises up like blood, for which Martí provides his own translation: like a horse "[m]y tortured verse rises up: / Yes; but it rises up: such as, / When the knife is thrust [?] into the / Neck of a bull, a thread of blood surges. / It takes Love to inspire melodies" (*Poesía completa* 98). The skeleton clacks, the lukewarm bones live and die again, and his verse gives a *salto mortale*.

Bodies in pieces have a long poetic tradition in *blazons*, the medieval practice of describing women through discrete body parts: lips, breast, eyes. It is not Woman, however, but Cuba that is continually dismembered, and reconstituted, by Martí's *blazons*. In "Isla Famosa" [Famous island], Martí writes: "Aquí estoy, solo estoy, despedazado. / Ruge el cielo: las nubes se aglomeran, / Y aprietan, y ennegrecen, y desgajan" [Here I am, alone, I am, torn to pieces. / The sky rumbles: the clouds rush together, /And darken, and blacken, and break apart] (*Obras completas* 16:163).[18] The island torn to pieces is Cuba as much as it is Martí. His well-known poem "Amor de ciudad grande" continues the theme. The rapid pace of the city forces a premature aging. A shattered lung reveals a petrified interior: "De gorja son y rapidez los tiempos / . . . / Si los pechos / Se rompen de los hombres, y las carnes rotas / Por tierra ruedan, ¡no han de verse / Más que frutillas estrujadas!" [Times of gorge and rush are these: / . . . If men's bosoms / were to open and their torn flesh / fall to the earth, inside would be / nothing but a scatter of small, crushed fruit!] (*Poesía completa* 89; *José Martí* 63).[19] The small crushed fruit suggest sterility: the petrified and shattered male poet anticipates a resurrection without reproduction.

In the suggestive lines of one notebook entry, "¿Qué es esto, que me penetra, y como bálsamo suave, dulcemente en mí se esparce? ¿Gozo de la tierra—o proximidad de la Muerte?" [What is this, that penetrates me, and like a smooth balm, sweetly scatters within me? Love of earth—or Death's approach?], Martí is penetrated by his love of earth, by the poet's ink typically directed at woman (*Obras completas* 21:170). He is impregnated by the chivalric (homoerotic) love of death that informs nationalism. The ejaculative connotations of *esparcir* recall the title of Petrarch's *Rima sparse* (in Spanish *Rima esparcida*), in which the Italian poet described Laura in *blazons*. So when Martí writes in the poem "He vivido: Me he muerto" that "mis restos propios

/ recojo" [I gather up / my own remains], we can read him as saying that his self-resurrection is the act of a simultaneous poet and muse, man and woman, dismemberer and rebuilder, living and dead. Martí/ Cuba alike are shorn of genealogies.

With woman factored out of Martí's birth of the nation, writing takes her place. Martí's poems re-member the war-torn, slavery-era, and immigrant nation. He summons the dead to life. In one poem the patria is a cadaver that "se levanta / Y a los ciclópeos golpes de su brazo / En tierra el opresor vencido rueda;— / Y, la avarienta muerte / En vida exuberante se convierte:—" [Arises / and from the circling blows of his arms— / the oppressor rolls defeated. / And avaricious death becomes joyful life— (*Poesía completa* 275). In this poem, written in Madrid in 1871, the nation torn apart by the ongoing abolitionist and anticolonial war (1868–78) arises from death to defeat its oppressors.[20] The dashes in the poem jerk to life the skeletal marionette of the patria.

Ada María Teja writes that Martí's dashes embody a "leap to freedom" (197–98). At other times, however, they seem spokes in the wheel of a history that spins but does not advance, as when Martí describes himself as a vulture eating itself: "Yo,—embriagado en mis penas,— me devoro, / Y sus miserias lloro, / Y buitre de mí mismo, me levanto, / Y me hiero y me curo con mi canto, / Buitre a la vez que altivo Prometeo" [I,—drunk on my troubles,—devour myself, / And cry their misery, / And, my own vulture, I raise myself up, / and I wound and cure myself with my song, / Vulture like arrogant Prometheus] (*Obras completas* 21:21). This strange hiatus, reminiscent of Prometheus or of the Egyptian *ouroboros*, the snake that eats its own tail, is a suspension of history, embodied in the poet. "Ugolino gnawed at his son," Martí writes, "but Dante, at himself: . . . Suspended, suddenly, historic life" (*Obras completas* 8:151). Martí spells his own death and his resurrection through self-cannibalism, yielding what Teja terms the "suspension of an oppressive law," a messianic suspension of time for judgment and redemption (197).

Rafael Rojas has argued that Martí's U.S. chronicles are defined by just such a time outside of time: parades, funerals, election day.[21] This makes Martí an unreconstructed romantic in Rojas's eyes and such episodes a "refugio vegetal," a retrenchment inseparable from a revolutionary zeal that is fully utopian—which has for Rojas here negative connotations (*José Martí* 23). In Rojas's reading, Martí's Republic can only be *por venir* [yet to come]: "Rather than the origin of all Cuban politics, the frustration of his republic represents the endpoint of all

Martí's poetics" (24). Martí's romanticism—political and poetic—*requires* a postponed, frustrated republic.

Martí's emphasis on a time outside of time mirrored his view of the Cuban republic as a space beyond the competing powers buffeting it. Martí wrote in his famous last letter to Manuel Mercado, "Every day now I am in danger of giving my life for my country . . . in order to prevent, by the timely independence of Cuba, the United States from extending its hold across Antilles and falling with all the greater force on our lands of America (*Selected Writings* 347). Martí's death, in his logic, leads to Cuban, Antillean, and finally pan-American independence. Cuba becomes the messianic savior of the Americas.

In typological thought the American continent itself had been conceived as a temporal hinge ensuring eschatological completion, a "threshold—new World to Old, mediate end to the Next" (Kadir 112). Martí's Cuba becomes a doubly *crucial* hinge in time and space. Millenarianism, whose name derives from the one thousand years during which Satan is locked in an abyss before rejoining the celestial apocalyptic battle, describes Martí's mission, too. For millennium is conceived as "a transitory phase of the future, an intermezzo between the old and the new world": Cuba's symbolic role for Martí and, arguably, for the later 1959 revolution.[22]

Messianism and millenarianism, products of crisis, are burdened with the task of convincing followers that new events confirm prior knowledge.[23] Martí, too, had to fill with belief the gap between death and resurrection, between 1868 and 1895. He was keenly aware of messianism's sublunary political drive, writing of the Jews that they call God that which they lack, a "liberator" and that Jeremiah "says the same thing I do: redemption will come to men via men" (*Obras completas* 22:45). Martí's exilic years allegorize a time that Arcadio Díaz-Quiñones locates precisely between the messianic and the political (261).

FROM NEW GRAMMAR TO NEW MEDIA

Building upon his signature use of the dash and the colon, Martí devised new grammatical marks to score new measures. He was frustrated that publishers ignored his deliberate attempts to alter punctuation and language in order to render "lo que veo, y lo veo todo en sus adjuntos, antecedentes y ramazones" [what I see, and I see it in all its connections, antecedents, and branchings] in a language that, he realized, must "appear new" to the typesetter (Marinello, *Obras martianas* 89). Martí mused about what kind of "material trace," or "huella material," thought leaves in memory (*Obras completas* 21:388). He followed this question with the understanding that a new grammar was needed to render thought and voice more accurately (see Figure 4):

> Ortografía.—
> Por lo menos, hacen falta dos signos:
> Coma menor, ,
> Por ejemplo:
> "Juntos de noche, Hafed , juntos del día."
> Así indico que la pausa en *Hafed* ha de ser más larga que en *noche*: si no ¿cómo lo indico? ¿cómo estorbo que otro pueda leer: "Juntos de noche,—Hafed, juntos del día," desluciendo el verso, y poniendo a Hafed en el segundo inciso, cuando quiero yo que esté en el primero?
> Y otro signo, *el acento de lectura o de sentido*, para distinguirlo del acento común de la palabra.
> Y otro mas, *el guión menor*. (*Obras completas* 21:388)

> [Orthography.—
> At least two symbols are needed:
> The small comma, ,
> For example:
> "Together at night, Hafed , together in the day."
> Thus I indicate that the pause after *Hafed* must be longer than that after *night*: if not, how to indicate this? How else prevent another from reading, "Together at night,—Hafed, together in the day," tarnishing the verse, and placing Hafed in the second clause, when I want him in the first?
> And another symbol, *the reading or meaning accent*, to be distinguished from the common word accent.
> And another, the *small dash*.]

This new punctuation, from the "small comma" and the "small dash" to Martí's signature long dash, was intended to create new measures.

We know from his notebooks that Martí had read Friedrich Hölderlin, though we cannot be sure which works. But independent of the question of influence, the two poets take a similar stance toward

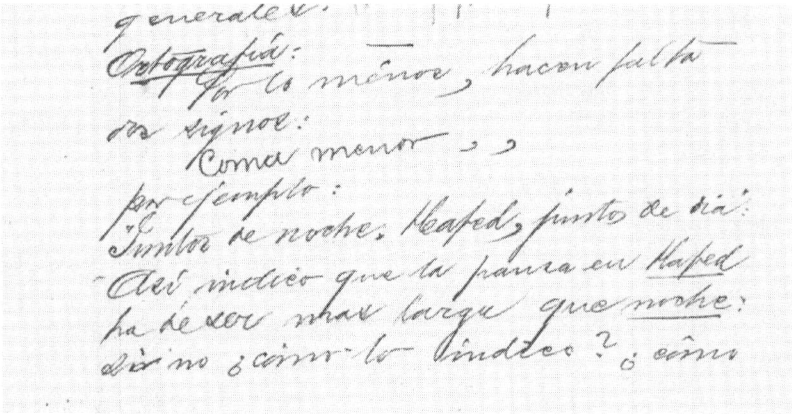
generales.
Ortografía:
Por lo menos, hacen falta
dos signos:
Coma menor , ,
por ejemplo:
Juntos de noche, Hafed, juntos de día:
Así indico que la pausa en Hafed
ha de ser más larga que noche:
dí no ¿cómo lo indico? ¿cómo

Figure 4. José Martí, "Coma menor." Courtesy of the Centro de Estudios Martianos.

poetry's relation to registering time and history. In a short prose piece, "Remarks on Oedipus," Hölderlin outlined a relation between punctuation and historicity. "Remarks" argued that poetic caesurae create counterrhythmic breaks that hinge two "moments." While a caesura normally refers to a break or joint in the metrical structure of a line of poetry, Hölderlin extended it to include suspensions in narrative.[24] Deleuze extrapolated from "Remarks on Oedipus" an entire theory of history and time as the measure of ethical or political acts.[25] In Deleuze's reading, Hölderlin's caesura is a messianic interruption on either side of which time is unevenly distributed and past and present fixed (*Difference* 89).[26] The past is the time in which one is not yet adequate to the task at hand. The present means readying for a future act.

Martí proposes something similar. He fashions past and future around breaks. The caesura—the utopian location outside of empire—fashions multiple temporalities. It cleaves into being a "before" and "after" crisis, two sides to an Atlantic *fosa*. In Deleuze's ethics of the caesura, the pause before an act explodes subjectivity to enable collective action. Martí similarly feels that times of transition demand an actor who subsumes the subjective in the communal.[27]

Media can facilitate alternative structures of time and community. Ramos sees in Martí's affirmation of the concrete a *modernista* who assimilated an ideology of specialization and autonomy, split into a writing of machines and a "reino interior." Instead of seeing the two as opposed complements, we might better understand Martí's poetics of concretude as exteriorizing the interior, just as his "coma menor" would materialize a pause in the voice or the moving eye. Martí often describes communication technologies as extensions, prosthetics, or *concretizations* of "voice," both literary and corporeal.[28] He celebrates protean, immaterial qualities of media and their new configurations of time as infinitely retrievable.

In "'Ciencia Loca y Sabia Locura'—Libro curioso y usos practicas del fonógrafo," published in the *Boletín de El Partido Liberal* in 1890, Martí notes the phonograph's utility for poets and businessmen alike. (Martí wrote these pieces for income, making him both the poet and businessman he describes.) The new recording technology allows one to swiftly channel oneiric thoughts in the heat of the moment, then restructure them in the cold light of day:

> [E]n las altas horas de la noche, cuando las ideas echan alas, y se tiñe la sombra de colores, y pasa una virgen llorando sobre su corazón roto . . . el poeta, que no puede perder tiempo en buscar fósforos, sacude a las sabanas fogosas, palpa en la oscuridad el fonógrafo que tiene a su cabecera, habla por la trompeta al rollo que recoge sus imágenes: y a la mañana siguiente, con poner en el fonógrafo el rollo, los versos salen cantando. El comerciante hace lo mismo. (*Obras completas* 13:509)
>
> [In the late hours of the night, when ideas hatch wings, and shadows are bathed in colors, and a virgin passes crying her broken heart . . . the poet, who cannot waste time looking for matches, shakes off the burning sheets, feels in the darkness for the phonograph he has at his head, speaks through the trumpet to the roll that collects his images: and the next morning, putting the rolls into the phonograph, the verses emerge singing. The businessman does the same.]

Later this heady subjectivity is processed by technology to arrive concretely on the page:

> Hay veces en que la mente está como encendida, y manda andar: la mano está para espada, más que para pluma: sentarse en la silla, es como sentarse en un potro: la cabeza,

> alta, padece de inclinarse: las ideas chispean: no se puede soportar presencia humana: se echarían abajo las paredes de la casa, y se le diría al sol, "¡aquí estoy!"—el fonógrafo, manso y veloz, recibe entonces la palabra impaciente del militar, del ministro, del abogado, del orador: el amanuense, allá donde no molesta su tecleo en la máquina de escribir, vierte al papel la frase vigorosa y fresca, sin los rasguños y torturas de la palabra escrita: se escribe menos y mejor, porque la idea sale como se la concibe. (*Obras completas* 13:509)
>
> [There are times that the mind is as if on fire, and calls for action: the hand is readier for the sword than for the quill: to sit in a chair, is to sit in a field: the head, high, suffers to be bent: ideas spark: human presence is intolerable: the mind would topple the walls of the house, and say to the sun, "here I am"!—the phonograph, docile and swift, receives then the impatient word of the military man, of the minister, of the lawyer, of the orator: the amanuense, there where his clacking on the typewriter does not irritate, sprays onto the paper the vigorous and fresh lines, without the tortured scratchings of the written word: one writes less and better, as the idea comes out as it is conceived.]

Over the course of this description, Martí's romantic poet gives way to a pragmatic businessman. The familiar chain of simultaneous sensations here experienced by the poet (winged ideas, colored shadows, burning sheets) is a romantic jumble given order by the phonograph, just as the chronicle's first example cedes to a second one in which the military man, lawyer, and orator turn to the machine for more concise writing.

We see Martí's interest in the phonograph's ability to fix language objectively in a chronicle that he wrote on the "glossograph" exhibited at the Vienna Electricity Convention.[29] Martí extols this forgotten invention, whose function is to translate speech directly into symbols on a page:

> El glosógrafo es un aparatillo ingeniosísimo, que puesto en lo interior de la boca, a la que se acomoda sin trabajo, no impede el habla, y la reproduce sobre el papel con perfección

> de escribiente del siglo XV. Sólo exige que se pronuncie con toda claridad; y cada sílaba, al punto que es pronunciada, ya es colocada sobre el papel que la espera, sin molestia alguna para el que habla; y sin confusion para el que lee, una vez que aprende la correspondencia de los nuevos signos.— . . . De tal modo está construido el aparato que una vez puesto en la boca, queda en contacto con el cielo de ésta, los labios y la lengua. Un registro electromagnético recibe los sonidos y los trasmite al papel.
>
> [The glossograph is an ingenious contraption, which, placed in the interior of the mouth, which it easily accommodates, does not impede speech, and reproduces it on paper with the perfection of a fifteenth-century scribe. It only requires that one speak with total clarity; and each syllable, as it is pronounced, is instantly put onto the paper awaiting it, with no bother to the person speaking; and without confusion for the reader, once he learns the correspondence with the new signs.— . . . The apparatus is constructed in such a way that it remains in contact with the roof, the lips, and the tongue. An electromagnetic register receives the sounds and transmits them to the paper. (*Obras completas* 8:418)]

Again the poet is interested in the transmission of rapid speech from the mind to concrete representation on the page. The glossograph materializes the voice. The famous opening lines from the poem "Amor de ciudad grande" are literalized: "De gorja son y rápidez los tiempos" [times of rush and gorge are these]. In these passages the voice—specifically the *recorded* voice—turns words into acts.[30]

FILOSOFÍA DE RELACIÓN

I have argued thus far that Martí uses prophetic, resurrectory imagery; typographical, grammatical, or narrative forms of caesurae; and descriptions of new media to render a moment in which changes were occurring in sovereignty and the global economy. Romantic tropes and ideas about time share space with an awareness of temporality as determined by material forces in financial capitals such as New York City. Similarly, Martí first describes *subjective* fragments or *retazos*—corpses and body parts that revive in order to yield a future, postindependence sovereignty—that are later complemented by more object-like *retazos* as well: products, fragments of buildings and of language. This compressed evolution from body parts to things recalls Walter Benjamin's connection established in *The Arcades Project* between baroque allegories of corpses and a nineteenth-century allegory of souvenirs.[31]

I would like to emphasize that Martí's later perspective is not a wholesale revision: he had a longstanding interest in philosophy's *vaivén* between subjects and objects. In an 1877 piece titled "La poesía" published in *El Federalista* in Mexico he ventured that a "subjective" poet is he who, in painting his "own self," "toma en sí mismo el motivo—*sujeto*—de sus inspiraciones, y no procura que del exterior—*objeto*—vengan las inspiraciones a su alma. . . . Y si copia el poeta los objetos, ya materiales o morales, debe para esto observar tanto, que en sí compendie todas las formas naturales, todos los medios de expresión de los objetos que en su poesía va a reproducir" [takes himself to be the motive—*subject*—of his inspirations and doesn't seek to derive from the exterior—*object*—his soul's inspirations. . . . And if the poet copies objects, be they material or moral, he must observe so closely that within him arise a compendium of all the natural forms, all the means of expression of the objects he will reproduce in his poetry] (*Obras completas: Edición crítica* 5:28). Here the young Martí believes in a sharp divide between subjective and objective aesthetics. A couple of years later he jotted down notes, probably from other philosophers, for a series of debates over realism and idealism held in Guanabacoa, on the outskirts of Havana. He describes one class of beauty that is objective and another subjective and writes, "there are plastic arts [*artes plásticas*], and subjective arts" (*Obras completas: Edición crítica* 6:44, 46). But in notes on the history of philosophy he commended thinkers who moved *beyond* such a divide. While Schelling confused subject and object, "the great" Hegel put them in relation, and Krause, "greater still," proposed an "intermediary" philosophy that would study how subjects examine objects, a philosophy Martí thought to call "Filosofía de relación" [Philosophy of relation] (*Obras completas: Edición crítica* 5:213).

Martí's "philosophy of relation" anticipates the poet's own transition from emphasizing the subject to emphasizing objects as vessels for historical import: "La cosa más pequeña, insignificante en sí, adquiere valor sumo, como símbolo del tiempo. El espíritu de los hombres afectado de uno o de otro modo, según las influencias que en él actúan, se refleja con todos sus accidentes en cada uno de los objetos que imagina para el adorno o para el uso" [The smallest thing, insignificant in itself, acquires the utmost value as a symbol of the times. Men's spirit, affected in some way or another, according to operative influences, is reflected with all its accidents in every one of the objects imagined for decoration or use] (*Obras completas* 19:296).[32] This is Hegel's *Aesthetics*, or perhaps Schelling, but translated into a kind of materialist poetics.[33] Yet it displaces a romantic rhetoric of agency with a historicist reading: "Men are products, expressions, reflections. They live either coinciding with or in marked differentiation from their era" (*Obras completas* 13:34). "Men," "the smallest thing," and poetry are made equal vessels for registering historicity (Martí writes elsewhere that "Poetry is, above all, the best method for embalming essential ideas") (*Obras completas* 21:403). All encapsulate contingency in materiality. As in Hegel, subjectivity and objectivity are reconciled in the concrete. In a passage in which Martí moves from Plato to Leibniz to describe the relationship between individuals, nations, and a historical moment, he ends with the statement, "concretion is divinity": "La individual es un resumen breve de la vida histórica; estudiando con espíritu analógico . . . se entiende el monismo de Platón y las Mónadas de Leibnitz [*sic*].—Todo, ascendiendo, se generaliza,—Todo; descendiendo, se hace múltiple. Reducir, concretar, es ascender. . . . La concreción es la divinidad" [Individual life is a brief summary of historical life; studying with an analogical spirit . . . one understands Plato's monism and Leibniz's Monads.—Everything, in ascending, is generalized,—Everything; descending, is multiplied. To reduce, to concretize, is to ascend. . . . Concretion is divinity] (*Obras completas* 19:441–42).

Against a Western philosophical tradition that posits a subject's appropriation of an object, critics such as Theodor Adorno have theorized poetic language as *anti*-appropriative, a shuttle between the subjective and the objective.[34] Martí sought to work out these relations both in his study of philosophy and in his own poetry. His readings in German idealism suggested to him the indivisibility of the subjective and the objective, even if he continued to ponder their relative weight in lyric. Adorno, a half century later, summed up the question of the "subjectivism" of lyric in his essay "On Lyric Poetry and Society" by arguing (in a modernist context, to be sure) that the subjective cannot *not* be objective, cannot *not* be shaped by societal forces (*Notes to Literature* 43).

In his notes on poets and painters Martí repeatedly praises a language of things. He italicizes a line from an English-language book review "*his words are things*" (*Obras completas* 22:89). Another entry ironically praises the effect of "despotism" on literature and adds drily, again in English, "One of the results of the terrors of the Russian penal code was that novelists learned compression and vigor" (*Obras completas* 22:88). Was Martí's exile, too, a laboring in terror that produced a concrete writing? Elsewhere he exhorts language to be "mathematical, geometric, sculptural" (*Obras completas* 21:255).

In Martí's work the thingliness of words is not only the flip side of the historicity narratable in things but represents his interest in language's condensation. His taste for others' terseness accounts for his interest in *dichos*, or sayings, scores of which he collected from throughout the Americas and which in his notebook immediately precede his celebration of concretude. Martí expressed an almost Heideggerian belief in the power of etymology, referring to linguistic use as a "layer" surrounding words behind which one had to peer to get at their "body": "Se siente en este examen que algo se quiebra, y se ve lo hondo. Han de usarse las palabras como se ven en lo hondo, en su significación real, etimológica y primitiva, que es la única robusta, que asegura duración a la idea expresada en ella.—Las palabras han de ser brillantes como el oro, ligeras como el ala, sólidas como el mármol" [One feels that something breaks apart in this examination, and depth revealed. Words must be used as they appear in such depths, in their real meaning, etymological and primitive, which is the only robust meaning, which assures the duration of the idea expressed in them.—Words should be brilliant like gold, light as a wing, solid as marble] (*Obras completas* 21:164). Martí believes in a "real" meaning, from which descends later uses.[35]

This interest in language's materiality earned Martí the label of baroque or neobaroque, "with its well-known characteristics of individualism and plastic concretion," an early modern imperial style repurposed during a period of late nineteenth-century imperial tensions.[36] Of course, the new moment was not reducible to changes in empire. The concept of "sculptural" language might have appealed to Martí for other reasons—his interest in the building blocks of contemporary cities, for example. Ramos has rightfully noted the poet's elitist recoil from urban abjection. But I want to emphasize that Martí also believed in the urban as a site of potential. We have evidence for this in the plans for what would have been a remarkable book of poems about New York's Fulton Market, the "book of landscape poetry: The Book of Work," as seen in the passage with which I opened the book. From the opening scene, Martí combines a chronicle's epigrammic snapshots of the city with a concise poetic sensibility:

> Fulton—allá van copia y lápiz del copiador poeta—limones italianos—naranjas de Valencia—enorme coliflor—plantas de América—en vasos de Pompeya—la muchedumbre corre—se estruja, avanza, vuela—flor de carnes tibias—asciende de las cuevas. (*Obras completas* 22:314)
>
> [Fulton—there go the copying poet's copy and pen—Italian lemons—oranges from Valencia—enormous cauliflower—American plants—in vases from Pompeii—the crowd runs about—squeezes by, advances, flees—flower of warm flesh—ascends from the caves.]

The temptation to read these notes as prose poems is not, perhaps, far-fetched if we consider an English-language piece published in *The Hour* in October 1880 shortly after Martí's arrival in New York, in which he used the same form to register a speech he associated with the rapid communication of the railway era: "among Americans . . . a sentence is an electric commotion. . . . We see that we are in the land of railroads. 'That's all'—'didn't'—'won't'—'ain't'—'Indeed'—'Nice weather'—'Very pleasant'—'Coney Island'—'Excursion.' That is all that I can seize": fragments of a language as difficult to arrest as the flow of goods in Fulton Market (*Obras completas* 19:122).

At Fulton Market American plants sprout from Pompeiian vases as old form cedes to new organicism, pulsing with life like the sexualized crowd. The market indicates the networks Martí depicts in other chronicles, the Italian lemons jostling against oranges from Spain like the anonymous members of a crowd he often describes as immigrant. The litany of objects and the style construct a poetics of global markets.

Martí's fascination with the market—not a necessarily modern one, to be sure—alternates with a critique of the role that products played in the transition from an era of colonial rule to a moment often termed neocolonial. U.S. products, he believed, were flooding Latin American markets, due to a U.S. economy erected on credit, overproduction, and "the hopes of selling dearly poor articles to the weak nations of Latin America" (*Obras completas* 22:256). Martí believed that surplus, inferior U.S. products incarnated a new threat distinct from Spanish colonial policy, which, on the other hand, he faulted for denying Cubans free trade.[37]

Martí's notes toward the *Libro del Trabajo* are undated. It is a pity they cannot be set in closer historical relation to his observations on the first Pan-American Congress, though they appear to be from roughly the same years.[38] In 1889, reporting on the conference, he provides impressions of a shift in regional hegemony materializing before his eyes:

> Jamás hubo en América, de la independencia acá, asunto que requiera más sensatez, ni obligue a más vigilancia, ni pida examen más claro y minucioso, que el convite que los Estados Unidos potentes, repletos de productos invendibles y determinados a extender sus dominios en América, hacen a las naciones americanas de menos poder. . . . De la tiranía de España supo salvarse la América española; y ahora . . . ha llegado para la América española la hora de declarar su segunda independencia. (*Obras completas* 6:46)
>
> [There has never been in America, since Independence to the present, an affair which requires more sensitivity, nor calls for as much vigilance, nor demands so clear and careful examination, as the invitation that the powerful United States, replete with surplus products and determined to extend its dominion over the Americas, makes to the less powerful nations of the Americas . . . from Spanish tyranny Spanish America knew how to save itself; and now . . . the time has come for Spanish America to declare its second independence.]

In the earlier nineteenth century, independence was sought from "tyranny"; now it had to be won from an inundation of products. Martí's concern with overproduction was common during late nineteenth-century monetary debates in the United States (Rosenberg 9). It dovetailed with discussions of capital's migration to new markets. An essay titled "The Economic Basis of Imperialism" (1898), for instance, argued that "advanced nations had invested in all the production that they could profitably accommodate and now faced a 'superabundance of loanable capital'" in search of new markets (Rosenberg 15). But just as it is impossible to reduce Martí's economic thought to a single position, so his reflections on such production do not stall at the merely pessimistic. Martí likely felt that his proposed *Libro del Trabajo* described promise as well.

ARCHITECTURE OF THE FUTURE

"The Book of Work" presumably referred to the work of those who sold wares at Fulton Market. But the title also suggests Martí's fascination with construction—of words as much as of things. His penchant for *retazos*, *pedazos*, and *trozos* is not reducible to merely a romantic attachment to ruins. He was concerned with building and edifying (*edificar*), with an architecture of the future. He preferred the *oficio* of the press and those of builder and stonecutter:

> yo rompí piedras para amasar edificios:—hay que tardar una eternidad en amasarse, porque son edificios de almas, mucho más duros a veces y más pesados que las piedras! Me enamora todo lo que se yergue y levanta. . . . Las casas en fábrica me son tan familiares como las desdichas de mi pueblo; siempre se me pintan en imágenes extrañas y nuevas las paredes a medio hacer, los fosos sombríos, las puertas boqueantes, los muros desiguales que se dibujan sobre le cielo oscuro como encías desdentadas. (*Obras completas* 22:252)
>
> [I broke stones to amass buildings:—one tarries an eternity in building them, because they are buildings of souls, much harder at times and heavier than stones! I adore all that is erected and raised. . . . Houses under construction are as familiar to me as the misfortune of my people; I always imagine, painted in strange new images, walls half built, the shadowy pits, the gaping doors, the uneven walls limned against the dark sky like toothless gums.]

The passage reverses the trope of the romantic ruin. The future, like real estate, is to be improved. Words and building blocks, respectively, create a future.

Martí links a taste for *retazos* and detail to the material abundance of a new world appropriating the ruins of the old. "Details are in fashion, in literature, in painting, in philosophy," he writes, and explains that as an old world "came crashing down," it is natural that new materials, "stone by stone," should be collected to build a new one (*Obras completas* 22:201). Men, "cegados con el polvo de la fábrica, encorvados bajo el peso de los materiales que allegan con sus manos y acarrean en sus hombros . . . no alcanzan . . . aún más que a presentar y bosquejar confusamente, en consecuencia de lo que tienen conocido, el resplandeciente mundo" [blinded by the factory dust, bent beneath the weight of the materials that they gather with their hands and ferry on their backs . . . can only vaguely present and sketch, drawing on what they already know, the gleaming new world] (*Obras completas* 22:201–2). A material language able to build the future defines his later poetics.

Fredric Jameson once wrote that the unfinished aspects of a building under construction are an allegory for the utopia "that ought to be present in all life and all activity, but which is at once forgotten and repressed when the project hardens over into a completed object."[39] Martí's notion of construction retains that utopian potential of building. Edification is not merely a progressive impulse toward the future.[40] The architecture of the future is processual, like writing, in which grammar metes out the reading process. The question for Martí, who died at the beginning of the war in 1895, was what the future might look like. He did his best, in any case, to read the writing on the walls. Cuba, he wrote early in his career, "sorprenderá a Baltasar en el festín" [will surprise Balthasar at his banquet]. Cuba would be "for the careless government the Mane, Thecel, Phares of modern prophecies. Spain regenerates? It can't regenerate" (*Obras completas: Edición crítica* 1:75). Overlapping with Martí in Manhattan the Brazilian poet Joaquim de Sousândrade (1832–1902) would use this very image of concrete writing, of a visual poetics of imperial change, to describe circum-Atlantic transitions under way.

CHAPTER 3

The Writing on the Walls

Babylon, Wall Street, Canudos

No entrecruzamento da referência a Iduméia (a "terra estéril" bíblica, tomada por Stéphane Mallarmé como símbolo da gestação solitária do poema), [eu quis] acusar uma coincidência curiosa, "discordia concors" textual, lembrando também que em 1897, o ano em que Euclides iniciava a árida saga da sua grande obra, Mallarmé lançava os dados do seu livro livre.

[In the intersection with the reference to Idumeia (the "sterile land" of the Bible, taken by Stéphane Mallarmé as a symbol of the solitary gestation of the poem), [I wished to] signal a curious coincidence, a textual "discordia concors," serving to remind also that in 1897, the year that Euclides began the arid saga of his great work, Mallarmé threw the dice of his free book.]
—Augusto de Campos

Las palabras son muros

[Words are walls]
—Severo Sarduy

Like José Martí, the Brazilian poet Joaquim de Sousândrade spent much of the time between 1880 and 1885 in New York City. The two writers together documented the rising importance of speculation on Wall Street while covering broader changes throughout the Americas. They published in New York–based Spanish- and Portuguese-language newspapers, respectively. Both were journalists and poets. They often wrote about the same figures of New York society and about the delayed arrival of abolition and republicanism in Cuba and Brazil. Both proselytized versions of pan-Americanism. No evidence has come to light that the two ever met, though it seems plausible that they might have, or at least that they might have attended the same lecture or other event of mutual interest.[1]

In their insights they are aligned, as they are, too, in their posthumous inclusion in a canon of proto-concrete writing. Martí's unattributed quotation "Everything, in ascending, is generalized.—Everything, descending, is multiplied. To reduce, to concretize, is to ascend. . . . Concretion is divinity" (*Obras completas* 19:441–42) even seems to share a source with lines by Sousândrade, who parodies Emerson's transcendentalism: "(EMERSON filosophando:) / —Descer . . . é tendência de principe; / Subir . . . tendencia é do vulgar: / Faz um stagnação; / Da nação / O estagno, o outro faz tempestar" [(EMERSON philosophizing:) /—To descend . . . is the prince's tendency; / To ascend . . . the tendency of the vulgar / It makes a stagnation: / Of the nation / The stagnant pool, the other makes a storm].[2] Here a possible convergence also yields a difference: Martí proposes concretude as transcendental; Sousândrade's comical passage purports to be a ventriloquism of period political debates and follows stanzas about the Paris Commune and general strikes: at stake is a revolt by the masses against reification in the form of a stagnated (still monarchical) nation.

In this chapter I revisit aspects of late nineteenth-century Brazilian literature that were recuperated for a subsequent concept of "concretude" as it was defined in the 1960s and retrospectively applied to Sousândrade. To some extent, I follow the concrete poets' analysis of several influences on Sousândrade's late poetry, including his engagement with communication technologies and with the rise of both monopoly and speculative capitalism. Augusto de Campos and Haroldo de Campos published these reflections as part of an edited and abridged edition of Sousândrade's epic *O Guesa errante* [The errant Guesa] (1873–1884?) titled *ReVisão de Sousândrade* (1964). But, now positioned from a vantage almost as many decades after the *ReVisão de Sousândrade* as was the abridged edition itself after the original *O Guesa*, I also go beyond the 1960s reading to ask both why such observations were important *then* and what their reading may have missed. I suggest that on the one hand, the concrete poets' interest in the poem reveals their investment—contrary to how many have read them—in nonlinear, antidevelopmentalist time, in the very year of a right-wing coup. But I also examine in what ways the poets bypass Sousândrade's critique of a technologically advanced but corrupt and discriminatory republic, juxtaposed unfavorably to more radically egalitarian Caribbean political projects. By reading Sousândrade alongside Martí, other literature from 1890s Brazil, and in light of geopolitical concerns raised in the previous chapters, I suggest new contexts within which to approach the better-known and most innovative portions of Sousândrade's oeuvre.

A satirical stanza from the delirious "Wall Street Inferno" episode of *O Guesa errante*, set in Atlantic locales from Brazil to West Africa to the Caribbean to New York City, serves as an illustrative example of how Sousândrade brought together meditations on technology, imperial change, and speculation.[3] Sousândrade's text places Brazil's emperor Dom Pedro II at a midnight soirée at the *New York Herald*. Suddenly an invisible visitor arrives:

> (*Sílvios* dedos rutilando ao typographar em vernaculo da
> "BANDEIRA-ESTRELLADA";
> POETA extactico; a Voz:)
>   —Grandes são graças e thesoiros
>   De Balthazar-Imperador! . . .
>   =Que treme ahi *sans-culottes*
>   Quijotes? . . .
>   —Manè-Tessèl-Pharès, Senhor! . . . (254)

> [(*Silvios* fingers flashing to the typesetter in vernacular
> of the "STAR SPANGLED BANNER";
> ecstatic POET, the Voice)
>   —Great are the graces and treasures
>   of Emperor-Balthazar! . . .
>   =*Sans-culottes* Quijotes
>   tremble there? . . .
>   —*Mane-Tessel-Fares*, Sir! . . .]

I see Sousândrade as engaged here in a sly rewriting of the Book of Daniel's scene of "writing on the wall," one in which Wall Street speculation and the information age loom as the true successors to the last days of the Brazilian Empire. In the Bible, of course, Babylonian prince Balthazar witnesses a disembodied *hand* writing the words *Mene,*

Mene, Tekel, Peres on the palace wall: God has numbered Balthazar's kingdom and ended it, the prince is judged wanting, and the kingdom is to be divided between the Persians and the Medes. In Sousândrade's version, however, it is notable that the eclipse of the Brazilian Empire (1822–89) is spelled out by a Wall Street *typesetter.* Both the medium and the place are significant. New communication technologies and the exteriorization of the romantic voice (a disembodied "Voz") are linked to new geopolitical divisions. *O Guesa*, critical of U.S. travesties of republicanism, racialized slavery, and economic inequality, mocks religious narratives of economic dominance following the decline of "quixotic" empires. This geopolitical narrative is folded into a poem that, incorporating hundreds of timely allusions taken directly from New York newspapers "and under the impression they produced," responds to the media and to the culture of speculation characterizing Wall Street (de Campos and de Campos, *ReVisão* 30).

"Wall Street Inferno" is the most famous canto of a poem that is largely read today because of what its image of the late nineteenth century meant to a 1960s generation of Brazilian poets. To write about Sousândrade today then almost necessitates a detour through the concrete poets and their context more broadly: Affonso Romano de Sant'Anna's rather stern poem "Empire State Building" (1968), for instance, also engages with *O Guesa*, while the artist Hélio Oiticica would, while living in New York City in 1972, make a film based on "Wall Street Inferno."[4] The de Campos brothers, along with the literary critic Luiz Costa Lima, celebrated Sousândrade as a modernist before his time. They praised his postromantic "objectivity," his Joycean portmanteaus, his engagement with advertising and new technologies, and his prescient critique of monopoly capitalism. In a 1960s climate of polemical cultural politics, the concretes poets, who had been accused of an apolitical formalism, announced a more "participatory" (politically engaged) phase. Now, in *ReVisão de Sousândrade*, they praised Sousândrade's Mayokovskian fusion of revolutionary form and content, his struggle against slavery, empire, and colonialism, his pan-Americanism, and his denunciation of capitalism's contradictions (76). "Like a seismograph for registering the political-social convulsions of its time," they proposed, "the poem communicates by nervous notations, almost telegraphic, extremely sensitive, and of a very modern sensibility, able, for example, to fuse in a quick flash the proletarian movements of the Paris Commune and North American strikes" (32).

Reissued editions are as much about what is of interest in a given moment as they are about recuperating past figures.[5] The evaluation of Sousândrade as extremely modern, then, reveals as much about the concrete poets and what counted as "modern" in 1964 as it does about the nineteenth-century poet. Thus in what follows I both shed light on what historical changes inform *O Guesa* and identify the twentieth-century problems for which Sousândrade's critique of speculative capital and embrace of an Atlantic emancipatory politics were especially resonant. In other words, I seek to answer the following question: what were the "discourse networks," to use Friedrich Kittler's concept, that came into being in the late nineteenth century, whose messages were still legible in the mid-twentieth?[6] What was at stake in the 1964 concept of the "moderníssimos" years of the 1870s through 1890s?

To begin to answer this question we can turn for a moment to the first epigraph of the chapter, which suggests that a "textual 'discordia concors'" occurs in 1897, since in that year the publication of Mallarmé's poem "Un coup de dés jamais n'abolira le hasard" coincided with the fourth and final Republican army expedition to Canudos and the beginning of da Cunha's writing on it. The epigraph, by Augusto de Campos, is taken from a 1997 book titled *Os Sertões dos Campos: Duas vezes Euclides.*[7] This slim volume is a centennial homage to *Os Sertões*. Despite its subject, however, *Duas vezes Euclides* is not a reflection on the great political stakes of this foundational conflict but instead a formalist paean to da Cunha's language.

Indeed, the careful attention to language in the epigraph that opens this chapter is the first key to understanding a series of concerns at stake in the 1960s' renewed interest in literature of the 1890s. Mallarmé's "Un coup de dés jamais n'abolira le hasard" had long represented for the concrete poets an event in verse, a response to the typography of the daily press that anticipated conceptual and visual poetry to come. But Mallarmé's application of newspaper aesthetics to poetry had an antecedent in Sousândrade, as Haroldo de Campos noted.[8] De Campos's epigraph thus puts Mallarmé's poetics, and by extension Sousândrade's, in conversation with the "literary" engagement with Canudos. While this barely implied connection seems willfully formalist, *O Guesa* and *Os Sertões*, in both their style and in the stories they tell—of the Atlantic, of the reverberations of the Haitian Revolution, of the battle between the state and a messianic community—constitute markedly different yet coincident late nineteenth-century struggles over both political and literary-technological representation. What did the two share? What does the *discordia concors* reveal?

As Nicolau Sevcenko has suggested, a current of writing from the late nineteenth century emphasized the visual and exterior over the lyric interior. I want to suggest that while visual poetry was the emblem of Brazilian economic and literary modernity in the mid-twentieth century—think of Augusto de Campos's 1963–65 poem "cidade-city-cité," a piece later printed as a massive sign in São Paulo—it has roots in the writing on the walls of Sousândrade's 1870s Wall Street, on the imperiled walls of Dom Pedro II's Empire, and on the vanquished walls of the separatist Canudos community.

Recently Adriana Campos Johnson has offered a rich reconsideration of the textual production surrounding the war of Canudos, arguing that the transition from monarchy to republic that immediately preceded the war should be seen "as a surface of inscription on which other tensions and changes were articulated."[9] We might go further to suggest that one of the changes the period witnessed included a shift toward privileging inscription itself. By this reading, da Cunha's book about a war in a largely illiterate region becomes one unlikely element in the *discordia concors* of which Sousândrade's collage of Gilded Age New York City and its media is the other, in an epochal shift toward a regime of visuality, of inscribing and fixing time and interiority.

As the stanza from "Wall Street Inferno" cited earlier suggests, the biblical scene of writing on the wall combined the theme of imperial succession (a division of territory and dynasties) with an allegory for reading practices: the future is announced as graffiti scrawled on a wall. The original scene from Daniel establishes that writing on the wall assures finitude. Historical change—imperial change—is written as a certain future. Writing is made akin to a fixing of history, of time. The nonprogressive time associated by an urban press with the millenarian predictions and purportedly communal lives of Canudos and the nonlinear time of Sousândrade's anti-epic both receive fresh interest in a 1960s context of nationalist developmentalism and military aggression, for which they offer a counterbalance.

Like the epic it celebrates, *ReVisão de Sousândrade* is *itself* a "seismograph," measuring a vibration running between the 1880s and 1960s. After several politically tense years, in 1964 Brazil suffered a right-wing coup and ensuing authoritarian regime characterized by both its use of mass media and its censure of information. Perhaps this explains why the relations between writing technologies, imagined communities, and temporality so charged in the late nineteenth century return in this moment.

ALL OF HISTORY IN HISPANIOLA

Sousândrade was born in Maranhão, on Brazil's northern Atlantic Coast. His family of planters owned slaves (some were sold to underwrite his university studies), and he was an ardent republican during the liberal empire of Dom Pedro II. After studying at the Sorbonne, he traveled to New York in 1871 to oversee his daughter Maria's education at Sacred Heart Academy; Sousândrade lived nearby at the Hamilton Hotel on 8th Avenue and 125th Street.[10] (Martí, as it happened, was the guardian for Cuban *autonomista* Miguel Figueroa's four daughters, all students at Sacred Heart.) (See Figure 5.) In 1878 Sousândrade traveled to South America but returned to New York in 1880. He moved back to Brazil in 1885 and after the establishment of the republic in 1889 became active in politics, serving as mayor in Maranhão (Williams, "Sousândrade: A Study" 45; Sousandrade, *O Guesa* 37).

While in New York, Sousândrade wrote several books of poetry as well as newspaper articles for José Carlos Rodrigues's newspaper, *O Novo Mundo* (1870–76). Immersed in the world of U.S. newspapers, Sousândrade has much in common with Martí: a quick cross-reference between the onomastic index of Martí's *Obras completas* and the names in the de Camposes' annotated glossary for only the "Wall Street Inferno" portion of Canto X of *O Guesa* yields more than 120 proper names shared between the two, spanning references from Alfonso XII and Henry Ward Beecher to Paul Bert, Antero de Quental, Johann Strauss, Zola's *Teresa Raquin*, and Sing Sing.

O Guesa, written over the course of forty years, recasts an Atlantic imaginary in light of changes in capitalism, politics, and media. It maps a route through the Atlantic by a pre-Columbian mythological figure, the Guesa; because the poem accrued as separate cantos over decades, this route in turn maps a stylistic move from romanticism to postromanticism.[11] As in Martí's writing, stylistic changes in *O Guesa* function as a kind of periodization: the romantic early cantos written by Sousândrade in the 1850s and 1860s narrate the first Portuguese conquest of Brazil through a romantic imaginary populated by jungles, Indians, and indigenous mythology, while later cantos mock romantic conventions and incorporate the language and rhythms of

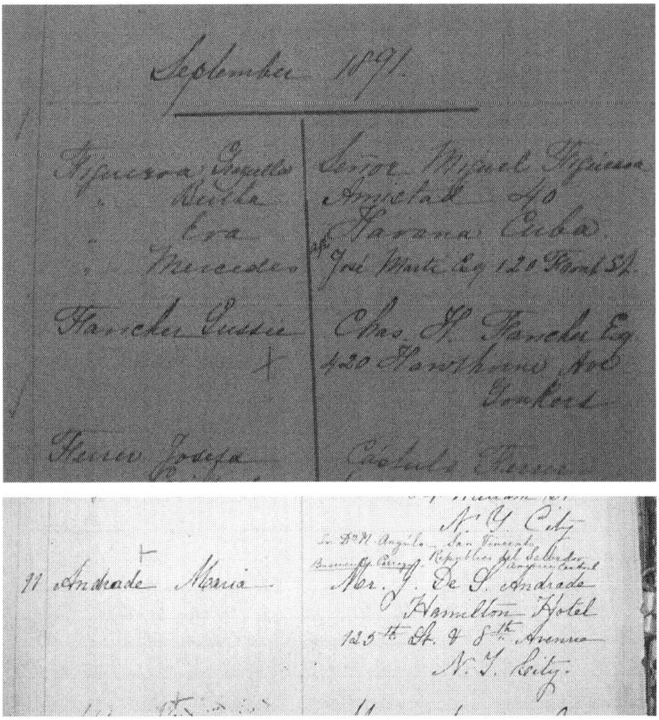

Figure 5. Ledgers identifying Joaquim de Sousândrade's address (1880–1889) and José Martí's role as guardian to Figueroa's daughters, Sacred Heart Academy (1891). Courtesy of Manhattanville College Archives.

late nineteenth-century speculation as witnessed by the writer in New York.

O Guesa theorizes both senses of the "object" of the Atlantic: teleologies of mutating empire as well as the media-inspired poetics of material language, developed against a background of speculation. The poem, which Sousândrade originally imagined would include an actual map of the Guesa's travels, reroutes the old transatlantic movement of empire (Williams, "Sousândrade: A Study" 132). As Idelber Avelar has argued, the poem undoes teleology through its form: whereas epics follow linear time toward a "transhistorical or eschatological finish line," the *errancy* of the Guesa flouts imperial teleology.[12] Indeed, the poem that aspired to be neither "lyrical, dramatic [n]or epic" does not tell a typical progress narrative but instead illuminates ramifying connections between capitalism, colonialism, and form *across* centuries (de Campos and de Campos, *ReVisão* 119).

Canto X's "Wall Street Inferno" episode has justifiably garnered the most critical attention for its innovative style, inspired by a language of speculation and print culture in New York City. This culture had its counterpart in Brazil, too, where speculation produced its own literature[13] and where the "belle époque" has repeatedly been described as one in which "interior values" were replaced with "the exterior, the material, the superficial, the mercantile," when "[t]he modern was the detail, something to be shown, the genteel exterior that hid coarse structures in art as well as in politics," and literature responded to print, reproductive, and distributive technologies.[14]

But just as Martí's interest in things was not a static aesthetics, here, too, behind a literature concerned with the superficial—with exteriors, facades, and new technologies—lay a preoccupation with time. Kittler contends that because writing technologies are themselves historical, what is perceived as artistic "style" in an author and time period is often no more than a given moment's "switchboard" orchestrating bits of "data and hence . . . time" (*Gramophone, Film, Typewriter* 3). Leaving aside the epistemological question of who or what controls the switchboard according to Kittler, we might ask what kind of "time" was being processed in late nineteenth-century Brazil and the United States that the 1960s concrete poets later excavate. The work of the concrete poets is often conflated with a general developmentalist spirit of the 1960s. But in *ReVisão de Sousândrade*, they are interested in a non-nationalist vision of time excluded from Brazil's teleology. Nations are imagined with hoary pasts and golden futures, but *O Guesa* is sensitive to other forms of time that are eccentric to nationalist narratives.

In the same year of Brazil's coup, *ReVisão de Sousândrade* recuperates this non-nationalist time. The poem is by turns mythic, pan-Atlantic, nonlinear, and, in its rhyme schemes, delirious, mimetic, and parodying of speculation and of colonial continuities. For instance, Sousândrade incorporates into his 1870s Wall Street a scene from Hendrick Hudson's journey to Manhattan and subsequent purchase from Algonquian Indians, for a song:

> (Ao fragor de JERICHÓ encalha HENDRICK-HUDSON;
> os ÍNDIOS vendem aos HOLLANDEZES a ilha de
> MANHATTAN malassombrada:)

—A Meia-Lua, proa p'ra China,
Está crenando em Tappan-Zee . . .
Hoogh moghende Heeren . . .
Pois tirem
Por *guildens* sessenta . . . *Yea! Yea!* (248–49)

[(HENDRICK HUDSON beaches to the din of
JERICO; the INDIANS sell to the DUTCH the haunted
isle of MANHATTAN:)
—The Half Moon, prow towards China,
Is careening in Tappan-Zee . . .
Hoogh moghende Heeren . . .
Well go for it
For 60 guildens . . . Yea! Yea!]

This sixteenth-century episode's insertion into scenes from 1870s Wall Street suggests that the latter-day hell is of a piece with colonial acquisition of the Americas.

But what the 1964 *ReVisão* does *not* reprint from the longer nineteenth-century poem is also telling: Canto IX (1871), set in the Antilles and Mexico and written in the same year that Sousândrade moved to New York City, is omitted in its entirety. This may well have been a question of space. But in my view Canto IX is crucial for appreciating *O Guesa*'s intervention into narratives of Atlantic modernity, for it narrates the Guesa's move from Senegambia (Sousândrade once passed through Dakar) through the Caribbean and on to New York, celebrating en route the Haitian Revolution and the Antilles as the "birthplace of modern generations."[15] By omitting Canto IX, *ReVisão de Sousândrade*, I believe, privileges the poem's interest in literary, financial, and technological modernity over its significant interest in political modernism—republicanism as well as the Haitian Revolution. When we read the original poem, we see a contrast emerge between the *political* modernity that the Guesa remarks upon as he passes through the Antilles (in Canto IX) and a *technological* and commodity-oriented modernity that enables the unfettered capitalism of the "Wall Street Inferno" episode to come.

As his boat passes Martinique, Guadalupe, and the Virgin Islands, the Guesa notes that it is the history of successful slave rebellions that guarantees the Antilles to be "'os jardins dos mares, / Onde houve berço a geração moderna!'" [the seas's gardens / Where the modern generation was birthed!] (173). Sousândrade offers here a revisionist version of the circum-Atlantic course of a modernity that has often been, as Sibylle Fischer notes, "disavowed."[16] Sousândrade defends *quilombos*—societies of runaway slaves—against those who would call them bandits: "Oh! lá vão pelos montes perseguidos / Da liberdade os magicos heroes! / Ninguem lhes ouve a dor, que 'são bandidos' / Eia briosa! engrandecei!" [Oh! There chased through the mountains go the magic heroes of liberty! / No one hears their pain, they are "bandits." / *Eia briosa*! Celebrate!] (179).

The Antilles as both revolutionary proscenia and progenitor are as "crucial" to Sousândrade as they are to Martí. The Guesa enters into the "grupo formosissimo das Virgens" [the strong group of Virgin (islands)] and the modern age is born bloody (171). The Guesa underscores the historic import of the Caribbean: Hispaniola is "a throne to Memory" in which "Toda a historia / Póde ler-se naquela ilha distante" [All history / Can be read in that distant island]. It is a romantic history, crowded with the usual cast of indigenous figures betrayed by Europeans: Guacanaguarí, Caonabo, Anacaona, and, later, Toussaint L'Ouverture (177). The Guesa and his daughter absorb in passing the Caribbean's "lesson" from a Saint Thomas slave revolt: "o escravo massacrava / Os senhores, e a pallida cabeça / De Soctman em tropheu alevantava" [the slave massacred / The lords, and Soctman's pale head was raised as a trophy] (172).

It is in Haiti, the Guesa remarks, where "—Alli primeiro o negro fôra escravo" and "Livre primeiro s'elevou dos erros" [There for the first time the black was a slave; first in freedom he rose above errors] (178). The Haitian Revolution thus appears in the poem not only as the scene of true enlightenment but as the realization of heretofore imperfectly realized French ideals: "Essa idéa que a França destruia, / Realisou-a o negro do Haytï" [That idea which France destroyed, / The black man of Haytï realized] (179). However much the Haitian Revolution may have seemed ancient history to many readers in the 1870s, it resonated for a poet from Brazil, where slavery had not yet been abolished and where the Haitian Revolution remained, as for much of the Caribbean, a model well into the nineteenth century.[17] Sousândrade's interest in celebrating the revolution runs counter to the Brazilian elite's *fear* of the revolution's enduring inspiration for Brazilian slaves, for whom the 1798 "Inconfidência Baiana" and declaration of a representative, race-blind republic constituted an instance of clear influence, as did early

1800s circulation in Rio de Janeiro of images of Jean Jacques Dessalines, an 1814 uprising in Bahia, and celebrations honoring the "King of Haiti" in 1820s Sergipe, no doubt among many others.[18]

O Guesa's structure of flashbacks and its rewriting of received genealogies—the Haitian Revolution salvages French travestics of republicanism—suggest that Sousândrade's notion of what was modern and what constituted progress (as Sibylle Fischer poses the question) was sophisticated (24). Many notions of radical emancipation were entertained in the early nineteenth century, and most of these were quashed by the nation (or republic). In *O Guesa* the committed republican Sousândrade situates his politics in a fully Atlantic history and future, drafting his final cantos at the dawn of a republic that did little to incarnate the liberation narratives sketched out in Canto IX. Sousândrade's book of poems written a decade after the republic, *Harpa de Ouro* (1898), addressed his disappointments.

Canto IX's Atlantic modernity stands as a precedent and a corrective, then, to the urban extremes depicted in Canto X. Canto X is set in New York City, to which the hero arrives after passing through a terrifying hurricane ("o inferno errante de Huração" [the errant hell of Hurricane]) in the Gulf of Mexico (185). We must read this hurricane as both natural and man-made, as political and climatic: the "fôrça muscular do oceano—" [ocean's muscular force] is called an "Onda rev'lucionária, independente" [rev'lutionary, independent, wave], evoking the histories of slave revolutions recently described in the preceding vignettes (185).

The question of which "modernity" presented in the two cantos should prevail is hinted at in the opening stanza of the "Wall Street Inferno" section of Canto X. The passage links the Antillean and New York episodes and concludes with a farcical question posed to the spiritualist Swedenburg: whether after the paradise of the Antilles, and inferno of New York, there remained any world to come—a question answered, equally tongue-in-cheek, later in the poem:

> (O Guesa tendo atravessado as ANTILHAS, crê-se livre dos XEQUES e penetra em NEW YORK STOCK EXCHANGE; a Voz, dos desertos:)
>
> —Orpheu, Dante, AEneas, ao inferno
> Desceram; O Inca ha de subir . . .
> =*Ogni sp'ranza laciate,*
> *Che entrate . . .*

—Swedenborgo, há mundo porvir? (231)

[(Guesa having crossed the ANTILLES, believes himself
rid of the XEQUES and enters the NEW-YORK-STOCK-
EXCHANGE; the Voice, from the wilderness:)
—Orpheus, Dante, Aeneas, to hell
Descended; the Inca must ascend . . .
Ogni sp'ranza laciate,
Che entrate . . .
—Swedenburg, do future worlds impend?][19]

Like Martí, Sousândrade locates a utopic republic in "future worlds," the present one being one of "patents":

(SWEDENBORG respondendo *depois:*)
—Há mundos futuros: república,
Cristianismo, céus, Lohengrin.
São mundos presentes:
Patentes,
Vanderbilt-North, Sul-Serafim (248)

[(SWEDENBORG responding *later*:)
—There are future worlds: republic,
Christianism, heavens, Lohengrim.
There are present worlds:
Patents,
Vanderbilt-North, South-Seraphim.]

The passage puns on the word "patent," since it can mean present, evident, but also a title or patent. The industrialist North and a dreamy South (of the Reconstruction-era United States? A global South?) are well established, while the future is located in a celestial world for whom justice—rather lamely equated with "republic"—can only come into being in some afterworld. These and subsequent lines also echo the conflation of geography and the future visible in Martí's notion of "tierras venideras": "E è do Guesa a existencia do futuro; / Viver nas terras do porvir" [and future existence is the Guesa's / to live in the lands to come] (282).

Also like Martí, Sousândrade renders figures from New York City as types or allegorical figures animated by a culture of speculation.

The *Xeques* appear disguised as "Railroad-managers, Stockjobbers, Pimpbrokers" and as "Vanderbilts, Jay Goulds, midgets" while elsewhere parade "people of Israel, Orangians, Fenians, Mormon Buddhas, Communists, Nihilists, Farricocos, Railroad-Strikers, All-brokers, All-jobbers, All-saints, All-devils, lanterns, music, sensation; Reporters" (Sousândrade, "From O Guesa Errante" 656; Sousândrade, *O Guesa*, 231, 248). The phantoms in Sousândrade's inferno are made of the same ethereal material as the fortunes created by speculators, whose human form the Andean spirits waiting to sacrifice the Guesa assume (de Campos and de Campos, *ReVisão* 283). This litany of types and personages recalls Martí's analysis of a parading striker's effigy or "allegory" of Jay Gould, a figure whose very being, Martí realizes, even before being turned into a puppet, allegorizes the condensation of the many into the one:

> Jay Gould es gran monopolizador, y sobre la espalda del trabajador de la alegoría va representado el Monopolio:—él lo representa bien, que ha centralizado en enormes compañías, empresas múltiples . . . el monopolio está sentado, como un gigante implacable, a la puerta de todos los pobres. . . . La tiranía acorralada en lo político, reaparece en lo comercial. Este país industrial tiene un tirano industrial. (*Obras completas* 10:84–85)
>
> [Jay Gould is a great monopolizer, and on the back of the worker [carrying] the allegory Monopoly is represented:—he represents it well, he who has centralized multiple businesses in vast companies . . . the monopoly is seated, like an implacable giant, at the doorstep of all the poor. . . . The tyranny contained in the heart of politics reappears in commerce. This industrial country has an industrial tyrant.]

Gould's effigy is an allegory of monopoly's abstractive properties: the condensation into allegorical form of a figure who managed to condense vast industries into monopolies. In writing about Gould, both poets seize upon the simultaneously abstractive and reductive properties of capitalism, which produces a system of types that, according to Baucom, emerge from a specifically Atlantic history of the development of finance capital, fed by the eighteenth-century slave trade and its attendant insurance apparatus (59).[20]

Just as otherworldly creatures in Sousândrade assume the form of stock-jobbers and "pimpbrokers," in Martí's prose, too, speculative value eventually assumes material form:

> El valor real a la larga se impone, casi siempre de un modo súbito y violento, y todo el orden falso de existencia edificado sobre estos valores huecos, viene a tierra, como una casa que toma dinero para negociar a un interés mayor que el que ella percibe, a la primera hora de arreglo de cuentas.
>
> [Real value in the end asserts itself, almost always suddenly and violently, and all the false order of existence built on these empty values comes down to earth, like a business that takes money to negotiate a greater interest than it earns, come the time to settle accounts.] (*Obras completas* 10:303)

Speculation can effect material and political change, Martí allows, but when the chips are called in, the fictitious world vanishes and reality comes crashing down: "Esperanzas y lujos son humo, y no es malo, cuando no tienen base, que desaparezcan; pero los pueblos de obreros son seres reales, que al caer a la tierra fría y sin pan, del seno de esa bomba de jabón, se levantan rugiendo y con los puños cerrados" [Hope and luxuries are smoke, and it's not bad, when they are baseless, that they should disappear; but the workers are real beings, which when they fall to the cold earth without bread, from the bosom of this soap bubble, rise up groaning and with fists clenched] (*Obras completas* 10:303). The false values are likened to bubbles or castles in the air that burst or crash down to take the form of a ruined business, or a people that rise up enraged.

CÓDIGOS

Where "Wall Street Inferno" really excels—and where it honors its author's claim that it was fifty years ahead of its time—lies in the fact that it perceives more than merely the concretization of the many into the one. Incorporating language from myriad newspapers and advertisements, Sousândrade's poem also replicates the blossoming *outward* of networks of information emergent with, and ultimately replacing, the surplus goods Martí saw as emblematic of the economic strategies of a neo-empire. Moreno Fraginals wrote of the period, "[i]n the process of the conversion of competition into monopoly, characteristic of the final third of the nineteenth century, the monopoly of information is a component of a monopoly of the market" (*El ingenio* 29). In fact, it was a time of growth of both monopolies and free trade, of concentration in certain sectors and in growing networks in others, and *O Guesa* grasps both of these moves.[21]

The poem's rhythm scores the stock exchange's risings and fallings, paralleled in the hero's ascent and descent into infernos (in the Amazon, on Wall Street). Poetry's originary function as memory-aid and enumerator, defined by time and measure, is used to multiply the effect of the calculus that characterizes speculation, as in the follow stanza:

> (NORRIS, *Attorney;* CODEZO, *inventor;* YOUNG, *Esq. manager;* ATKINSON, *agent;* ARMSTRONG, *agent;* RHODES, *agent;* P. OFFMAN & VOLDO, *agents;* algazarra, miragem; ao meio, o GUESA:)
> —Dois! Trez! Cinco mil! se jogardes,
> Senhor, tereis cinco milhões!
> =Ganhou! ha! haa! haaa!
> —Hurrah! Ah! . . .
> —Sumiram . . . seriam ladrões? . . (231)
>
> [(NORRIS, *Attorney;* CODEZO, *inventor;* YOUNG, *Esq. manager;* ATKINSON, *agent;* ARMSTRONG, *agent;* RHODES, *agent;* P. OFFMAN & VOLDO, *agents;* shouting, mirage; in the middle, the GUESA:)
> —Two! Three! Five thousand! By gambling,
> Sir, you'll five thousand win!
> =He won! Ha! Haa! Haaa!
> —Hurrah! Ah! . . .
> —Vanished . . . were they confidence men? . . .]
> (Sousândrade, "From O Guesa Errante" 656)

Here numerousness is as much a quality of people (lists) and of poetry as it is of sums traded. Poetry, more than other genres, encodes temporal consciousness. Rhythm beats out meaning in oral performances; rhyme schemes direct a reader through written verse via a score of pauses, advances, quickenings, and full stops. Here Sousândrade links verse both to meter and to calculation and code in a manner that we will see again in mid-twentieth-century concrete poetry's attention to information science and cybernetics. Certainly the nineteenth-century poet seems to anticipate concerns about the supercession of religious meaning by informatics or, as a 1973 poem by Augusto de Campos puts it (examined later), the supercession of *God* by *Code*.

First, though, it is worth noting the poetic economy with which Sousândrade suggests a lineage from American slavery to modern capitalism:

> (*White-girl-five-years* ao linchado luisiano negro C. ATKINSON:)
>   —Comer pomo edêneo (má fructa)
>   É morte e o paraíso perder!
>   Nem mais Katy-Dids
>   Nas vides
>   Ouvir do inocente viver.
>
> (OSCAR-BARÃO em domingo atravessando a TRINDADE, assestando o binoclo, resmirando, resmungando de *tableaux vivants*, cortejando: o povo leva-o a trambolhões para fóra da egreja:)
>   —Cobra! Cobra! (*What so big a noise?!* . . .)
>   Era o meu relógio . . . perdão! . . .
>   São "pulgas" em Bod. . . .
>   Me acode!! . . .
>   =*God? Cod! Sir, we mob; you go dam!*
>
> [(*White-girl-five-years* to the lynched Louisiana negro C. ATKINSON:)
>   —To eat the edenic apple (evil fruit)
>   Means death and to lose paradise!
>   Never more Katy-dids
>   In the vines
>   And innocent life to hear.
>
> (OSCAR-BARON on Sunday crossing TRINITY [CHURCH], adjusting his binoculars, refocusing, muttering about *tableaux vivants*, strutting about; the people lead him stumbling out of the church:)

—Cobra! Cobra! (*What so big a noise?! . . .*)
It was my watch . . . pardon! . . .
They are "fleas" in Bod . . .
Help Me!! . . .
=*God? Cod! Sir, we mob; you go dam[n]!*]

This infernal New York stages a modern scene of the Fall, which refers back to Canto II (the "Taturema" episode), set in the Amazon.[22] Here a black man in Louisiana has been lynched for tasting of a forbidden fruit, becoming in turn that "strange fruit," a lynched man. Meanwhile, slavery's link to the market has already been identified in Canto II's Taturema "inferno," where Sousândrade calls slavery "live gold" (60). The hanged man is like a Christ on the altar as the poem turns to "Oscar Baron" (according to the de Campos brothers, Sousândrade's fusion of "robber baron" and Prince Oscar), who muses on "*tableaux vivants*" as he wanders through Trinity Church. The rigor mortis becomes a tableau (*mort*), while the *tableaux vivants* are allegorical types, like the Baron himself, or Jay Gould.

Capitalism's abstraction combines with racialist reason here to freeze into being rigid people-things: *tableaux vivants* (allegorical types) and *tableaux morts* (sculptures of a dead Christ; a hanged man). The Baron is interpellated as "Cobra": a snake in this post-lapsarian garden, a semi-anagram of Oscar-baron, and an allusion to money/charges—*cobrar*—while the tick of his watch marks the order by which he earns his money, signaling the eclipse of religious temporality by labor-time as measurement. "Religião" is replaced by "relógio," the Baron's watch.[23] His inscrutable pleas for rescue occasion a biting reply from "the people": "God? Cod! Sir, we mob; you go dam!"

In their analysis of this passage, the de Campos brothers submit that "cod" is a reference to a period usage of "Cod-fish aristocracy," a slang term for men who made their wealth in business (de Campos and de Campos, *ReVisão* 339). But "cod"—very nearly the English "code"—might also suggest that "God" has been substituted for by code, by the intricate urban language of advertising and newspapers that Sousândrade incessantly quotes from in the poem (he puns on English sounds and words throughout this canto). The play with syllables—cobra, *acode*, god, Bod, cod, mob—prefigures the recombinatorial algorithms of concrete poetry, which often included permutations on a single word. Sousândrade's wordplay also prefigures Augusto de Campos's poem "Código" (1973), published nine years after *ReVisão de Sousândrade*. (See Figure 6.)

Figure 6. Augusto de Campos, "Código" (1973). Courtesy of Augusto de Campos.

With "Código," Augusto de Campos overlays *Código* [code] and *Digo* [I say], to create a modern symbol in which "God" is also clearly legible. The poem calls up a Christian tradition of the word: the word made flesh, or at least visible. It also suggests the religious word's supercession by code in a period (the 1970s) that saw the rise of computing, a trend closely followed by the de Campos brothers.[24] A line from a poem in Sousândrade's *Harpa de Ouro* seems to echo here: "No anagrama Dog, God estava" [In the anagram *Dog* was *God*].[25]

Sousândrade thus anticipates not only the turn toward things but also the 1960s' turn within concrete poetry *away* from "thingliness" toward the virtual, toward code. To be sure, Augusto de Campos's emblem was for the magazine *Código*: clearly the immediate occasion for the design. But the name of the magazine was itself evidence of converging design, advertising, and cybernetics. "Code" was crucial to the concrete poets for its role in graphic design, computing, and structuralism alike. Haroldo de Campos, for instance, believed that Ferdinand de Saussure's theory of a "skeleton of code" would free readers from the laws of versifying.[26] In 1965, Décio Pignatari, who penned "poemas códigos," posited a supercession of objects by language and by "code," the "new reality": "the world of objects, of things-in-themselves, is a world in the phase of being superseded. We are entering into the era of language. From the code [*código*] to the message. To information and communication. Language is the new objective reality of our time, the new universal reality. Time of signs."[27] And in 1971 a member of the post-concrete *poema/processo* movement, Wlademir Dias-Pino, composed the manifesto/dictum "Código": the didactic stage of the poem.[28] In these years, computing, linguistics, and poetry all turned to the concept of code to theorize how language worked.

Sousândrade anticipates by a century this moment when "the world of objects" was approaching the world of information transmitted electronically: an electronic era. One stanza of the 1867 "Taturema" section (Canto II) features a "BEAR" (a figure that Canto X will intertextually recuperate to refer to bear markets on Wall Street) and a "CHICKEN" snuffing out candles to make way for electricity:

> (Um *URSO* e um *GALO* apagando a última brasa e
> consolidando-se duo in uno tatus:)
> —São de eletricidade
> Tempos, mundo do fim
> =São as manchas solares,
>   Dos ares,
> A aluminar tudo *assim*! (de Campos and de Campos,
> *ReVisão* 256).

> [(A *BEAR* and a *COCK* snuffing out the last ember
> and consolidating two into one *tatus*:)
> —Electric are the
> Times, world of the end
> =They are sun spots,
>   From the air,
> Illuminating all like *this*!]

"São de electricidade tempos" looks forward to the speedy times evoked some fifteen years later in Martí's ode to New York, "Amor de ciudad grande" (1881), mentioned in Chapter 1: "De gorja son y rapidez los tiempos."

CANUDOS AND THE PETRIFICATION OF ROMANTIC NATIONALISM

In an essay appended to *ReVisão de Sousândrade* Luiz Costa Lima contrasted favorably Sousândrade's "poetics of concretude" to the mawkish and formulaic romanticism of "sentimental states" typical of the poet's contemporaries (407). Costa Lima's essay is subtle and recognizes that hackneyed romantic tropes themselves constitute a reality, albeit one that registers poets' distance from "real" reality. Concretude in Costa Lima's essay indicates that in the 1960s the term referred to some kind of realism: sounding rather Adornian, or indeed Hegelian, Costa Lima writes, "Sensibility is only achieved when the creator is able to move beyond himself. . . . Art realizes itself by becoming objective" [*A arte realiza-se por objetivar*] (407). Costa Lima proposes the concrete—in opposition to romanticism—as a precipitation of *reality* out of (mere) ideology, echoing Marxian notions of the concrete debated in the period (by 1975 the poet and critic Moacy Cirne would invoke Alain Badiou and Pierre Macherey to describe concrete and post-concrete poetry, concluding that a "work does not translate an ideology, it concretizes it. And it concretizes it [we say] through historically determined aesthetic meaning.")[29]

Still, concretude is something more tangible or architectural, too. It is significant that Costa Lima opposes romanticism's "degrees of emotional openness" and "sentimental states" to what he sees in Sousândrade as visual structures that borrow from the external world (397). For this typically modernist stance ignores the fact that romantic lyric (whose "interiority" Costa Lima anyway finds false, hence not truly emotional or sentimental) depends on codes that translate reality as much as those that index visual or objective reality. This contrast between a metaphorical "interiority" in which feelings and subjectivity are bound "inside" the subject and an objective world imagined as lying outside some figural walls is not new: Sloterdijk even speculates that the walls of ancient cities were what permitted philosophical notions of interiority in the first place (268). But it was a division insisted upon in postromantic writing.

We see Sousândrade making the transition from romantic tropes to a poetry that directly indexes a "reality" via reproductions of news items, in the forty years it takes him to write *O Guesa*. The poem itself thematizes this evolution. By Canto X the poet is mocking a vocabulary employed in earlier cantos in a scene that suggests the literal petrification of sentiment. Satirizing romantic tropes as well as their transformation into postromantic stylizations, Sousândrade writes in Canto X:

> (Sentimentes *doctoras* carbonisando o coração do GUESA:)
> —Que escorra sangue, não veneno . . .
> =Um "morango"!—Oh . . . todo oiro e dor . . .
> =Fossilpetrifique!
> —Ai . . . não fique
> Sem glória o Inca e o astro sem flor . . . (254)

> [(Sentimental *doctoras* carbonizing the GUESA'S heart:)
> —Let it bleed blood, not venom . . .
> A "strawberry!"—Oh . . . all gold and pain . . .
> =Fossilpetrify!
> —Ay . . . may he not remain
> Without glory the Inca and the star without flower . . .]

Gold and pain, emblems of a flowery verse, are petrified. Sentimental doctors convert the Guesa's organ of feeling into a fossil of Incan history: a critique of sentimental Indianism that relegated indigenous peoples to a past incompatible with the modern nation. (Ramón Gómez de la Serna once wrote that romanticisms live on posthumously, as classicisms are nothing more than "the fossilization of romanticisms that have died.")[30]

Coining the word *fossilpetrifique*, or "fossilpetrify," Sousândrade hints at a new temporality. If, as W.J.T. Mitchell has argued, the discovery of fossils meant for romanticism the introduction of "new orders of temporality" beyond the historical or biblical,[31] *fossilpetrifique* may invoke the new orders of temporality ushered in by fossil fuels and petrochemical industrialization, a revolution for which Latin American economies were, in the late nineteenth century, unprepared.[32]

The fossilization of the Guesa's innards also allegorizes a transformation in nationalist iconography. The transition from a romantic to a postromantic ideology entails a transformation from the location of national essence within an organic body (*Iracema*/America; palm trees, Indians, and so on) to a spectacularization of national progress on the walls of the nation—of Rio de Janeiro and of what was probably Bahia's second largest city, Canudos. The turn-of-the-century reimagination of the nation as a republic sought an elimination of difference that was broadcast on both urban and natural walls. As an article dating from the demise of Canudos put it, "Nas paredes escuras das rochas abruptas, foi escrita com o sangue dos sertanejos a história de um povo redivivo!" [on the dark walls of steep rocks was written in the blood of *sertanejos* the history of a people reborn] (Nogueira Galvão 105). In other words, the rebirth of the nation was written with the lifeblood of the *sertanejo*, whose epitaph was scrawled on the rocks of Canudos.

In different ways, Sousândrade and Euclides da Cunha both document a changing language of nationalism. Sousândrade, before the 1889 founding of the republic, gestures toward a fully supranational, *Atlantic* imaginary in which new print technologies forecast a postimperial future, but one that situates republicanism in an Atlantic context. Da Cunha's work, published a decade after the final edition of *O Guesa*, is a melancholic reflection on a massacre that, viewed from today's vantage point, seems to document the mediated erasure and museification of the *sertanejo* or backcountry person, in a war with the infranational—a war, Campos Johnson argues, in which political struggles were written about and, in so doing, written over; as she conceives of it, "sentenced" to a kind of oblivion.

Canudos (about which Sousândrade does not seem to have written) was a glaring instance of how the republicanism the poet dreamed of was easier to extol when it remained in the future.[33] Sousândrade's subsequent disillusion with the first decade of the republic was not unusual in the region, where widespread critique was common, particularly among black Brazilians.[34] The republic arrived saddled with a system of patronage and structures of power inherited from slavery. Indeed, many saw it as a threat to liberties, not an arbiter of them. Some former slaves, having gained emancipation under the monarchy, feared a republican reinstatement of slavery.[35] Canudos, variously cast as a struggle between civilization and barbarism, urban centers and the rural northeast, progress and messianic anachronism, also represented at the time what Robert Levine termed a "flash point" for contests between monarchism and republicanism (*Vale* 23).

In the poor, drought-ridden *sertão*, a devout, millenarian leader named Antônio Vicente Mendes Maciel (known as Conselheiro [the

Counselor]) established a religiously based community during the first years of the republic. This city of an estimated tens of thousands was eventually destroyed by the Brazilian army between 1896 and 1897.[36] While Maciel preached against the republic, favoring the city of God, even contemporary commentators recognized that the community in Canudos neither militated against the republic nor was monarchist.[37] If anything it was separatist. The assault on "Canudos," the name of an abandoned ranch that became synonymous with the community (which called itself Belo Monte), became a foundational national narrative in which an excessively brutal state massacred its own citizens in the name of civilization.

The most famous and controversial writing on Canudos was da Cunha's *Os Sertões*. Da Cunha, an engineer who accompanied the republican troops, wrote a study (later canonized for its literary merits) that was influenced by post-Darwinist, pseudoscientific theorists of degeneration and progress. For da Cunha and the media at large, Canudos embodied an alternative temporality to that of the Nation. It was *out of sync* with the nation, at once backward and millennialist.

And yet the temporal imaginations contrasted in this case—millenarianism and progress—spring from a single branch. Michael Walzer has traced ideologies of progress to medieval millenarian thought, seeing contemporary radical politics as a secularization of a political messianism dating back to Joachim of Fiore.[38] Canudos threatened the state because it arguably offered an alternative politics—albeit one in many ways hierarchical and conservative—realizing, in modest form, what the republic failed to achieve.[39] This promise goes far toward explaining why the myth of Canudos, evolving with changing contemporary needs and hopes, has been abiding.

In addition to persistent, varied investments in Canudos as a space of alterity, a practice of reading surfaces also survives the moment. It transitions from positivism to postexpressionism. As in the farcical hell mocked in *O Guesa*, *Os Sertões* describes a regime of visual interpretation in which "types" (e.g., "the *sertanejo*") are decoded from exterior traces. Types, of course, are not particular to this moment; they populate medieval allegories, eighteenth-century sketches, and nineteenth-century naturalism. Baucom has suggested that in the Atlantic world the "culturally representative type," in conjunction with historicist thinking, arose in the eighteenth century as a form for representing the abstract logic of finance capital and insurance. And physiognomic readings were part of pseudo-Darwinism and early criminology everywhere. Yet Kittler suggests that the turn into the twentieth century in particular saw the eclipse of a romantic view that imagined writing to be an expression of "the inwardness and voice of man" by a regime of representation, extending from modernism into the digital era, more indebted to communications technology (*Discourse Networks*, 212).

The "essence" of the *sertanejo* thus registers as a set of characteristics legible in blood on the walls of the national bedrock, while Sousândrade renders the end of empire as legible in the words of an invisible typographer on the walls; for both historicity is visualized. If da Cunha's campaign memoirs depict a Canudos that seems more wretched than the realization of a putative space of equality, he seems to translate into phrenological terms the same empty sameness and erasure of difference that the nation is premised upon. He describes a perfectly racialized, "mixed" "Brazilian" subject: "there was a rare and striking uniformity in the more characteristic facial features of these prisoners. There were few whites or pure Negroes among them; an unmistakable family likeness in all these races pointed to the perfect fusion of three races" (*Rebellion in the Backlands* 473).

The Canudos war played out on the level of bodies starved, massacred, and deciphered. It also played out on the level of representation. (It was a moment of national codification, of Ángel Rama's lettered city, redux: the *Academia Brasileira de Letras* was also founded in 1897, in part to define Brazilian Portuguese.) The conflict unfolded through newspapers, telegrams, and poems (Levine, *Vale* 24; Nogueira Galvão 33). Printers believed to be sympathetic to monarchists found their offices trashed by pro-republican mobs. Newspapers even turned Canudos into a commercial event, with advertisements invoking Canudos's alleged asceticism to sell products: "Canudos ao alcance de todos!" [Canudos within everyone's reach!] (Nogueira Galvão 49–53, 4).

Canudos was an event of narration, and the mysterious sect's secrets had to be deciphered by the press for urban readers. Da Cunha writes

> Não vimos o traço superior do acontecimento. Aquele afloramento originalíssimo do passado, patenteando todas as falhas da nossa evolução, era um belo ensejo para estudarmo-las, corrigirmo-las ou anularmo-las. Não entendemos a lição eloqüente . . . os patriotas satisfazeram-se com o auto de fé de alguns jornais adversos. (*Obra completa* 2:347)

> [We failed to grasp the larger significance of the event. This most unusual efflorescence of the past, revealing all the cracks and fissures in our evolution, afforded us a fine opportunity to study, correct, and do away with those faults; but we could not understand the eloquent lesson that it offered . . . patriots were satisfied with making an *auto-da-fé* of a few hostile journals.] (*Rebellion in the Backlands* 281)

Canudos constituted a lesson in national reading practices. But what lesson was discerned in Brazil's history (or "evolution")?

It proved hard to decipher. Da Cunha saw in the war connections to the anachronistic Sebastianism of a decadent Portuguese empire. The purported fanaticism of the backlands is simultaneously derivative of Portuguese messianisms and somehow unintelligible. The *sertão* itself is "a geographical category Hegel failed to mention." Canudos is "a parenthesis, a hiatus . . . a vacuum. It did not exist" (*Rebellion in the Backlands* 444). As a geologist reads the land for its past, so da Cunha reads the material culture—and the literal walls of the city—for clues to the psychology of its inhabitants. The buildings themselves, "as if by a stereographic process," evinced the society's moral attributes: "Era a objetivação daquela insânia imensa. . . . Se as edificações em suas modalidades evolutivas objetivam a personalidade humana, o casebre de teto de argila dos jagunços . . . sugeria paralelo deplorável: . . . a decrepitude da raça" (*Obra completa* 2:227–28) ["It was the objectivization of a tremendous insanity. . . . If our edifices in their evolutionary manifestations are to be taken as objectifying the human personality, then the clay-roofed hut of the jagunços . . . suggests a deplorable parallel: . . . that decrepitude which is due to race"] (*Rebellion in the Backlands* 145). Interiority and moral attributes are projected doubly: the built environment of Canudos is likened first to a "stereograph" and then to an "objectivization" of decrepitude.

The decrepit facades, however, not only expose but also mask interiority. Da Cunha calls Conselheiro an "automaton" [*autômato*] and a "puppet" [*títere*], types utterly devoid of interiority (*Obra completa* 2:214.) It was, perhaps, this opacity that incited attempts to read what little exteriors remained of the city after its destruction. After the final siege, republican soldiers sacked the decimated settlement, exhibiting, to da Cunha's eyes, "covetousness" and "insatiable curiosity" about the scrawled documents they found there, "especially the terrible verses" that seemed a conduit to the voice of a mysterious, vanquished enemy

(*Obra completa* 2:245). The inhabitants of Canudos are recognized only in their posthumous words. Da Cunha writes elegiacally of the destruction: "it was the very core of our nationality, the bedrock [*rocha viva*] of our race, which our troops were attacking here, and dynamite was the means precisely suited. It was at once a recognition and a consecration" (*Rebellion in the Backlands* 464; *Obra completa* 2:504). The posthumously discovered documents are an epitaph that lives on in place of the dead: da Cunha calls them "bem vivos documentos" (lively—or quite alive—documents) (*Obra completa* 2:245).[40]

Nevertheless, it is worth heeding Sara Castro-Klarén's reminder that Maciel was no unspeaking subaltern.[41] Similarly, Campos Johnson finds period descriptions of his rise as a regional religious figure to reveal a "jockeying for power within a shared domain" rather than portraits of the Counselor as a fanatic beyond engagement or comprehension (55). An accomplished and literate preacher, he gave the region's priests a run for their money; the Bishop of Bahia forbade him to preach. This struggle over language was echoed at the level of communication networks. The telegraph guaranteed the republican army unique narration of the event. But we can also see it as a metaphor for the linkages that the nation sought to forge, a sign of the lettered city that imagined Canudos as its opposite. Paradoxically, even *literatura de cordel*—popular verse written on small pamphlets and read aloud publicly, a format allegedly derived from medieval scribal practices—celebrates the power of the telegraph in vanquishing Canudos.[42]

THE STEREOGRAPHY OF NOTHING, OR EVERYTHING

To return to the figure of the puppet or automaton: what, exactly, was inscrutable about the *conselheiristas*? We might say that what the republican soldiers coveted in Conselheiro's posthumously discovered papers were others' desires. Lacanian psychoanalysis suggests that our hatred of others is ultimately a hatred of how others *enjoy*, which is in turn a veiled discomfort with our own enjoyment. Jacques-Alain Miller developed Lacan's notion of "extimacy," the strange position of otherness within us: an exteriority within or an interiority without; a fear of others within ourselves. Campos Johnson similarly argues that *sertanejos* more generally were placed in such a position (135). For Miller, it is our discomfort with the other's pleasure that fuels chauvinisms: "Racist stories are always about the way in which the Other obtains a *plus-de-jouir*: either he does not work or he does not work enough, or he is useless or a little too useful, but whatever the case may be, he is always endowed with a part of *jouissance* that he does not deserve."[43]

Canudos was derided both for not honoring religious weddings (too pagan) *and* for preaching too ascetic a Christianity (too true to the early Church). Poor, the community was nonetheless resented by non-members for what it possessed. In other words, the inhabitants of Canudos, lumped together as inhuman, were resented both for what they were and for what they were not. Similarly, da Cunha is only able to recognize and elegize the people of Canudos's "humanity" after he reinserts them into a scheme of civilization/*barbárie*, within which their former inscrutability morphs into illegibility or, to be precise, illiteracy. The Counselor is humanized in the same stroke of the pen by which he is re-barbarized, now not as a fanatic but as a rube. The *desires* imputed to Canudos, once feared, are now mocked:

> Pobres papéis, em que a ortografia bárbara corria parelhas com os mais ingênuos absurdos e a escrita irregular e feia parecia fotografar o pensamento torturado, eles resumiam a psicologia da luta. Valiam tudo porque nada valiam. Registravam as prédicas de Antônio Conselheiro; e, lendo-as põe-se de manifesto quanto eram elas afinal inócuas, refletindo o turvamento intelectual de um infeliz. (*Obra completa* 2:245)
>
> [Poor bedraggled sheets of paper on which the barbarous orthography paralleled the most naïve absurdities, while the irregular and unsightly handwriting seemed to be a photographic reproduction of the twisted way of thinking of these people; it appeared to sum up the psychology behind the conflict. These scraps of paper were worth everything in the world for the reason that they were worth precisely nothing. On them the sermons of Antonio Conselheiro were written down; and, as one read them over, one realized just how innocuous his preachings really were after all, reflecting simply the poor fellow's intellectual turmoil.] (*Rebellion in the Backlands* 162)

The sermons are worth everything because they are worth nothing: their value lies precisely in their exposure of the lack in the other, their confirmation of the safe ignorance of the defeated. They prove the emptiness of the desires imputed to them. Yet they remain unrecognized on their own terms. Instead they are rendered barbaric and harmless, worthless.

Da Cunha not only describes barbarous handwriting from Canudos but analyzes the vernacular accounts of the battle related in the graffiti scrawled on the wrecked walls. Da Cunha calls these crude writings "outrageous palimpsests" [*palimpsestos ultrajantes*]:

> em cada parede branca de qualquer vivenda mais apresentável . . . se abria uma página de protestos infernais. Cada ferido, ao passar, nelas deixava, a riscos de carvão, um reflexo das agruras que o alanceavam, liberrimamente, acobertando-se no anonimato comum. A mão de ferro do exército ali se espalmara, traçando em caracteres enormes o entrecho do drama; fotografando, exata, naquelas grandes placas, o fácies tremendo da luta em inscrições lapidares, numa grafia bronca, onde se colhia em flagrante o sentir dos que o haviam gravado. (*Obra completa* 2:457–58)

> [on every white wall of ever more presentable dwelling . . . the Marshal's party encountered a scrawled page of infernal protests. Every wounded man on passing by had left there, daubed with lumps of coal, a reflection of his own bitterness of heart. They had all expressed themselves with the utmost license, taking refuge in a common anonymity. The army had there flattened its mailed fist to trace in enormous characters the plot of the drama. The result was a photographically exact reproduction of the outward aspect of the formidable conflict; that was the true significance of the monumental inscriptions with their crude handwriting, so glaringly expressive of their authors' feelings.] (*Rebellion in the Backlands* 411)

These purportedly indexical—*photographic*—writings are taken to be both unmediated expressions and allegories of the conflict: the outward *expression* of interiority and the *reproduction* of the "outward aspect" of the conflict. The writing, in other words, is interpreted according to *both* a romantic theory of literature *and* an objectivist one. It is both expression and snapshot, reflecting the changing nature of nationalism between sentiment and external architecture.

But the move is not unique to da Cunha or to depictions of Canudos. Kittler dates to the 1890s the acme of graphology, the "science" of reading interiority through handwriting, which coincided with a transition from handwriting to typewriting (*Discourse Networks* 262–63). Like the architecture of Canudos, which was called a *stereographic* objectivization of its anachronism, handwriting is likened to photography in its visual reproduction of "the psychology behind the conflict." Both handwriting and photography were, at the time, understood to function similarly as systems of representation that involved the translation of information from one form into another, a process during which human agency was imagined to be removed and meaning automated.[44]

Here again I would argue that the increasing visuality of writing is inextricable from changing reflections on temporality. In his Seminar titled *The Ego in Freud's Theory and in the Technique of Psychoanalysis*, Lacan discusses cybernetics and psychoanalysis with relation to Daniel's scene of writing on the wall. He likens writing on the wall to attempts to regulate time, to measure the unmeasurable, and to cybernetics' reduction of the world to 0s and 1s to attempt to order time and the unknowable through inscription:

> [M]an has tried to join the real in the play of symbols. He has written things on the wall, he has even imagined that things like *Mene, Mene, Tekel, Upharsin*, get written all by themselves on the walls, he has placed figures at the spot where, at each hour of the day, the shadow of the sun comes to rest. But in the end, the symbols always stayed where they were intended to be placed. Stuck in this real, one might think that they were just its landmark. (300)

Lacan argues here that codifications of that "real" that lies beyond signs—that is, the time that a clock *measures* or the meaning that writing *renders*—manipulate the real. For Heidegger, "the true question of time" is its ability "*to be fixed*, to be inscribed."[45] If writing always encodes a time, then these passages in da Cunha attempt to reorder Canudos's "time" (anachronistic, messianic, etc.) and control its writing.

Given the ways in which interiority, exteriority, and alternative temporalities were at stake in the Canudos struggles, it is perhaps not surprising that Maciel's corpse became subject to interpretation as well, as its examiners sought insight into an enigma. The most far-fetched romantic phrenologies were deduced as his skull was severed from his trunk and analyzed by psychiatrists. The skull was discussed in much the same terms as were the papers worth everything, because worth nothing. The skull became a "precious relic": "the sole prize, the only spoils of war this conflict had to offer!" (*Rebellion in the Backlands* 476). The papers gained their worth from their ridiculousness; the skull gained its worth from the abjection of a war without any true spoils to collect.

The cranial analysis was widely covered in the press. When the novelist Machado de Assis left his post as *cronista* at the *Gazeta de Noticias* in 1897 it fell to Parnassian poet and journalist Olavo Bilac to cover the final moments of Canudos.[46] Bilac joined an urban majority in deeming Maciel a fanatic and his followers "furious nuts exalted by religious delirium," yet remained skeptical of phrenological (or graphological) modes of "reading" interiority, as evidenced in his witty piece titled "Cérebro de fanático" [A fanatic's brain]. "Cérebro de fanático" satirizes the news that Conselheiro's skull had been sent to the National Museum for analysis. It fantasizes a comic analysis of Maciel's verbal abilities—spoken and written—as discovered in the recesses of his skull.[47]

The satirical narrator of "Cérebro," presumably Bilac, grows curious about the brain of "that fanatic, long the director of the satanic cult of Canudos." The text then takes a turn as Bilac hits upon a way to access these secrets: he will channel the spirit of Paul Broca, the French anatomist who discovered the speech production center of the brain and who used his purported analysis of skulls to promote racist theories (396). Bilac contacts Broca via a medium who palpates the Conselheiro's brain:

> Aqui temos a circunvolução da palavra, enorme, inchada, exuberante. . . . Falava bem, o maluco! e com que fogo! e com que poder de convicção! Quando ele falava, os homens abandonavam as boiadas e as lavouras, as mulheres abandonavam as casas, e todos vendiam quanto possuíam, e lá se iam em pós ele, ardendo em fé e em loucura.
>
> Aqui temos a localização da palavra escrita . . . nula: não sabia escrever o Antônio . . . também, se tinha tantos secretários, em Canudos, em Minas, na Bahia, na rua do Ouvidor! (399–400)

> [Here we have the word curl, enormous, swollen, exuberant. . . . He spoke well, the madman! And with what fire!

> And with what power of conviction! When he spoke, men abandoned their cattle and fields, women abandoned their houses, and all sold whatever they possessed, and they went off with him, burning with faith and madness.
>
> Here we have the location of the written word . . . null: Antônio didn't know how to write . . . he had so many secretaries, in Canudos, in Minas, in Bahia, in Ouvidor Street!]

The fictive medium, in palpating the cranium, provides access to that which is otherwise presented as beyond mediation: the allegedly illiterate, crazed Conselheiro. Yet the scene simultaneously gives the lie to phrenological reading practices. If the dead Conselheiro's interiority is visibly legible in the interior of his skull, why is a medium necessary? Here we might agree with Campos Johnson, Costa Lima, and others that Canudos and its Sebastianist/messianic temporality were precisely *not* beyond the pale (or grave) but constituted the "*internal* limit to the state's hegemony" (Campos Johnson 70). But if, as Kittler stresses, media are "flight apparatuses into the great beyond," then the medium channeling Broca to penetrate Conselheiro's brain, and period depictions of Conselheiro as a ghost, seem to confirm the extent to which Canudos emblematized a feared but desired otherness or beyond (*Gramophone, Film, Typewriter* 13).

THE DISCORDIA CONCORS OF 1890S BRAZIL

"Wall Street Inferno" and "Canudos" are two sides of what Slavoj Žižek calls a parallax view: two events or perspectives that do not so much complement each other as add up, through their constitutive but irreconcilable differences, to a more comprehensive picture of a situation. Žižek's classic example is quantum physics' famous wave/particle theory of light: light can be understood as a particle or as a wave, but it cannot be measured as both simultaneously.[48] The parallax view is similar to a *discordia concors*, a harmonious discord, a tension internal to a larger whole or truth like the *discordia* that Augusto de Campos identifies in *Duas vezes Euclides*.

To conclude this chapter, I would like to revisit the versions of *discordia concors* sketched out earlier, as well as the subtle differences between them. Two discrete bodies of writing—Joaquim de Sousândrade's *O Guesa errante* and literature about the battles of

Canudos—share a quality that characterizes them as "writing on the wall" and an ability to assimilate changes in capitalism, geopolitics, and communication systems into their own literary form. This writing is also an attempt to fix time and simultaneously an acknowledgment of alternative temporalities. Both *O Guesa errante* and literature about Canudos describe temporalities alternative to the republic: *O Guesa errante* reaches back into Atlantic history to connect Muisca mythology, Portuguese colonialism, Atlantic slavery, the radical modernity of the Haitian Revolution, and late nineteenth-century capitalism. Canudos is read as gesturing ahead to an apocalyptic messianism while being branded—for this same reason—an outdated anachronism.

Campos Johnson has suggested that today's increasing postnationalism allows for a renewed interest in Canudos as an exemplary place of both political possibilities and the ways that such possibilities are judged (173). I would suggest that the appeal of the 1890s' temporalities alternative to the juggernaut of teleological developmental nationalism returned also in 1964 when, for instance, Glauber Rocha makes *Deus e o diabo na terra do sol* [Black god, white devil], a film about a messianic leader in the *sertão*, and when *ReVisão de Sousândrade* is reedited.[49] Yet while refuting a nationalist teleology, 1960s concretism in many ways spatialized temporalities, a move that the concrete poets traced to Mallarmé and Sousândrade, of fixing time on the page, even if wholly contingently—Mallarmé's "chance" that a throw of the dice cannot abolish. The subsequent moment of neoconcretism, as we will see in Chapter 6, abandons fixity altogether for process in a move that makes time itself the subject of art.

CHAPTER 4

Ramiro de Maeztu's Primacy of Things

The 1890s wars in Brazil and Cuba, and the literature produced during that time, remained touchstones for political and aesthetic debates in the mid-twentieth century. In Spain, too, the legacy of the 1890s was enduring and seems at first clear enough: after all, an entire so-called Generation of '98 was defined by the imperial loss of Cuba, the Philippines, and Puerto Rico. Yet if Cuba in particular is iconic in Spanish regenerationist thought, its independence (or loss) is but one event in a dense web of multiple, interrelated movements throughout the Atlantic world, spanning abolition, Latin American independence movements, Spanish economic development, and North African occupations, among others. In this chapter I argue that the work of Ramiro de Maeztu, knitting together these circum-Atlantic struggles, provides an exemplary instance of one way in which twentieth-century developmentalisms emerge out of nineteenth-century Atlantic debates.

Ramiro de Maeztu is emblematic of the ways in which a strain of twentieth-century Spanish thought—at first liberal, then right-wing—develops a philosophy of things, objects, and development out of the imperial crises of the 1890s. For Maeztu, the loss of Spain's American and Pacific colonies in 1898 spurs an increased investment in North African colonialism, a mystical theory of money, and a rejection of sovereignty in favor of proto-fascist states organized around things. Maeztu was perhaps the most infamous member of the Generation of '98: he supported the dictators Miguel Primo de Rivera and Francisco

Franco, and was murdered in 1936 by republican soldiers. But recently he has been the subject of new intellectual biographies.[1] Why this return to Maeztu?

For the intellectual historian José Luís Villacañas, comprehending twentieth-century Spain depends upon understanding Maeztu's thought. Villacañas calls Maeztu the most important ideologue of the twentieth-century Spanish right and sees much of post-transition (but presumably pre-2008 crisis) Spain to be a "realization of Maeztu's idea and project" (13, 18–19). Aesthetically, Maeztu's dialogue with—and even possible influence upon—his British friend T. E. Hulme and other Imagists is little remarked, yet these movements would be a reference for other objectivists, including the Brazilian concrete poets. If, as I suggest, Maeztu's objectivism emerges as a reaction against abolitionist and anticolonial movements in Cuba and North Africa, it seems important to reintroduce this Atlantic history into histories of modernist aesthetics in Madrid, London, São Paulo, and beyond.

Maeztu is hardly a consistent thinker; he wrote thousands of newspaper articles over the course of forty years. And yet a roughly coherent history and ideology inform his positions. Throughout his work, imperial Spain serves as a model for a postcolonial Spain unsure of its future. Economic development remains an elusive but obsessive goal. Maeztu repeatedly reaches back into Spain's Golden Age and ahead to Franco to explicitly yoke the millenarian zeal of the Inquisition and conquest of the Americas to twentieth-century colonialism in North Africa and to fascist developmentalism.

Abiding connections emerge in Maeztu's work between: (1) his writing on the Spanish/Cuban War of 1895; (2) his writing on "Africa," South and North; (3) his theories of value, both economic and aesthetic; and (4) his rejection of subjectivity, sovereignty, and romanticism. Uniting these four areas is an ideology most explicitly articulated as "The Primacy of Things." In this chapter I show how this synthetic theory of Things serves as a bridge between concerns voiced in Maeztu's first book, *Hacia otra España* (1899), and his 1930s defense of authoritarian Spanish developmentalism and "hispanism," as articulated in his book *Defensa de la Hispanidad* (1934), underscoring how debates over nineteenth-century emancipatory struggles were, in the twentieth century, transfigured and contained in aesthetic, developmentalist, and neo-imperial ideologies.

SELF-PORTRAIT AT A CRITICAL AGE

Maeztu's own life story serves as an allegory for the version of Spanish history that he narrates. He was born in 1874 in the Basque country. His father, Manuel, was born in Cuba, where Manuel's father, Francisco de Maeztu y Eraso, operated an *ingenio*, the sugar mill El Pelayo.[2] Maeztu's mother, Juana Whitney, was raised in France, the daughter of the English consul.[3] In a piece titled "Autorretrato en edad crítica" [Self-portrait at a critical age], Maeztu recalls an early childhood of leisure and tutors. In a strange but telling splitting of his own subjectivity—his is not a singular but a generational narrative—he describes in the third person the disappearance of this privileged world when the Cuban *ingenio* began to fail and his family fortunes were thrown into peril:

> [P]or causas ajenas a la voluntad de nadie, hubo de quebrantarse la disciplina educativa, y a la opulencia sucedió la medianía, y a la medianía la pobreza, y a la pobreza la miseria. Su adolescencia se desarrolló entre los incidentes de la almoneda de su casa. Primero se marchó el padre a América, en defensa del capital amenazado; luego fueron desapareciendo profesores particulares, sirvientes, caballos, coches, arneses, libreas, casa lujosa, mueblos de precio, alhajas sedas, libros, mientras de diez en diez días se aguardaban del correo de Cuba pliegos de valores, que no llegaban nunca. Se hundió el crédito de la casa, algunos acreedores se insolentaron, se vivió una vida falsa durante años, sin otro aliciente que las cartas de Cuba, llenas de ilusiones; y del esplendor de la infancia no quedaron más restos que algún látigo roto y una vieja criada con la lealtad de los criados del régimen antiguo. (*Autobiografía* 25–26)

> [For reasons beyond anyone's power, the educational regimen was broken, and opulence gave way to a middling state, and that to poverty, and poverty to misery. His adolescence unfolded amid the auctioning off of his house. First his father left for America, to defend imperiled capital; then tutors began disappearing, and then servants, horses, carriages, harnesses, livery, a luxurious house, fine furniture,

> jewels, silks, books, even as every fortnight the mail from Cuba promised bills of real value, which never arrived. The house equity sank, creditors threatened, a fraudulent life continued for years, without any real hope beyond that provided by letters from Cuba, filled with illusions. And of the childhood splendor nothing more remained than some broken whip and an old servant with the loyalty of those of the *ancien régime*.]

This narrative of class declension presages Maeztu's later obsession with *Spain's* historical "decadence" and possible regeneration. As Maeztu claimed elsewhere, his life as a writer was "consecrated almost exclusively to the problem of my patria Spain, which was great and later declined [*decayó*]" (*Autobiografía* 221).

In an essay on the dialectical workings of class, Fredric Jameson once described how Flaubert learned his class affiliations through a ricocheting between the alternatives offered by his two parents. As a result the French writer hated his father's middle-class empiricism as much as his mother's aristocracy, but above all hated his own boorishness, an "interiorization of what he imagined to be his own class (i.e., himself) seen from the outside." For Jameson, Flaubert's family traits are placeholders in an attempt to resolve class conflict "under the guise of problems of a psychological order."[4]

The scraps of Maeztu's autobiography written about himself in the third person—in other words, as "seen from the outside"—similarly fuse personal history and class affiliation, psychological and national traumas. Thus Maeztu frequently marshals the specifics of his genealogy—a Cuban-born Basque father and a French-born British mother—as the fortuitous preconditions for, or proof of, his sensitivity to geopolitical issues. The otherwise unremarkable failure of the family's Cuban sugar mill becomes a benchmark along a Möbius strip around which Maeztu will continue to march his entire career. Sometimes he departs from the personal to end up at the political: the "psychological" childhood trauma of familial decline motivates his concern for Spanish economic success. At other times he moves in the opposite direction: the loss of the *ingenio* in the 1890s and, before it, the abolition of slavery occasion the demise of a family idyll. This early self-portrait notably indicates a repeated connection between Maeztu's life and a particular version of *fin de siglo* Spanish imperial history.

In the 1890s Maeztu went to Cuba to try to save the mill. In the same period that Martí was writing in New York of the dangers represented by the Pan-American Monetary Commission and feverishly preparing for war, Maeztu was experiencing firsthand the tensions in Havana between *autonomistas* (who sought limited local representation and power without breaking from Spain), *separatistas* (pro-independence Cubans), and the power of U.S. capital in a society subject to Spanish trade restrictions. These tensions, Maeztu claimed, would be formative for his subsequent intellectual and personal interests.

In Cuba Maeztu worked a number of menial jobs typical of Cuba's sugar- and tobacco-based economy, including that of reader in a tobacco factory. He also (as he described it in the third person) "weighed sugar, painted chimneys and walls beneath the sun, pushed carts of cooked dough from six in the evening until six in the morning, collected bills in the streets of Havana, worked for a money changing kiosk . . . and plied another thousand jobs, until one day, summoned by his family, he returned to the Peninsula in the hold of a transatlantic ship" [*en la bodega de un barco trasatlántico*] (*Autobiografía* 26–27). This last detail, like the *látigo*, or "whip" in his autobiographical fragment (surely for horses but remembered as the sole remains of wealth alongside an "old servant"), carries with it in inverted form ambiguous echoes of his family's slave-owning past.

The return to the Peninsula, too, was typical of the era. In a literary essay on *Don Quixote*, Maeztu once proposed a symptomatic reading practice in which Don Quixote's fantasies bespeak "the sense of the epoch in which he lived"; if read through these same hermeneutics, the loss of the Maeztu property, the fall from upper-middle to laboring class, the circuit through Cuba and return to a stagnant Restoration Spain all sow the seeds from which will sprout a regenerationist ideology, common to his "epoch," designed to compensate for such humiliations.[5] The Maeztu family's loss of Cuban capital—writ large a few years later in Spain's loss of its colonies—will produce Ramiro's subsequent fixation on "things": the servants, horses, silks, and books, now elevated to an economic and philosophical level.

Spain's material and affective losses, in Maeztu's calculus, must be compensated for by the production of (industrial) things and by renewed imperial expansion into Morocco. Likewise, his desire to return to a childhood moment before the Fall is echoed in attempts to recall the golden years of the Spanish empire.[6] And Maeztu's pseudo-philosophical rejection of the category of subjectivity, as we will see, has roots in a transatlantic history of slavery.

Maeztu attributed his intellectual and political formation to "los años decisivos" spent in Cuba (1891–94).[7] There he formed his lifelong obsession with perceived differences between Iberian and North Atlantic economies. He dates his turn to journalism, born of economic necessity, to just before the "grito del Bayre" [*sic*] that inaugurated the 1895 Cuban War of Independence—or, as he translates it, the "beginning of the colonial catastrophes" (*El sentido* 201). And he attributes his own plans for pan-Hispanism to having witnessed firsthand in Cuba the contrast between nationalist (that is, Spanish) sentiments and their critique by Cubans.

There is, however, another angle to the colonial conflict, one that he paints as a family feud and one that he, "son of a Cuban," feels uniquely situated to describe. It is an angle that locates his biographical narrative of decline within a more complex history of the multiple factors driving Cuba's independence struggles: namely, slavery in the Atlantic world.

In an article published in Argentina's *La prensa* in 1917 titled "El egoísmo contemporáneo," devoted to discussing Bertrand Russell's *Principles of Social Reconstruction*, Maeztu critiques liberal subjectivity and deems inadmissible any a priori "right" to personhood. What draws notice, however, is that his example is a slave—not the abstract, Greek slave of Western political theory but a Cuban slave owned by the Maeztus. It is worth quoting the passage in full so that we may see how he frames the issue and how this simultaneously personal and national anecdote will be used to shore up allegedly abstract philosophical positions.

> Mi familia sufrió quebrantos de fortuna al abolirse la esclavitud de los negros en Cuba. Si la esclavitud es injusta en sí misma, o, cuando menos, si era injusta cuando se abolió, porque ya había entonces manera de asegurar la disciplina social por métodos más justos que los de la esclavitud, podré resignarme a una medida que ha privado a mi familia de sus medios de acción; pero si la justicia o la injusticia dependen meramente de su relativa relación positiva o negativa con el crecimiento de los hombres, no veo motivo para que el crecimiento de los otros me interese más que el de los míos. . . . [M]íster [Bertrand] Russell no logrará

interesarme en la libertad de mi esclavo si me dice que el esclavo no me pertenece porque se pertenece a sí mismo. Vale más que un hombre sea mi propiedad, si yo me doy en propiedad a Dios o a la ciudad, que no dejarle que se encierre en la cáscara impenetrable de su propio egoísmo. Afirmar que cada hombre se pertenece a sí mismo, y nada más que a sí mismo, no puede ser principio de reconstrucción social. Si tanto el amo como el esclavo son capaces de ciudadanía, lo justo es que ambos sean ciudadanos. Si lo es uno sólo, éste debe ser el amo, aunque sea actualmente el esclavo. Y si no lo es ninguno de los dos, no debemos interesarnos ni por el amo, ni por el esclavo, ni por su relación.[8]

[My family suffered a great loss of fortune upon the abolition of black slavery in Cuba. If slavery is unjust in itself, or, at least, if it was unjust when it was abolished, since by then there existed the means of assuring social discipline by methods more just than those of slavery, I can resign myself to a measure that deprived my family of its livelihood; but if the justice or the injustice depend merely on their relatively positive or negative relationship with the development of men, I see no reason that the development of others should interest me more than that of my kin. . . . Mr. [Bertrand] Russell will not succeed in interesting me in the liberty of my slave if he tells me that the slave does not belong to me because he belongs to himself. It is better that a man belong to me, if I give myself to God or to the city, than it is to let him lock himself in the impenetrable shell of his own egoism. To affirm that every man belongs to himself, and only to himself, cannot be the principle of social reconstruction. If both master and slave are capable of citizenship, what is just is that both be citizens. If only one may be it, he should be the master, even if he is at the moment the slave. And if neither is, we should not be interested in master, slave, or their relationship.]

In this passage, Maeztu turns Hegel's ostensibly abstract relationship between lord and bondsman—itself recently shown to have been influenced by the Haitian revolution—into a historical example based on his own family's history of owning African-descended slaves in order to refute liberalism's claims for absolute liberty.[9] He places a reactionary Catholic universalism above individual claims to liberty. And with a preview of the fascist capitalism that Franco's regime was to embrace, Maeztu implies that slavery was unjust at the time it was abolished perhaps *only* because by then other more effective means of extracting labor had been achieved.

Nowhere more clearly than in this example does Maeztu link what would become his post-1915 philosophical rejection of "subjectivity" or "personality" to the historical conditions that gave rise to both his familial "quebrantos" in the 1890s and Cuba's motives for seeking independence from Spain—first in 1868, when abolition was a key issue, and again in 1895. The anecdote should remind us, as we turn at the end of the chapter to the "primacy of things," that Maeztu's otherwise canny critique of romantic subjectivism has its roots in a reactionary denial of emancipatory struggles. These struggles, moreover, were not confined to Cuba but were scattered throughout the Atlantic. In the writings of some Spanish authors from the period, Cuban, Puerto Rican, and North African anticolonial movements are even conflated. Thus "1898," itself a continuation of sorts of the slavery-era War of 1868–78, is the impulse not only for Maeztu's objectivist philosophy but also for renewed occupation in North Africa.

"AFRICA" AND 1898

As Maeztu would repeatedly demonstrate throughout his career, the events of 1898 were what most indelibly, indeed "transcendentally," marked his thought (*Autobiografía* 65). The conflict represented for him not merely Spanish military defeat but confirmation of a perceived Cuban preference for U.S.-modeled industrialization rather than Spanish development. His articles on the topic were collected in *Hacia otra España*,[10] and what distinguishes the collection today is not so much its inclusion of hallmark preoccupations of its generation (ruminations on Spanishness, reflections on Don Quixote) as its economic analysis of the "Disaster."[11] One of Maeztu's enduring obsessions, rooted in 1898, was his belief that Spain needed to industrialize its agricultural heartland. As the articles make clear, the drive for industrialization was spurred in large part by the disappearance of a crucial market: Cuba had been not only a great producer for Spain but a principal market for Spanish exports.[12] With the loss of the colony, Spain had to develop internal markets.

But if for the young Maeztu "1898" above all underscored the need for Spanish economic development, in his later writings economic loss is converted into symbolic loss.[13] Spain's loss of Cuba, Puerto Rico, and the Philippines has to be compensated for by new incursions in North Africa. This was not only Maeztu's position but the government's as well. As José Piqueras argues, "[F]uture endeavors [*empresas*] in North Africa, before the Antillean wounds had even closed, confirm this outward-moving vocation of a capitalism that did not resign itself to the retreat imposed upon it by the capitulation at [the 1898 Treaty of] Paris."[14]

Spain's loss of Cuba following the Treaty of Paris must, indeed, be situated within a longer history extending back to the fateful 1860s, which saw a significant war in Tetuán, Morocco, in addition to a Cuban war of independence (1868–78). In 1893, just two years before the outbreak of the second independence war in Cuba, fighting in North Africa had again become a thorny national issue. The Cuban war two years later raised the specter of unresolved conflicts in Morocco. As Francisco Márquez Villanueva has keenly observed, the regenerationist discourse of Spanish renewal typically associated with the *post*-1898 period actually precedes it.[15]

Spanish discourse of the 1890s sometimes played nineteenth-century imperialism in Africa and the sixteenth-century conquest of the Americas off one another. Period writers show an awareness of this conflation of imperial reason. Ángel Ganivet parodied colonial explorers' writings in his figure of Pío Cid, who set up a kingdom in Africa among a people called "the Maya."[16] In 1905, scant years after the loss of American and Asian colonies, Benito Pérez Galdós published *Aita Tettauen*, a historical novel about the 1859 war in Morocco. A character in the novel, eager for a Spanish invasion of North Africa, cites a colonial history in which he confuses Cortés's conquest of Mexico with the conquest of "an empire of blacks" in Havana (127).

This was, after all, the Age of Empire, and the affective (and literal) economy by which American and African colonial exploits were fused or substituted for one another was not unique to Spain. Portugal's experience with Britain and the 1890 Ultimatum similarly ushered in a rhetoric of modernist regeneration against proleptic postcolonial melancholy and *saudade* for former imperial might. In literature and in political writing the Ultimatum was cast as a millenarian break after which Portugal would rise again. Like Spain's North African occupations, dreams of further Portuguese expansion into Africa (curtailed by the Ultimatum) compensated for the loss of Brazil. The idea of an immense Portuguese Africa, Maria Pinto Coelho contends, transferred the lost dreams of American riches to Africa, in an association between the 1890s and Golden Age Portugal: "Africa becomes the messianic kingdom in the national imaginary."[17]

But "Africa" meant something special in post-'98 Spain. Uprisings in the Spanish protectorate in 1893 and 1897 set the stage for the subsequent 1909 *semana trágica*, during which Catalan soldiers revolted against an unpopular colonial war, catapulting Spain into civil strife. Meanwhile, the loss of the American colonies was to be made up for by expansion into North Africa, now termed the Reconquista (Nerín 52). Empire-obsessed *africanistas* (the military men who served in the Moroccan campaigns) carried with them the experience of former colonial campaigns in Morocco, Puerto Rico, the Philippines, and Cuba. They saw twentieth-century expansions into North Africa as a chance to rebuild national pride (Nerín 26, 52). As Xavier Casals Meseguer puts it concisely, once the overseas colonies were lost, the Protectorate constituted "'the last frontier' of a waning empire for officials in search of promotion, the bulwark of an Army frustrated by its 1898 disaster."[18] The fighting in Morocco and the *semana trágica* in turn animated Franco.[19] While the loss of Cuba provoked a compensatory penetration into North Africa, a libidinal economy that foreshadows a masculinist fascism, *africanista* rhetoric reached back *before* 1898 to Spain's Catholic empire. Units in the 1927 battles in Morocco were named in honor of soldiers who had fought against the Revolt of the Netherlands (Nerín 52).

Maeztu, for his part, staked on Moroccan victories the recuperation of Spain's global reputation. He believed North African colonization would reenergize *Hispanism*, his post-'98 campaign for a Latin American spiritual connection with Spain that was in many ways reminiscent of Arielism (Villacañas 268). Morocco, Maeztu believed, constituted an organic link in this genealogy since it had shaped the military men—Franco most famously among them—who were to form the newly powerful, fascist Spain, a Spain that ought rekindle Latin American allegiance with the motherland (Nerín 92). *Defensa de la hispanidad* was published in Maeztu's final years, when he was a cultural attaché in Argentina. But early on, the conflation of American and African exploits, fused in the burning issues of the 1890s, had already yielded a peculiar result: a pseudonymous novel set in South Africa.

South Africa is not as strange a choice of setting as it might first appear. After all, "1898" for the young Maeztu represented a crisis of global proportions, the imagined movement of empire we have seen announced elsewhere. Between March 1900 and May 1901 Maeztu published five articles on the South African or Boer War. In 1905, and with apparent collaboration from Pío Baroja and other members of the Generación del '98, he adopted the persona of a Boer journalist, "Van Poel Krupp," and published *La guerra del Transvaal y el misterios de la Banca de Londres* as a serialized novel in *El País*.[20]

La guerra del Transvaal is a forgettable romance set in South Africa during the Boer War, which stands in at points for Spain's relations with its overseas territories. A kind of reverse black legend, the novel features British avarice and anti-Semitic theories about banking.[21] In this romance about hard-working Boers overwhelmed by greedy British financiers and their devilish concubines, native South Africans appear only as shifty aides to the warring white camps. The absence in the novel of any real treatment of non-settler Africans is notable given a context in which Spain was alternately exhorted to "Africanize" or "Europeanize." Of course, Cape Town is a continent away from Ceuta, and "Africa" at the turn of the century more immediately connoted a millennium of North African exchange, rule, and war. Still, it is in these same post-'98 years that the continent as a whole—"Africa" (significantly, the military's name for the Spanish protectorate of Morocco)—was invoked to symbolize the antithesis of desires to assimilate to "Europe." And in fact "Africa," while frequently signifying Morocco, sometimes referred to sub-Saharan Africa.[22]

Maeztu's interest in the Boer War stemmed from his critique of British imperialism during an early period in which he was also critical of Spanish colonialism in the Caribbean. In *La guerra* strained identifications are intimated between Boers, Cubans, and post-1898 Spaniards. Although the novel is set in the Transvaal, its readers are interpellated as Spanish: a British mining company lays claim to as much land as "Spain and Portugal together," sums are reckoned in Spanish currency, and the South African fields yield "sugar cane, coffee, and tobacco"—typical export crops of Cuba and Puerto Rico, not South Africa (251–53). As E. Inman Fox points out in his introduction to the 1974 edition of *La guerra*, the novel's fictional Dutch protagonist, who, after being educated in Holland, returns to South Africa to save his uncle's farm, is much like Maeztu, who went to Cuba to try to rescue his father's *ingenio* (17). The subtitle of the book, suggestive of antibanking conspiracy theories, echoes the anti-Anglo, *resentimentist* tension that Maeztu felt with respect to Cuba's pro-U.S., anti-Spanish alliances.

Maeztu/Van Poel Krupp positions Spain as both colonizer and colonized (with respect to northern Atlantic economic hegemony) when he intimates a commonality between Cubans and Boers. He writes: "The sons of those English who today invade the margins of the Vaal will find themselves exploited by the Metropole's avarice and will rebel against her. They are sons, like us, the Boers of those Dutch Belgians who, though few in number, knew how to stand up to the fearful Spanish Inquisition and vanquish the armies of Felipe II. The Afrikaners will triumph!" (16). Speaking as a fictitious Boer, Maeztu critiques Spanish and British imperialism alike. In adopting the Boer perspective he is simultaneously a colonial subject (like Cuba with regard to the metropole; like the Dutch under Felipe II) and colonial envoy (the author is actually a Spaniard, writing for a Madrid newspaper; his mouthpiece Boer is a settler colonialist among native Africans).[23]

But if Maeztu's 1905 novel serves as a soapbox from which to critique colonialism, by the 1920s and 1930s he spouts a racist civilizing discourse barely dusted off from the annals of early modern empire. In a section of *Defensa de la hispanidad* titled "Contra Moros y Judíos," Maeztu claims that the Spanish character is the subtractive, purified result of a centuries-long battle to exclude the Moors and Jews (253). The war in Morocco, he writes, is "a civilizing war of a backward people" and "there can be no more justified wars than colonial wars, whose virtue it is to bring the good(s) [*bienes*] of our Western civilization all across the face of the earth" (*Con el directorio militar* 19–20). He cites with approval a book that depicts Algerians from a "Spanish" point of view: as "savages who never had any more civilization than that from the people they dominated: Syrians, Egyptians, Persians, and Spanish" (*Defensa de la hispanidad* 242). European colonization in Africa is a necessary last resort: "America was lost, economically, for Europe, as a consequence of the war; Asia was at serious risk; the future of Europe was in Africa; but Africa could not be wholly exploited, colonized, and civilized without the concert of all the European powers: some by their technology, others with their capital, others with their population, all with their arms. That concert had to be" (*Con el directorio militar* 296).

One of the most urgent news stories of the day was the struggle between the Rif resistance leader Abd-el-Krim and the Spanish general Manuel Fernández Silvestre (described by the Spanish press as more "barbaric" than Krim). In a 1927 article in Madrid's *La Nación* criticizing class struggle, nationalism, imperialism, and racialism as products of liberalism, Maeztu described the North African conflict as not one between "persons." Instead, "each button" on a Spanish soldier's uniform represented "all Europe, Christianity, and Civilization, while Abd-el-Krim's cause . . . was the desert, slavery, polygamy, and Islam" (*Con el directorio militar* 178). From such talk of a clash of civilizations it was but a short step to color-based racism: a month later Maeztu wrote that "there must be some reason that black Africans are ruled by Europeans" (*Con el directorio militar* 210).

In Maeztu, then, the black legend of Spain's unique colonial cruelty is rebutted in a civilizing discourse that transfers blackness to Africa. For Maeztu, the history of Spanish involvement in the transatlantic slave trade is never far from, but is only opaquely admitted into, his theories of Spanish empire, civilization, and progress. Here, for instance, Abd-el-Krim's independence struggle is described as a fight *to maintain* slavery. Maeztu's own defense, a decade prior, of Cuba's racialized slavery—as a means to secure labor and capital—is now omitted. His retrieval of an early modern imperial discourse will have ramifications, too, for his economic and philosophical ideologies.

THE REVERENTIAL SENSE OF MONEY

Maeztu's revival of an early modern language of *moros y cristianos* and of civilization and barbarism is not his only invocation of that era in which purity laws fed a racism directed against both *moros* and sub-Saharan Africans (Martin-Márquez 14). His entire oeuvre is haunted by the early Spanish empire. His call for economic modernization, for instance, echoes an early seventeenth-century *arbitrista* tradition that takes aim at court waste, at the failure to develop the local agriculture and economy, at the diversion of American specie into foreign hands, and at luxury. The *arbitrista* era was a moment of particularly rapid economic expansion, when Spanish colonization of the New World yielded riches for Genovese and Dutch bankers, while the Spanish court allegedly wasted income on luxurious splendor. Echoing the *arbitrista* Martín González de Cellorigo, Maeztu laments, "Spain would be the richest nation on Earth had it invested the money from the American galleons in exploiting its natural resources, instead of wasting it on the incredible luxury of those great houses, that counted in the dozens of thousands their silver plates!" (*El sentido* 111).

Maeztu's economic thought is rooted in this earlier moment. He increasingly comes to frame his economic writings in moral and religious parameters. His 1926 articles published in Madrid and Havana and collected as *El sentido reverencial del dinero* [The reverential sense of money] narrate the consummate conjunction of the material and the mystical. The eponymous "reverential sense" is not to be understood as a secularized fetishization of specie but as a desire to reinvest money with religious rather than merely "sensual" meaning. Openly indebted to Max Weber's work and informed by a 1925 visit to the United States, *El sentido* claims that Spaniards on the whole lacked this coveted "sense."[24] One promising exception exists, however: the "indianos," men who made their money in the Americas (often Cuba) and used it to underwrite Peninsular development. Maeztu believed that the reverential sense, although proper to historically puritanical or Calvinist cultures, nonetheless burned brightly in the *indianos*. They indeed might enable Spain's eclipse of Britain: whereas the British Empire was ruined by a taste for "luxury" borrowed from Indian rajs, Spain could borrow from its *indianos* the values of philanthropy and investment, the traits of hard work and abstinence (*El sentido* 25).

In *El sentido* Maeztu presents economic thought as religious, or at least moral, in a system cobbled together from the thought of Weber, Adam Smith, and perhaps Werner Sombart. By returning to Smith, and, further back, to the Catholic Monarchs, Maeztu evoked that moment in which, as John Guillory has shown, "value" had not yet split into two different and often opposed meanings: economic value versus moral, spiritual, or aesthetic value. Maeztu thereby fit in with his London peers, on both the left and right, who fantasized about a more holistic, medieval world.

In 1896, reflecting on his experience in Cuba, Maeztu had thought he perceived "the enormous potential of the United States, the irremediable catastrophe; saw it coming, but bemoaned it with much bitterness, and took from it the substance of a new idea of regeneration, of progress, of national strength" (*El sentido* 200–201). Anxious to understand the roots of what he saw as North Atlantic economic power, he moved to London in 1905, where he would remain through 1919 as a foreign correspondent for Spain's *La Correspondencia* and the Argentine *La Prensa*. He soon befriended prominent Fabians and writers gathered around Alfred Richard Orage's *The New Age*.

The New Age had been important under editor Joseph Clayton for prodding the British working class to reflect on its own subaltern position within purported British "democracy" and for highlighting native South African oppression in the Boer War. But after Orage took over in 1907, the journal renounced its Christian socialist agenda and embraced first a Fabianist, then a fascist tone.[25] It showcased authors Katherine Mansfield and George Bernard Shaw, as well as T. E. Hulme and Ezra Pound, who promoted a poetics of Imagism.

It was in *The New Age* that Maeztu spelled out his rejection of romanticism in favor of what he termed "the primacy of things." The theories laid out in these articles have economic as much as aesthetic, formal, and political implications.[26] They detail a program that Maeztu had already intimated in 1897, one of progress meted out through economic measure and *in opposition to* a (democratic) romanticism (Villacañas 189). The "primacy of things" proposes a theory of subjectivity and objectivity that intentionally conflates economic, human, and aesthetic ideas of value, or *valor*, as the word signifies doubly in later Spanish translations of these English-language essays. As Guillory has argued, both economic and aesthetic discourses of value share eighteenth-century roots.[27]

Although Maeztu only rarely uses Marxist terminology, his celebration of artisan guilds and his disdain for what we might understand as the *subjective* nature of exchange value—a value that depends on other commodities and other people—leads him to prefer the purported "objectivity" of use value. But as several scholars have noted, the very notion of use value can emerge only in contradistinction to—with or *after*—that of exchange.[28] And yet Maeztu not only believes in objectivity but immediately invests the apparent "objectivity" of the artisanal thing with theological meaning. He argues, leaning on homonyms, that "el dinero merece reverencia porque es bueno, porque es un bien ligado intrínsecamente, como todos los bienes, al bien en general, que es la unidad del bien" [money deserves reverence because it is good, because it is a good linked intrinsically, like all goods, to the general good, which is the unity of the good] (*El sentido* 61–62). Maeztu links *goods* to the good, *value* to Christian values.[29]

Elsewhere Maeztu wrote that "1898" spurred his generation to attempt a reconciliation between Kant's idealism and Marx's socialism (*Autobiografía* 314–15). In 1911 he went to Marburg to study with the neo-Kantians who would shape thinkers such as Husserl and Heidegger. Maeztu himself, in a talk given at the Unión Iberoamericana and published in *Revista de las Españolas* in 1926, the same year that Heidegger finished *Being and Time*, mentions the concept of *aletheia*, which is, of course, central to Heidegger's magnum opus: "Not for nothing did the Greeks give to truth the name *aletheia*. It is something that surges from forgotten things, or better, neglected things . . . because the circumstances are lacking that would put it in the right place" (*El sentido* 201). Maeztu had likely heard Heidegger discuss the concept in lectures that preceded the publication of *Being and Time*.[30] However Maeztu encountered the concept, *aletheia* was in keeping with his lifelong efforts to redeem the overlooked greatness of Catholic Spain.

In Marburg Maeztu grappled with the relationship between the subjective and the objective. Kant's thesis concerning a priori concepts confirmed a counterintuitive "primacy" of spirit that Maeztu would retroactively imbue into the "things" and materialism he had extolled the year before (*Autobiografía* 224–25). Indeed, Maeztu's "thing" comes to look more like what Lacan calls a *Ding*, with a capital D: a transcendental, immaterial entity that invests with meaning the more mundane, earthly things (*dings*) filling our lives. The "primacy of things" becomes an objectivization of theological transcendentals—a combination that anticipates Maeztu's later embrace of a Catholic, fascist capitalism.[31]

The primacy of things thus depends upon a simultaneous theological and capitalist notion of the thing. Maeztu's is truly an object of the Atlantic: that good (*mercancía*; *bien*) that carries within itself the metaphysical niceties of a messianic history of transatlantic salvation shrunk to the size of an industrial object. For Maeztu links the very idea of "the good" to both goods and "geographical discovery," which cannot but conjure 1492 and its legacy: "Every new and true thought, like every geographical discovery, increases the number of good things" (*Authority, Liberty and Function* 14). As Villacañas observes, Maeztu "identifies the objectivization of society with its theologization" (201).

Proof that this slippage between the *Descubrimiento* and neo-objectivism was not unique to Maeztu can be found in the use by the Russian avant-garde of similar paradigms. The same connection is made in 1928 by El Lissitzky, who wrote, "Several centuries ago our ancestors had the good fortune to make the great discoveries. We, the descendants of Columbus, are creating the age of the most splendid inventions. They have made our globe quite small, but have enlarged space and lengthened time."[32] And Maria Gough has shown that Russian Constructivists' insights into the simultaneous materiality and immateriality of non-objective art was shaped by reflections on the geopolitical, specifically by Oswald Spengler's theories of financial speculation and civilizational decline (144).

In Maeztu, objectivity turns into the transcendental. The desire to earn more money is a symptom of the divine. The eschatological, transcendental project of pan-Hispanism that Maeztu will advance in the pages of the magazine *Acción española* manifests in the things themselves. (*Acción española* took its name from Charles Maurras's reactionary *Action Français*, the inspiration for much of Maeztu's antiromanticism.) Things are to fill what Maeztu describes as an "immense void that the literature of the Disaster created in the Spanish soul" (*Autobiografía* 84).

I would argue that there is a further connection between Maeztu's use of economic meanings of "value" and the guild preferences he shared with his London friends. As Guillory and Mary Poovey have observed, not only did properly "aesthetic" value not exist as such before the distinction between use value and exchange value, but there was no model for "value" in general.[33] To this end, Poovey emphasizes the importance of the course of Adam Smith's development of ideas of value (Smith was an important influence on the nineteenth-century Spanish liberals Maeztu read and cited).[34] In *The Theory of Moral Sentiments* (1759) Smith emphasized "the imaginative 'pleasures' attendant on the possession of certain objects," but he shifted, in *The Wealth of Nations* (1776), to the concept of a use value founded on production (Poovey 288–89). In this shift, Smith developed his idea of aesthetics "as a theory of consumption, but a consumption whose object was the commodity conceived as a 'work of art'" (Guillory 313).

Maeztu's reflections on value are profoundly defined by this split. And yet he seeks to return to a time *before* "value" described different spheres. Against the so-called Viennese school of economics, which espoused subjective understanding of value—according to which one pound sterling is "worth" more to a penniless beggar than to a millionaire—Maeztu argued for absolute value. He blamed the seventeenth-century economist Nicholas Barbon for popularizing the theory that the market was the best arbiter of a thing's value. Barbon, he thought, had spread the erroneous idea that "[t]he value of a thing is no longer the objective value of its utility but the subjective value given to it by the market" or "the caprice of man" (*Authority, Liberty and Function* 88–89). "Utility," however, is a red herring. Things are meaningful for Maeztu not only because of their use value but because they are an index of spiritual progress. Maeztu wants to link economic, transcendental, and aesthetic value.[35]

In a passage from his book *Authority, Liberty and Function in the Light of War* (1916) in which he rejects the Viennese school, Maeztu segues into a discussion of Victorian novelist George Meredith's *The Egoist*, deliberately using an *economic* language of value to describe the novel's *literary* merits: "An entire school of economics—the Viennese—was based on this subjective relativity of the value of things. . . . In this conceptual sense Meredith's novel tells us nothing new. Its value lies in the wealth of its words, the subtlety of its descriptions, the fluidity of the narrative, the consistency of the scenes and characters—in short, its imaginative veracity; for even on the plane of imagination there is truth and falsehood" (143). The choice of *The Egoist* is significant: the Victorian realist novel derives its value from eschewing liberal, individualist ("egoist") musings to represent the panoply of society. According to Maeztu, the reader is supposed to identify with these figures and lose her own desire for happiness, emerging cleansed. The novel allegedly succeeds in disabusing readers of the subjective notion of appropriative desire.

Maeztu's own analysis moves between economic and aesthetic notions of value. He slips from a description of the content—what the story teaches about money—to an evaluation of its form. The fact that the subjective nature of desire is a *theme* of the novel means little to him. The novel instead proves its worth through fluid narrative, consistent characters, and so on, which redeems it as an *objectively* good novel. If the novel's *theory* of value is unoriginal, its *aesthetic* value is confirmed through suprasubjective evaluation. For Maeztu, a novel is valuable when the subjective response to it concords with those of a community of like-minded readers: "Once or twice a year I read a novel, too—one of those novels, as a rule, which after ten or twenty years of criticism, have been acknowledged to be good. In doing this I find two kinds of satisfaction. The first consists in feeling, as I almost invariably do, that my own judgment is in agreement with that of the authorities of my profession. . . . The second satisfaction, and the more important, is that of purification" (141–42). Literary classics for him provide a standard for thinking about value, and Meredith's novel does so especially, in its denial of subjectivity and individuality, the purification of egoistic financial desires through catharsis, the respect for authority and for objective value. In this way, literature and its consumption stand in for Maeztu's politics more generally.

Maeztu's antiliberal, guild-based theory of artisanal production is mirrored in his lament that no one at the time read the "objective" theory of French jurist Léon Duguit because they were too busy reading lowbrow literature. Exchange value has ruined use value. The golden age of classicism is gone. The difference between the eighteenth century and the twentieth, Maeztu writes, is that in the eighteenth century Rousseau and Paine were read by thousands, while "there is no Syndicalist, so far as I know, who has read the books of the theorist Duguit. The multiplication of silly books and silly newspapers has stultified, among the general public, all sense of intellectual values" (*Authority, Liberty and Function* 212). (Maeztu's aversion to the culture industry in the form of the *folletín*—"there is a form of literature which can scarcely be called art: the *folletín* novel"—is especially striking as it was the very format in which he published *La guerra del Transvaal* [*Don Quijote* 30].) Maeztu's theory of the "primacy of things" will finally link these analyses of "value" and veneration of money and things to his critique of sovereignty, rejecting subjectivity in both spheres.

THE PRIMACY OF THINGS

Maeztu's most famous book, *Authority, Liberty and Function in the Light of the War* (translated as *La crisis del humanismo*) comprised and extended the article series "On the Primacy of Things."[36] In *Authority, Liberty and Function* Maeztu argues against national sovereignty and subjective humanism and for a society organized through a kind of guild socialism: not a society mediated by political goals but an "objectivised society, in which the classes would be exclusively constituted around things."[37] Although the phrasing of the title—"in the Light of the War"—indicates the seismic import of World War I for Maeztu's thinking on sovereignty and nationalism, in fact much of the content of the volume connects his concerns back to the same circum-Atlantic histories that preoccupied him earlier. In "On the Primacy of Things" Maeztu blamed Renaissance humanism for emphasizing subjectivity, and he sought to correct the idea that "man" was the measure of all things—a rejection of anthropocentrism—by inverting it: "things are the measure of men" (515).

In his essay "The End of Romanticism" (1915), Maeztu declares romanticism "dead" and "[a]n objective conception of social life . . . clearer. . . . [E]very human society . . . is an association of men in things."[38] Maeztu is disillusioned with sovereignty as a horizon of emancipation or politics and presses for a community based around things. He claims that "men" will soon lose their love of "absolute sovereignty" and instead "seek their salvation in a conception of law founded on things" (*Authority, Liberty and Function* 231). Despite its nostalgia for a medieval, organic relationship between producer and product, this theory of men associated through things works as a description of social relations under late capitalism. Marx, indeed, saw capitalist society—as *opposed* to feudalism—as defined by "connection by means of things."[39] Georg Lukács's description of people as but parts in a mechanical system in an era of mass production in his essay on reification likewise resonates with a description of Maeztu's ideal, militaristic society.[40]

Maeztu's rejection of romanticism is crucial for understanding the connection between his aesthetic and political positions. *Aesthetically* he rejects personality in favor of things and objectivism. *Politically* he rejects claims to sovereignty or emancipation in favor of suprasubjective systems of control. In "The End of Romanticism" and in other essays, romanticism's travesties are attributed to two events: the Renaissance overturning of the belief in original sin, and Rousseau. The former prompts Maeztu's call for a return to Christian authoritarianism. The latter underlies his critique of nineteenth- and twentieth-century national liberation struggles.

According to Maeztu, Rousseau's pernicious legacy is a cult of personality. Maeztu may have taken this reading of Rousseau from Hulme or, like Hulme, from Pierre Lasserre.[41] According to Maeztu, anyway, the philosophe paved the way for a society that privileges the "'sacredness of personality'" (*Con el directorio militar* 53). Personality means the imposition of inner sentiments upon the world of things, rather than the deduction of selfhood from external, universal categories. Romantics, Maeztu rebukes, "forget that things do exist" (184). He rails against "personality" not merely because the latter bears a link to a despised romantic individualism but because he fears that it prevents men from sacrificing themselves for the nation, while inducing in women the desire to be something more than mere reproductive machines (*Authority, Liberty and Function* 123). Maeztu's critique of personality was elaborated in England, where in early modern times a woman gave up both her property—technically called her "personalty"—and her personality in marriage: "in giving up her personalty, she gave up her personality, the two words which originally meant the same thing."[42] Maeztu's banishing of subjectivity, then, depends upon an objectivity at least partially derived from a particular structure of gendered subjectivization. And if for Lukács "personality" is that which is sacrificed to commodity culture's forms of production, for

Maeztu personality is what must be purged from commodified society (Lukács 98).

But personality was not merely a Rousseauean or British legal concept at this moment. It had a particular resonance within Spanish colonial history. "Personality" is a legal term and fiction applicable to states, dating to Hobbes and Pufendorf, and, before them, to Roman law.[43] The emergence of Westphalian sovereignty and attendant notions of state personality were shaped by European empires' creation of colonies. Antony Anghie has argued that sovereignty doctrine was "forged in the colonial encounter" and built on an "intent to erase the non-European world from any subjectivity or personality." He finds that notions of cultural difference between Spain and the Americas in particular determined the legal theorist Francisco de Vitoria's ideas of "personality, just gentium and, indeed, sovereignty itself," principles upon which Spanish empire drew.[44]

The laws governing the earlier transatlantic Iberian empires and their colonies recognized that nations had juridical personality, which could be asserted in the face of colonial rule.[45] In Roman law a slave's "personality" was also acknowledged, and nineteenth-century Spanish law, while defining slavery as the state of man reduced to property, did not confuse slaves with things.[46] As Fernando Ortiz observed, slaves in colonial Cuba, for instance, had limited rights but rights all the same: "One could not, in short, deny personhood to an enslaved man."[47]

"Personality" was also at stake in the Cuban independence wars and in the quest for abolition, as acknowledged by Spanish statesman Francisco Pi y Margall in 1870, when he presented to the courts a proposal for reforming government: Spain's "integridad territorial" (the union of the Peninsula and its overseas colonies) could not continue, Pi y Margall maintained, since "[l]as libertades individuales . . . 'forman parte de nuestra personalidad y donde quiera que haya hombres sometidos a nuestras leyes, allí debemos llevar nuestras libertades.' Debían, además, abolir la esclavitud" [individual liberties . . . "form part of our personality and wherever there are men subject to our laws, there we should bring our liberties." They had, moreover, to abolish slavery].[48] Such debates over *national* personality, inseparable here from the question of slavery, echo even in postindependence Cuba when, for instance, the vanguard magazine *Revista de avance* declared in 1927, in its quarter-century reevaluation of the young republic, that a protest against corruption evinced "The highest ideal of the Revolution: liberty to think, to be, to affirm personality [*afirmar la personalidad*]" in contrast with a "pseudo-colonial" attitude the magazine decried as prevalent.[49]

Maeztu's dismissal of subjectivity and personality must, then, be read against this history of the concepts and terms. And while Rousseau's romanticism was indebted to noble savage imagery frequently referencing the Americas, Maeztu bemoans the romantic discourse behind Latin American republicanism. He studies key documents from the U.S. and Latin American independence revolutions only to find that in the latter "motivo económico de la independencia no aparece para nada" [No economic motive whatsoever appears] (*El sentido* 204).

Maeztu is a keen but reactionary critic of nationalism, which he sees as a "sentimental, and romantic ideal" (*Authority, Liberty and Function* 92). Separatists' will to self-determination is a "passion, a nineteenth century madness" (*Con el directorio militar* 177). Sovereignty in the wake of World War I is a dangerous romantic illusion best quashed by supranational associations—the Church or *hispanidad* itself. As Villacañas points out, Maeztu had first to destroy "the ideal of sovereignty" in order to begin work constructing a Hispanist community of nations (399).

Meanwhile, as Maeztu's critique of romanticism and subjectivity informs his aesthetic theory, it is worth noting the extent to which his theory dovetails with views held by his British contemporaries. (Maeztu acknowledges their influence on him.) Maeztu's articles "On the Primacy of Things" and "The End of Romanticism" are clearly similar to an article by Hulme titled "Romanticism and Classicism," published sometime between 1911 and 1914, which rejects romanticism for what Nicholas Brown describes as a literature of "'small, dry things'" (18).[50] This would make Hulme's essay the likely inspiration for Maeztu's rather than the other way around—although it is impossible to know at what point Maeztu began frequenting Hulme's salon and hence how the shared ideas may have developed in conversation.[51]

How does this objectivist poetics connect to the great imperial concerns undergirding Maeztu's positions? Lynn Festa has argued, with respect to French and British eighteenth-century authors, that in a world of expanding empire, oriented toward commodity extraction and production rather than settler colonization, objects mediated relations more than did sentiment.[52] She implicitly suggests these positions echo in twentieth-century aesthetics when she invokes T. S. Eliot's concept of an "objective correlative" to describe things' relation to emotions

(118). Maeztu appears to recuperate such neoclassical preferences in his attempt to recuperate a prior moment in empire.

Liberal subjectivity in the early twentieth century is, for Maeztu, the baleful extension of a romanticism whose sin is to have stirred colonized peoples to desire their own freedom. This romanticism is indissociable for Maeztu from the imperial 1890s. Subjectivism, in his reckoning, is a direct result of the tension between the desires fueling global expansion (Iberian expansion into the Americas) and the late nineteenth-century exhaustion of colonial possibilities. In a single move he both acknowledges and denies the rights of colonized peoples to sovereignty and subjectivity when he calls "subjective rights" the result of a Renaissance discourse of "the free development of human personality" enabled by the Iberian discovery of the Americas and of the East Indies.

Maeztu argues that the Age of Discoveries led to a sense that the world was of "inexhaustible dimensions," permitting the conception of right as privilege. In 1916 he writes, "the world has been explored. There are now titles of property or sovereignty to the whole cultivable extensions of the planet" (*Authority, Liberty and Function* 273).[53] The implications are surprising: "To-morrow the subjective rights of the coloured races will be opposed to the subjective rights of the white races to-day. So long as these subjective rights are not limited, there can be no remedy for the injustices arising from the fact that some nations and individuals possess everything, or almost everything, and other nations and individuals possess nothing, or hardly anything" (*Authority, Liberty and Function* 273).[54] Although Maeztu argues here for a limit to the "subjective rights" of "coloured races" in advance of a future in which whites are not in power, he in the same breath acknowledges that a clash of "subjectivities"—also class struggle and anticolonial struggle—is unavoidable when gross inequality is operative.

Maeztu thus acknowledges the material conditions that motivate anticolonial revolt, warning Europeans that there is no philosophical justification for their appropriations. Put simply, he does not want formerly or presently colonized (or "coloured") peoples to claim independence, "personality," or "subjectivity." Sovereignty's emptiness becomes an excuse for denying it to past and present colonized peoples. José Rizal, the great Philippine nationalist, is dismissed as a romantic artist *racially* incapable of serious thought, for a true thinker would wonder "whence came his spirit of justification for his desire and pretension that his country, the Philippines, should figure in the circle of free and sovereign nations on earth, and that his race, Tagalog, should be one of the ruling races" (*Defensa de la hispanidad* 176). Maeztu concludes: "No one will again believe honestly in the cause of oppressed peoples after having seen how easily they become the oppressors. This is the crisis of nationalism" (*Don Quijote* 122). A critique of nationalism leads to a bad-faith dismissal of the cause of "oppressed peoples."

It comes as no surprise that Maeztu's final articulations of a philosophy of "objectivism" should unfold under the banner of a Catholic universalism in the same moment that Schmitt was developing his theory of the nomoi of the earth and Heidegger his notions of a historical people and "worlding." As Maeztu himself exemplifies, this historical consciousness was the product of imperial thought. He understood geographical notions of universalism to be historically contingent, earthly translations of a more spiritual form. They were a "territorial ideal that substituted in Hispanic nations for the Catholic one" (*Defensa de la hispanidad* 105). Inverting this, Maeztu formulated Hispanism as an extension of Christianity and defined it as a shared spirit among nations that had once belonged to the Spanish empire. Through the twofold defense of global exploration and religion, the Spanish, he boasted, were "the creators of universal history, which without us would only have been a series of histories of continents" [*una serie de historias de continentes*] (*Autobiografía* 101).

Atlantic histories of empire and slavery undergird Maeztu's aesthetic proposals, which, in their Anglophone objectivist versions (to which Maeztu was indebted and perhaps influenced), were taken up by concrete poetry in the 1950s. Maeztu, deeply influenced by the late nineteenth-century wars in North Africa and Cuba, continued to publish in Havana in the 1920s. A 1927 article in *Revista de avance* thus responded to one of Maeztu's prior articles in the same journal by calling his Hispanist universalism precisely (and ironically) "subjective" since, like Roman Empire, it believed itself to be the hero of universal destiny.[55] In *Revista de avance* and elsewhere in Cuban periodicals other aspects of late nineteenth-century conflicts continued to reverberate. In the next chapter I return to Cuba in the 1920s and 1930s to track how a discourse of things unfolded in literature from early twentieth-century Cuba.

CHAPTER 5

The Spirit of Martí in the Land of Coaybay

"Famous Toasts: 'Long Live the Republic!' At an enthusiastic banquet, this independence cheer has a double meaning." So begins an advertisement in a 1926 issue of the Cuban society magazine *Carteles*. The ad hurries to explain its "double meaning": "He who is the victim of bad digestion will never truly feel free without Hepatic Salt, the body is slave to the pernicious caprices of the stomach. Emancipate yourself! You must enjoy the table's pleasures with plenitude and without scruples!" (See Figure 7.) One can hardly imagine a more apt illustration of what Žižek has described as a transition from old-fashioned authoritarianism—here, colonial rule and slavery—to modern liberal capitalism, with its injunction to *enjoy* ("hay que gozar con plenitud y sin escrúpulos!").[1]

The advertisement appeared amid the young Cuban republic's sugar-fueled boom, though a few years after disturbing bank crises.[2] It parodies the language of independence and abolition—the principal causes in Cuba's nineteenth-century wars—in order to sell a digestion aid that facilitates more and better consumption. The ad copy confirms a common charge levied against the republic by Cuban intellectuals of the 1920s: namely, that nineteenth-century struggles for independence and abolition, and for postabolition racial equality, had given way after 1902 to a booming but corrupt, discriminatory, and dependent society of consumption, and that a quarter of a century into its existence the longed-for republic had fallen short. These 1920s writers contributed to an enduring, though reductive, narrative that the island had merely

Figure 7. Advertisement for Sal Hepática, "Viva la República," *Carteles*, May 16, 1926, p. 33. General Research Division, The New York Public Library, Astor, Lenox and Tilden Foundations.

passed from Spanish colony to U.S. neocolony, from formal dependence to economic dependence and a compromised sovereignty in the form of the Platt Amendment (1901–34), which gave the United States the right to intervene militarily in the island.

Cuba emerged from the nineteenth-century wars destitute: fighting between 1868 and 1878 had consumed two-thirds of the nation's wealth (Pérez, *On Becoming Cuban* 101). The subsequent 1895 war, with its reconcentration camps for civilians and scorching of land, further ravaged farms and businesses. Against this background, Louis Pérez Jr. argues, consumer culture's "new forms" were a "principal means through which a multitude reassembled their world and resumed their lives" (*On Becoming Cuban* 143).

In the literature of the postindependence republic these new forms of consumer culture featured prominently, and writers frequently used debates over thingliness and immateriality to gloss the transition from formal independence to economic dependence. In numerous literary works, we find that objects, relics, and products hint at the island's dependent status, while immaterial specters return to argue for a different future. At other times a ghostly evanescence depicts a vanishing economy, territory, even a fantasized "essence," while material things take on the reassuring resilience of the homely, tactile, and intimate—a coziness that yet becomes unhomely and haunted by invisible forces (foreign markets, debt restructuring) that rearrange everyday life.

To return to the advertisement, we might note that after such ruin, it is not surprising that the arrival of abundant wealth would occasion toasts. The world summoned in the advertisement and in the social pages of *Carteles*, where socialites participate in sports at the Havana Yacht Club or receive wisdom about how to best furnish "el living room," hums with wonder at newfound affluence. Who wouldn't rather worry about how to most enjoy food "con plenitud" than how to escape from literal enslavement or disenfranchisement, a reality for many Cubans of the prior generation? Yet the audience to whom the magazine was directed was mainly white, *habanero*, and upper class; for very few in this group were "emancipation," "enslavement," or possibly even "independence" real concerns.

The 1920s and 1930s also saw the most pointed targeting by writers, artists, and other intellectuals of the nation's ills of racism, class divisions, corruption, and undue connection to the U.S. economy and military. For no one was the republic that Martí had imagined realized. A 1930 essay from *Revista de avance* confessed that "In this moment, we have all felt a bit under the sign of Martí."[3] Again and again, popular authors emphasized the distance between Martí's ideals and the reality of the republic. Of course Cuba was not unique in seeing its wealth migrate to foreign-owned banks or its dreams of radical postslavery emancipation cede to bitter racial antagonisms. But the sense that its wars should have brought more radical change made the postindependence letdown particularly sour (Fernández 165). The targets of this disappointment and critique shift with evolving geopolitical conditions in the first decades of the twentieth century, as do the ways by which the critique is rendered in literature; these are the focus of this chapter.

The writings of José Antonio Ramos, Bonifacio Byrne, Alfonso Hernández Catá, and other authors discussed in this chapter constitute a particular corpus known for depicting a state that has jettisoned sovereignty for consumption. Many other kinds of literature were published in these decades, of course. Literary histories of the republican period identify a series of trends: a first period distinguished by historical novels about the previous independence wars, naturalist novels about the city and country, and *modernista* poetry. A second era begins in 1923 and ends in 1958, in which an avant-garde—mainly white and male, though associated with an emerging "afrocubanismo" that counted among its members Nicolás Guillén and Regino

Pedroso—formed the Grupo Minorista (1923–28). These writers published in the magazine *Social* and then in the *Revista de avance*. Following the avant-garde a wider variety of styles flourished, including a sparser literature by women: Aurora Villar Buceta, Carmela Nieto de Herrera, Graziella Garbalosa, Ofelia Rodriguez Acosta, Dulce María Loynaz, Mariblanca Sabas Aloma. Although many were leaders in the era's feminist movements, with few exceptions the literature that they produced contested women's rights and roles only timidly.

These periodizations are admittedly arbitrary, and other dates and watersheds could have been chosen—the 1912 massacre of the Afro-Cuban political party Independientes de Color, for example; the 1933 revolution; or the 1940 constitution.[4] Nevertheless, most writing from the first half of the century can be characterized as a *costumbrista* realism, whether in portraits of *guajiros* or life on the sugar *centrales*, historical novels treating the wars of independence or urban novels of a naturalist bent. Much of this literature also testifies to the experiences of immigrant groups and contending classes assembled in the new state in a period in which a racial order intensified: Chinese, Afro-Cubans, Jamaicans, Haitians, Italians, and "Gallegos."[5] These novels serve to explicate the new social map of the republic. A trenchant line from Miguel de Carrión's *Las impuras* (1919) defends this role of fiction (with echoes of Marx's estimation of Balzac over social science): "Latin America has not yet produced the patient and modest historian of private life that might help explain the genesis of those grand and lunatic movements of rebellion and reaction that almost continually rock our societies."[6]

Amid these works, the subgenre of the novels, poems, and plays describing the "new forms" that the republic was taking thematizes a shift from a romantic 1890s generation represented by Martí toward a new era of technology and commodities (which Martí himself, as we saw in Chapter 2, both critiqued and embraced). This literature enjoins readers to remember Martí's lessons, particularly the importance of literary "concretion" and the dangers of U.S. informal empire in the wake of Spanish formal empire.

From the *Revista de avance* writers to the eponymous group of authors associated with the magazine *Orígenes* in the 1940s, avant-garde writers saw in Martí a prescient concretude, in much the same way that the 1950s and 1960s Brazilian concrete poets looked back to Sousândrade.[7] In 1927, for instance, Raúl Roa wrote against literary critics who mistakenly identified Martí as a precursor to *modernismo*

Figure 8. Westinghouse Electric—La electricidad en la casa. *Social*, June 1922, p. 43. General Research Division, The New York Public Library, Astor, Lenox and Tilden Foundations.

(here, precious or symbolist poetry). Unlike the *modernistas* Julián del Casal, José Asunción Silva, Manuel Gutiérrez Nájera, or Rubén Darío, all of whom Roa describes as "locked in a hermetic Bastille of subjectivism," Martí's *Versos libres* marked for Roa a prescient avant-garde indebted to Martí's rendering of life through a "purely plastic prism" [*prisma puramente plástico*] that produced "surprising crystallizations" in which were united, "as if in a miraculous concretion [*concreción*], verbal richness and the suppleness of procedure."[8] Martí and his "concretion" were precursors to a Mallarméan imagism born, Roa writes, from the "condensation of new times" (254). Roa congratulates Martí for having comprehended, before the transatlantic vanguard movement of *ultraísmo*, a simplicity of form and for celebrating the beauty of bridges. In short, Roa places Martí in a tradition of concrete writing born of a dialectic between immateriality and materiality, change and construction.

More influential than Martí's aesthetics, however, were his moral, political, and prophetic texts. His warning against a potential wave of "surplus products" from the United States serves as an antecedent for critiques of an "American way of life." But both facets of Martí were important. An interest in Martí's style and a concern with a perceived transition from romantic anticolonialism to complacent consumerism focused attention on the new "forms" that republican life brought.

In this chapter I explore how Martí haunts republican literature in two significant ways: (1) in literary works in which Martí appears specifically as a specter or spirit rebuking a nation that does not measure up, and (2) in the treatment of things in republican literature and history, approaches that intersect in their use of Martí's body and spirit as vessels for materiality and immateriality. I contend that an immaterial, ghostly Martí haunts early post-1902 literature, later complemented by increasing attention to the thingliness of goods, furniture, and Martí's bones themselves.

The works that I read here thus chart a progression: in the years just after the 1895 war the spirit or remains of Martí echo his messianic discourse of jeopardized sovereignty. But these themes evolve into depictions of economic dependence and consumption as the former Spanish colony becomes more deeply connected to what Victoria de Grazia has termed, in reference to a European context, "market empire."[9] Martí haunts works by authors who believed the republic had traded territorial sovereignty for economic dependency. Martí appears as a specter—a material form of the immaterial—to protest the island's "dematerialization" by foreign capital.[10] At the same time, a cult of Martí celebrating both his ideas and his relics fuses with concerns about an influx of commodities and capital, as well as the dissolution of republican "spirit." For Walter Benjamin, commemoration is a secular version of worshiping relics that reveals the deepening alienation "of human beings, who take inventories of their past as of lifeless merchandise" (in Jameson, *Marxism and Form* 73). Martí and other war heroes' fetishized bones return in the early republic alongside merchandise as if inversions of Hamacher's "messianism of commodities."

THE SPIRIT OF MARTÍ

Martí's remains led the itinerant life of so many political corpses, interred and exhumed repeatedly. After being buried in a common grave in Dos Ríos in 1895, his body was moved in 1907, 1947, and 1951, when it was to be transferred to an elaborate tomb in Santiago de Cuba. But the architects of the new tomb found Martí's coffin empty, the remains dissolved by a dribble of water that had entered the tomb.[11] This historical accident morbidly mirrors what Alfred López has documented as the Cuban state's desire to both monumentalize and disperse Martí: to render him in ubiquitous marble busts on the one hand and to project him as an intangible spirit or "geist" on the other.[12] This vacillation between his absence and presence, his materiality and immateriality, also served as a model for other discussions of material culture and national "spirit."

In 1921 the government passed legislation authorizing how Martí was to be commemorated.[13] Busts were produced throughout the country and a lock of his hair placed in a museum. Lillian Guerra interprets this legislation as an attempt to control readings of the past that would highlight discrepancies between his writings and reality (252). We might also see this obsession with his bones as a compensation for a lack: for psychoanalyst Pierre Fédida, the materiality of relics summons the absent body in order to defy death.[14] Here the absent body is not just Martí or only his idea of the republic but a radically egalitarian vision that emerged from the nineteenth-century wars.[15] Martí's corpse represents a more inclusive nation that did not come to be. The Cuban republic restricted liberties for former slaves and for black Cubans—those who had fought for more than merely the goal of attaining independence from Spain. Black and white Cubans alike stressed the postwar betrayal of Martí's "vision of a racially fraternal nation" (de la Fuente, *A Nation* 33). Martí as a symbol and as a physical relic served, then, both as a way to control visions of the past and as a fetish compensating for a disappointing present.

A charm against absence and disappointing presents, Martí furthermore occupied a place in which dreams of the future played out. Marial Iglesias Utset has found that the coincidence between the establishment of the Cuban republic and a change of century heightened its strikingly *temporal* valence, spectacularly manifest in a Jacobinesque proposal for a new calendar whose year zero was to be 1895 (55–56). The centennial hope and growing disillusion apparent in many works from the early republican period produce a strange, jagged temporality, mixing future and past. We see this in Bonifacio Byrne's play *Matanzas en 1920 o el espíritu de Martí* (1908).[16]

Byrne, a poet who bridges the anticolonial and postcolonial generations, wrote romantic, insipid verse and owes his fame to the poem "Mi bandera," which recounts dismay at seeing the U.S. flag alongside the Cuban one in 1899. *Matanzas en 1920 o el espíritu de Martí*, however, is different. It purports to take place in a future time, although it actually alludes to its present (Martínez Carmenate 199–200). The play addresses the plight of the republic as a failure of Martí's "espíritu." Two years before the play debuted, a 1906 U.S. intervention had influenced "official commemorations of José Martí as the embodiment of the myth of social unity achieved during the 1895 War" (Guerra, *The Myth* 221). Byrne's play thus conjures a future (1920) to illuminate a present (1908) that responded to events in the recent past (1906), creating jags in time that echoed tensions between formal independence and the disappointments of postindependence reality.

In *Matanzas en 1920 o el espíritu de Martí* Byrne alludes to the island's debates about sovereignty by invoking Cain. In the biblical story, Cain murders Abel—the prototypical martyr—because Cain's gift is not accepted. (One wonders, too, whether Byrne was aware that one of Martí's noms de guerre was Abel.) A character warns: "¡Conservad mi reliquia! ¡Mi bandera! / Que el abatido espíritu reanima / Desde la azul esfera, / La miro cual profusa cabellera, / Flotar al aire en la empinada cima! / . . . Si una mano extranjera / La llegase a ultrajar ¡que una hoguera / Calcinada esa mano se suprima!" [Conserve my relic! My flag! / Reanimated by a depressed spirit / From the blue heavens, / I see it like thick locks, / Float in the air on the steep peak! / . . . If a foreign hand / Managed to defame it, let a charring bonfire / suppress his hand!] (Martínez Carmenate 200). The speaker challenges a usurper from beyond the grave, demanding that his flag, which he calls "my relic," be preserved. Alluding intertextually to Byrne's earlier poem "Mi bandera," the passage calls for a reanimation of spirit in the face of compromised sovereignty.

Byrne's play carries the subtitle *o el espíritu de Martí*, which can mean both "what Martí stood for" and "Martí's ghost," or better, specter: in

Specters of Marx, Jacques Derrida claims that what distinguishes Marx's *specter* from mere *spirit* is a "paradoxical phenomenality, the furtive and ungraspable visibility of the invisible . . . that non-sensuous sensuous of which *Capital* speaks."[17] Byrne's *espíritu* is such a specter, an invisibility that makes something visible, perhaps the ungraspable work of an influx of capital itself. The audience is reminded of a lost cause worthy of renewed pursuit with a "depressed spirit."

Disrupted temporalities, again linked to Martí, return seven years later in *El traidor,* a play by José Antonio Ramos (1915).[18] *El traidor* takes its plot from three stanzas of Martí's *Versos sencillos* (no. XXVIII) that serve as an epigraph and narrate a conflict between a dead father and his son, on opposing sides of Cuba's independence wars:

Por la tumba del cortijo
Donde está el padre enterrado
Pasa el hijo, de soldado
Del invasor: pasa el hijo.

El padre, un bravo en la guerra,
Envuelto en su pabellón
Álzase, y de un bofetón
Lo tiende muerto por tierra.

El rayo reluce, zumba
El viento por el cortijo.
El padre recoge al hijo
Y so lo lleva a la tumba. (*El traidor* 6)

[By the tomb on the estate
Where the father lies buried
The son passes, a soldier
For the invading army: he passes.

The father, brave in the war,
Wrapped in his flag
Rises, and in one blow
Strikes his son dead

The lightening flashes, the wind
Screams through the estate.
The father gathers up his son
And carries him to the grave.]

Ramos adapts Martí's poem about the Ten Years' War into a one-act drama set during the 1895 war. By assigning to the son and father participation in the two different wars, Ramos establishes a continuity between them but also a generational difference. The father and son have the same common name, Juan García, a sameness that underscores their radical moral divergence, sealed by the father's rebaptizing of his son as "traitor" (25). The doubling is echoed in a superfluous repetition early on in the play, in which two soldiers fighting for Cuban independence notice a strange man (the father, now a ghost), recalling the opening scene of *Hamlet*. They comment, "Que hombre más extraño este hombre" [what a strange man this man].

The play presents haunting doubles in both its content and form. The two Juan Garcías embody a political splitting of the masculine genealogy of the patria across years of independence wars. The conflict echoes something that Martí wrote about his own Spanish-born father: "Y si a los esp. / por ser españoles, los ataco, mi padre saldría de la tumba, y me diría: parricida" [And if I attack the Span. / for being Spanish, my father would arise from his tomb, and tell me: parricide] (*Obra completa* 22:11).

The ghostly father that drags his son into his tomb seeks to right the flaws of an insufficiently "Cuban" son, but as the two fall into the same tomb, the differences between them collapse. Marc Redfield has observed that the apparently generic tombs of the Unknown Soldier commemorate in fact a particular death: a male, military death that cancels out other forms of loss and identity, all of which are subsumed into the national.[19] In *El traidor* the tomb represents such a militant, male, national subject, but in the play other differences persist: for instance, the Cuban soldiers discuss their Spanish grandfathers' cruel treatment of both "cubanos" and "esclavos," suggesting a mutual exclusion of "Cuban" and "slave" that highlights how this unresolved past haunts the republic, a literary reflection of how the postindependence constitution literally did not count African-born citizens (who had, of course, been slaves) as either Cuban or foreign.[20]

Another doubling occurs in the literary resurrection of Martí through his *Versos sencillos* and, more specifically, his verses about specters. One poem by Martí begins, "He vivido: me he muerto: / y en mi andante / fosa sigo viviendo" [I have lived: I have died: / and in my walking / grave I go on living] (*Poesía completa* 91).[21] Ramos confirms this vision of Martí as a living dead, as resurrected or as a ghost that haunts because that for which he was ostensibly "martyred" did not come to pass.

THE REPUBLIC FURNISHED FORTH

By the 1920s evocations of national essence and spirit cede to critiques of the material conditions of the republic. Spirit no longer meant Martí's message; material no longer meant his bones. Now the intangible was equated with an invisibly manipulated economy, the tangible with new material culture. In a 1940 letter to the Communist Revolutionary Union within Cuba's constitutional assembly Ramos conjured a materialist Martí: "Martí is with us, comrades. Martí, today, would be accused of being a communist. Communist today is anyone who feels repulsion for this indecent grab of public posts . . . in order to rob: to create those ephemeral fortunes we have seen made and unmade in thirty-eight years of republic, without their leaving a single concrete industry, without leaving anything Cuban, nothing constructive or solid—even if capitalist!"[22] For Ramos, foreign investment and internal corruption had eroded Cuban industry.[23] The nation itself is ghostly, bereft of "concrete industry." Seven years earlier, Ramos had written that he felt he was witnessing "la disolución de nuestro espíritu nacional!" [the dissolution of our national spirit!][24] The critic Emma Álvarez-Tabío Albo suggests that much republican literature advanced a cultural nationalism meant to compensate for lost sovereignty; yet she herself employs such language when she writes that "the great latifundios in the hands of foreign capital and dependence on the United States began to literally dematerialize the national being" (145–46).

The hypostasization of "culture" against disappearing finances that Álvarez-Tabío Albo identifies can be seen in Ramos, who returned throughout his career to discussions of materiality, materialism, and immateriality. In a presentation at the Sociedad de Estudios Afrocubanos in 1937 titled "Cubanidad y mestizaje," published in the first issue of Fernando Ortiz's *Estudios afrocubanos*, Ramos framed a discussion of national and racial theories as a casting aside of romanticism to discuss the "burning" topic of "materialism and spiritualism." He called for a true economic history of Cuba to replace the image of a "romantic colonial past" that, in reality, had been rife with "untold ferociousness," greed, inhumanity, and "sadism and crimes" and had continued on in republican racisms (93).[25] His own essay, however, turns *mestizaje* into a thing against evanescence.

Ramos's discussion of materiality and materialism against ephemeral finances or racial discrimination unfolded against other debates in which consumerism replaced struggles for more significant material changes. As the advertisement discussed at the start of this chapter demonstrates, a simplistic, but not incorrect, opinion prevailed that the wars begun in 1868 for independence and abolition—to remove humans from the status of commodity—had yielded minimal democratic advances but a greater access to consumer products.

To a certain extent, the symbolic struggle over the meaning of the republic now played out in more quotidian realms, where the United States' increasing power in the region registered in its abundant material culture, as Louis Pérez Jr. documents exhaustively in *On Becoming Cuban* (1999). American products were not uncommon in Cuba before the 1895 war, and Pérez even suggests that consumer goods may have been a destabilizing factor for Spanish empire, "undermining some of the most fundamental social assumptions of the colonial order" and instantiating a kind of democracy of mass consumption (66). But in postwar Cuba, he claims, they became so central that "democracy and political liberty . . . acquired a material dimension" (84).

Between 1895 and 1920, U.S. imports soared from $10 million to $404 million (Pérez, *On Becoming Cuban* 129, 327), while the post-1914 period in particular saw "a seemingly endless flow of commodities of every imaginable type" (281). Yet if these products were signs of Cuba's increasing incorporation into U.S. markets, historians have questioned the narrative that describes Cuba's independence from Spain and subsequent neocolonial relationship with the United States as the simple result of restrictive Spanish economic policies or inevitable U.S. hegemony.

Antonio Santamaría García and Alejandro García Álvarez, for instance, find that Cuba's particular role in an evolving international economic system "better explains its independence process than the hits or misses of Spanish policies and politics" (48). José Piqueras, for his part, is skeptical of descriptions of a nineteenth-century split whereby Cuba was a political colony of Spain but already an economic one of the United States, a bifurcation "that invariably and perhaps also imperceptibly establishes a fatalist (and fatal) union of both conditions under semi-sovereignty or North American tutelage" (31). Piqueras finds textual evidence in 1890 Spanish government pamphlets that Spain still remained the significant metropole (19). Indeed, he finds that in the years leading up to the 1895 war Spanish economic interests were stronger than ever, and, even allowing for the "overwhelming dependence of Cuba on the North American market," they ensured Spain was a metropole "in all senses of the term, including that without which colonialism loses its meaning: material gain" (121).[26]

Why, then, has a narrative endured (perhaps first advanced in republican literature) in which a colony stifled by Spanish economic policy is so dependent on the U.S. market that it merely transitions from empire to neocolonial state? Piqueras argues that nationalist historiography has blinded us to the propagandistic nature of the claims put forth by late nineteenth-century Cuban business interests, who articulated a resilient but intellectually dishonest narrative in which the Cuban economy was portrayed as captive to Spanish law. This narrative, Piqueras claims, was designed to pressure the Spanish government to obtain a treaty with the United States to allow for free export of Cuban sugar to North America, benefiting sugar barons (241).[27] The rhetoric of victimhood advanced by the island's late nineteenth-century *burguesía* favored their own pockets but "trickled down throughout Cuban society and fostered socially convergent interpretations" (241–42). According to this narrative, Cubans wanted access to better-made and more expensive U.S. goods but were crippled by Spanish tariffs. In truth, however, Piqueras claims, it was the inferior Spanish goods that were sought after by the "popular" classes, whose ranks had swelled in the 1880s and 1890s with recently emancipated slaves and recently arrived Spanish immigrants (241–42). In Cuba, as in Brazil, imports were minimal under slavery (when slaves had little purchasing power) but surged after abolition (Bulmer-Thomas 44–45).

Piqueras thus turns on its head an argument used in the 1890s to justify Cuban independence and referenced ever since to explain the late nineteenth-century wars: namely, that Cubans were deprived of access to basic goods due to Spanish restrictions. At the same time, however, his findings confirm the rhetorical place of "products" and consumption in the rationale and discourse of both the 1895 and, eventually, the 1959 revolutions.

The story of a Spanish policy of limited consumption, under formal empire, followed by a U.S. era of mass consumption, during a mediated sovereignty, was well cemented by the 1920s when a nativist anti-imperialism emerged among both popular sectors and the lettered elite. *Atuei*, *Revista de avance*, and other publications by *minoristas* discussed anti-imperialism, "afrocubanismo" (often little more than folkloric fantasies of *mulatas de rumbo*, *comparsas*, and so on), and fears for the masculine vigor of *cubanidad*. Much as the *sertanejo* was transformed into the bedrock of the Brazilian nation, so "the black Cuban" became in these years "the firmest base, the richest and most infallible repository from which the feeling of Cubanness sustains itself" (Ramos, "Cubanidad y mestizaje" 107).

This telluric repository was imagined as a bulwark against the "disappearance" of *cubanidad*. But if such imagined "dematerialization" was enacted by foreign capital and dependence on the United States, as Álvarez-Tabío Albo suggests, and meant the swallowing of smaller national sugar plantations by larger U.S. corporations, the question remains, whose Cuba was disappearing? For black Cuban and West Indian sugarcane cutters, it surely mattered little who in particular was exploiting them. And though the United States indisputably brought a more virulent form of racism to the island, protests against it were also a cover for Cuba's homegrown versions. A *Revista de avance* piece about West Indian and Haitian immigration uses anti-American nationalism to cover for Cuban racism, in which it was not exactly the "blackness of the skin" of Haitian and Jamaican laborers that bothered the authors, but the fact that "non-Cuban mouths are crying out to the world the drama in our canefields." Jamaicans and Haitians, "semi-enslaved on Yanqui sugar latifundios," were in the same breath accused of "blackening Cuba"—equated with "intellectual ruin"—and of speeding the island's conversion into an "enormous plantation run—directly or indirectly—by a dozen North American landowners."[28] Indeed, such articles hint at the enduring legacy of a broader Caribbean antiracist struggle *beyond* nationalism. The "specter" of a second Haitian revolution, more than a century after its success, was not only invoked as a justification for U.S. military interference in the war of 1895 but imagined in the North American black press as an inspiration for the 1912 protests over the abolition of the Partido Independiente de Color.[29]

Black Cuban culture was seized upon in these years by the primarily white vanguard as a mark of authenticity against economic dependency. Carpentier's *Écue-yamba-ó* thus brandished "Afro-Antilleanness" against a monstrous U.S. sugar industry, summed up in affirmations such as "El bongo: Antídoto de Wall Street!" [The bongo: Antidote to Wall Street!] (119).[30] The novel narrates sugarcane worker Menegildo Cué's initiation into the secret society of Abakuá. Anke Birkenmaier has illuminated the connections between the novel's inclusion of photographs of Afro-Cuban ritual objects and a surrealist, ethnographic gaze. We might, however, connect the novel's attention to objects to Carpentier's language itself.

The book's reproductions of Abakuá signs are visual codes beyond the vocabulary of the white lettered society for whom the vanguard "objectivist" prose is directed. Carpentier complements these *anaforuana*, which concentrate visual, nonverbal meaning in a symbol, with a comparable reading of the material culture of different immigrant groups on the sugar *centrales*: Galicians, Chinese, Jamaicans, Poles, and Haitians, as well as of the furnishings of the American hotel, in which wares and brands become emblems:

> El hotel American hace barnizar su bar de falsa coaba. Hay cigarrillos extranjeros con las figuras de príncipes bizcos. . . . Marcas que ostentan escudos reales, khedives o mocasines indios. Los cafetuchos y cantinas se aderezan. Cien alcoholes se sitúan en los estantes. La caña santa, que huele a tierra. Los rones "de garrafón." . . . Carta blanca. Carta de oro. Las estrellas de coñacs se vuelven constelaciones. . . . Medallas. La Exposición de París. El preferido. (*Écue-yamba-ó* 19–20)
>
> [The American hotel varnishes its bar of fake mahogany. There are foreign cigarettes with figures of cross-eyed princes. . . . Brands that brandish real shields, khedives, or Indian moccasins. The coffee stands and cantinas dress up. One hundred kinds of alcohol line the shelves. The holy cane, which smells of earth. The "jug" rum. . . . *Carte blanche*. Gold card. The cognac's stars become constellations. . . . Medals. The Paris Exposition. The preferred one.]

In this passage we note that finished products of an export economy (cigarettes and rum, products of tobacco and sugar) are displayed beautifully, their content dressed up with symbols of gold, stars, constellations, medals, brand names. The writing itself creates a staccato beat of objects—a rhythm that returns, now more sinuous, forty years later in Carpentier's description of princely things with which he opens his *Concierto barroco* (1974): "De plata los delgados cuchillos, los finos tenedores; de plata los platos donde un árbol de plata labrada en la concavidad de sus platas" [Of silver the slender knives, the delicate forks; of silver the salvers with silver trees chased in the silver of the hollows].[31]

Carpentier employs the style later in the novel in what seems an antecedent to Sarduy's "Mood Indigo" and the latter's general obsession with circles, orbits, *anillos* (discussed in this book's epilogue). Carpentier writes: "[P]ececillos de cristal, tirados por un elástico, saltaban de ola en ola. Punto. Anillo. Lente. Disco. Circo. Cráter. Órbita. Espiral de aire en rotación infinita. . . . Cilindros palpitantes, discos de luz, elipses con cola, emigraban en la noche de la tormenta" [small crystalline fish, catapulted by an elastic, leaped from wave to wave. Tip. Ring. Lens. Disk. Pit. Crater. Orbit. Spiral of air in infinite rotation . . . palpating cylinders, disks of light, ellipses with a tail, emigrated in the storm's night] (39). The passage ends with an attempt to visually render a billboard torn asunder by the wind and with an announcement of the "ciclón" itself, which serves as an allegory of both natural cycles and the cycles of harvest and dead time (*zafra* and *tiempo muerto*) that the sugar industry imposes on the novel's characters: "CI. A. ROS. Las letras que caen cortan el asfalto como hachazos [. . .] CI . . . C . LON, dicen todavía los rótulos. CI . . . C . LO, dirán ahora" [CI. A. RETTES. The letters that fall cut the asphalt like ax blows. [. . .] CY. . . C. LONE the signs still announce. CY. . . C. LE they must now say] (40).[32]

Carpentier critiques the republic through his treatment of objects in the American hotel. Byrne, too, although he hails from an older generation, turns from his flags and patriotic poems to household things to indicate larger historical forces at work. His poem "Los muebles" (1914), which was included in Félix Lizaso and José Antonio Fernández de Castro's canon-building 1926 anthology *La poesía moderna en Cuba (1882–1925)*, ostensibly depicts a world of bourgeois interiority, but in which critique appears in spectral form. The poem begins lightly enough, "¿Por qué no? Cada mueble puede hacernos alguna confidencia" [Why not? Every piece of furniture can reveal something to us], but turns strangely morbid:

> ¿Habéis visto los viejos escritorios?
> Semejan, por su aspecto, emperadores
> Que yacen en sus vastos dormitorios,
> Pensando que la pompa y los honores
> Son pálidos fantasmas ilusorios.

. . . .
¿No habéis visto en los espejos
Pavorosos perfiles
De rostros demarcados
Que acaso llegaran desde muy lejos,
Tristemente impulsados
Por ráfagas errantes y sutiles?

Si veis a media noche los estantes
En donde los infolios permanecen,
Notaréis que los libros se estremecen
En poder de unas manos vacilantes,
Que en aire se alargan, y parecen
lirios que van por el espacio errantes.
. . . .
Hay efigies muy bellas
En las paredes próximas pendientes,
Que nos hablan de espíritus ausentes
Cuando fijamos la mirada en ellas.

Pero hay otras de ceño cejijunto . . . ,
¡esas parecen que se están odiando!,
y, al verlas, me pregunto:
¿en qué estarán pensando? . . .
¡tal vez en las pupilas de un difunto
que desde lejos las está mirando![33]

[Have you seen the old desks?
They seem, from their appearance, emperors
Lying in vast bedrooms,
Thinking that pomp and honors
Are pale illusory phantoms
. . . .
Have you not seen in the mirror
Angry profiles of marked faces
That perhaps arrive from far away,
Sadly urged onward
By errant, subtle gusts?

If at midnight you look at the shelves
Where folios are kept,

You will see the books tremble
Possessed by quivering hands,
Which stretch away in the air, and seem
Lillies lost in space
. . . .
There are beautiful effigies
Hanging on the nearby walls,
That speak to us of absent spirits
When we gaze at them.

But there others with a frowning brow . . . ,
Those seem hateful!
And, looking at them, I wonder:
What might they be thinking of? . . .
perhaps of the pupils of a corpse
watching them from afar!]

The function of the furniture in "Los muebles" alternates between a materialization of spirit and an animation of things, in which "hateful" (or hating) effigies are studied by a far-off corpse (Juan García *padre*? Martí?). Do the pupils perhaps belong to the corpse of a recent and dismal past of slavery and colonial rule not yet buried, as do a corpse's pupils in Regino Pedroso's poem "Dos poemas chinos" (1933), which tells of generations of Chinese Cuban men separated by the wars of independence? (A deceased grandfather's pupils stare from the abyss between the wars and the grave.)[34]

In Byrne's poem the books are "en poder de unas manos vacilantes," manhandled invisibly as if by a *mort main*, an echo of the hand in Byrne's *Matanzas en 1920* and an allusion to the presence of an unwanted other. His unhomely interior belongs to a literature of postwar: many men returned from years fighting in the swamp trenches of the war, or in exile in Florida, to a place that was unrecognizable and subject to military interventions. As a 1903 Miguel de Carrión short story puts it, "The furniture, the clothes, the buildings, the streets, the customs and the women underwent a transformation as radical as the political change had been."[35] The most familiar references were as new as the state itself.

Of course, furniture is a staple prop in any realist writing. But a number of authors in the first decades of the twentieth century used it to channel historicity. Examples in the Anglophone tradition include

Henry James's *The Spoils of Poynton* (1896) and Elizabeth Bowen's *The Death of the Heart* (1938). For Frankfurt School critics, furniture encoded meaning: Benjamin read turn-of-the-century European culture in its "plush—the material in which traces are left especially easily" (22), while Adorno speculated that "ultimately, perhaps, even carpets, ornaments, all nonfigural things longingly await interpretation."[36] Among Latin American *modernistas* and vanguard poets one finds Darío reading British racial attributes in furniture styles on display in Paris at the Great Exposition of 1900[37] and César Vallejo writing metaphysically of furniture in *Trilce*: "buena guardarropía, ábreme / tus blancas hojas: / quiero reconocer siquiera al 1" [good wardrobe, open for me / your blank pages / I want to recognize at least the 1].[38] Later, in "Viaje a la Semilla" (1944), Carpentier would use furniture to illustrate how the homely becomes strange as time runs backward and a man turns into a child.[39]

If furniture serves as an index of class among realist authors or as a hieroglyph to be decoded in critical theory, Byrne's "Los muebles" and a homonymous short story by Hernández Catá—also the author of a book titled *Mitología de Martí* (1929)—suggest unhomely exchanges between subject and object, thingliness and spirit, in republican literature. Hernández Catá writes of the dark forces nestled in the most intimate spaces of home and nation. His short stories feature infidelity, murderous rage, and class conflict. In one, a babysitter scares her charge to death ("Cuento de amor" [1927]). In another, field hands hailing from all sectors of an immigrant underclass—Haitians, Jamaicans, Italians, Germans, Spaniards—"escorias de raza" [scum of the races] (42)—murder a group of Chinese workers because they are willing to work for lower wages than their Antillean peers ("Los Chinos" [1933]). In "Los muebles" (1931), Hernández Catá describes a man's descent into madness, manifest as a dawning fear of the furniture in his home.[40]

The malady begins in a furniture store. A cabinet catches the attention of the protagonist for its imposing weightiness, its "odious solidity!" (*Mejores cuentos* 94). The cabinet seems to look at him funny: "'Las cosas tienen una actitud de mofa cruel para los hombres, y los ven pasar entre crujidos de sarcasmo . . . ¡Aquel armario nos miraba de una manera . . . !" [Things have a cruel mocking attitude toward men, whose comings and goings they punctuate with sarcastic wisecracks . . . that chest looked at us in such a way!] (95). Like the protagonist of Byrne's poem, Hernández Catá's protagonist feels watched by a vaguely malevolent spirit. As he descends into madness, it is no longer the enduring furniture that mocks the protagonist's mortality, but, in a sudden flip and reversal, it is the protagonist who, as if the furniture, sees himself as a dead man:

> En la pared ví mi sombra en una silueta rígida, yacente. . . . Me ví muerto como he de estar un día. . . . Y al mismo tiempo todos los muebles de la habitación—la mesa de noche, el lavabo, las sillas—empezaron a gritarme odiosamente: "¡Nosotros no necesitamos ser tan fuertes como el armario de la almoneda para vivir más que tú, pobre hombre. Afánate, lucha, que nosotros te hemos de ver como te has visto ahora: muerto, ¡muerto!, ¡muerto! . . . ¡Ja, ja, ja!" Y se reían. (96)
>
> [On the wall I saw my shadow in a rigid, prone silhouette. . . . I saw myself dead as I will be one day. . . . And at the same time all the furniture in the room—the night table, the sink, the chairs—began to cry out hatefully: "We don't need to be as strong as the chest to live longer than you, poor man. Rally, fight, we must see you as you've just seen yourself: dead, dead! dead!, ha ha ha!" And they laughed.]

Driven into a murderous rage by their taunting, the protagonist smashes the furniture to pieces, landing himself in a sanitarium. The thingliness of the furniture and its transformation into spirit mock the man's mortality (disappearance) and suggest an invisible and unwanted visitor in his home.

I want to suggest that Byrne, Hernández Catá, and Carpentier choose furniture as an instantiation of the most "at hand" of objects that have become most unhomely in a moment in which furniture and theories about the ideal home were being pushed on Cuban readers. The 1920s magazine *Social*, for instance, ran a series of articles about new ways of arranging furniture and inhabiting rooms. One article gave tips on how to decorate the bedroom, while another, "La saleta o 'Living Room,'" advised readers on how to inhabit the new space: "When thinking of the *saleta* or 'living room,' our first thought should be of repose and comfort . . . comfort, in the armchairs and 'chaise-longue', chairs, tables, lamps and other appropriate details, all grouped in a pleasing intimacy";[41] living rooms, the article advises its readers, served to avoid kitchen odors. Here we see the Cuban home undergoing changes to better reflect U.S. hygienic theories and consumer taste in the very years, Susan Buck-Morss writes, when "the ideology of the private home came to bear a tremendous burden, that of legitimating the entire system of industrial capitalism."[42]

In a moment in which domestic space was the arena for battling ideological claims to modernity, political economy, and what counted as the republic's achievements, the spirits of Byrne's or Hernández Catá's furniture replace the overt symbolism of Martí in *Matanzas en 1920 o el espíritu de Martí* and other works. Their use of furniture to thematize philosophical questions of death, temporality, change, and alienation is consistent with a long tradition in which furniture represents the most concrete things against deceptive appearance. Plato invoked tables and beds as the real against which he could dismiss the mere semblance of poetry; Marx's famous passage from *Capital* on the commodity fetish argues that an "everyday thing, wood," once it becomes a commodity, begins to produce "out of its wooden brain grotesque ideas, far more wonderful than 'table-turning' ever was," recalling the spirits of republican furniture.[43] Meanwhile, coeval with Hernández Catá's story, Van Doesburg's manifesto for concrete art offered as its example of the concrete a representation of a piano.[44] Strikingly, the illustration accompanying Hernandez Catá's "Los muebles" in its original anthology *Manicomio* (1931) is a sketch by Galician artist Arturo Souto Feijoo of an enraged man attacking a piano with an ax.[45] (See Figure 9.)

These 1930s reflections on furniture would continue in neo-avant-garde philosophy and art. In Brazil, Waldemar Cordeiro made several works about chairs in 1964, including *Subdesenvolvido* [Underdeveloped], a severed chair and table affixed to a door, and then, as if allegorizing concretude's disappearance into a post-concrete virtual period, a chair half disappearing into the wall titled *Tudo Consumido* [All consumed]. (See Figure 10.)

Cordeiro's works were made in dialogue with observations by Max Bense, who described Brazilian constructivist works as characterized by "an interpenetration of two states of things—things of practical consumption and things of theoretical consumption, for instance chair legs and polygons."[46] And everyday furniture, as we will see in Chapter 6, was invoked by Brazilian poet and theorist Ferreira Gullar in his influential 1959 definition of the "non-object." Cordeiro's chairs, moreover, anticipate seminal U.S. conceptualist furniture pieces: Joseph Kosuth's "One and Three Chairs" (1965) and Vito Acconci's

Figure 9. Illustration by Arturo Souto Feijoo for "Los muebles," by Alfonso Hernández Catá (1931).

"Step Piece" (1970).[47] Both artists took to heart John Cage's rejoinder to Clement Greenberg's lament that anything was considered art ("including a door, a table, or a blank sheet of paper"): "'We must bring about a music which is like furniture'" (Kotz 38).[48] Cordeiro's popcretes and conceptual art, of course, come decades after the early twentieth-century meditations on things. What is significant about the representations of spirited furniture in the earlier moment is that they document the replacement of the overt symbolism of Martí. The messianism associated with a spectral Martí dissipates, and critique

Figure 10. Waldemar Cordeiro, *Tudo Consumido* (1964). José Serber Collection. Courtesy of Analívia Cordeiro.

becomes as materialist as a new material culture that nonetheless remains haunted by a feeling of the *unheimlich*.

COAYBAY

We can track this shift clearly in Byrne's and Ramos's work. Byrne followed his "mano ultrajante" in *Matanzas en 1920 o el espíritu de Martí* with a meditation on an uncanny hand rifling through furniture, while Ramos followed his overt morality play *El traidor* with a more intricate political allegory in his novel *Coaybay* (1926), where again a patriarch accuses his son of being a traitor. *Coaybay* is the story of failed revolutions, dictatorship, and dependency in "Coaybay," an imaginary Latin American nation, neighbor to "Norlandia." Its capital is the "gran ciudad moderna y norlandizada" [great modern and northlandized city] that yet maintains Spanish colonial palaces; the two styles are described equally in the novel as examples of "industria extranjera" [foreign industry] (30). Again we are presented with a narrative of transition between Spanish and U.S. empire.

The novel is essentially a satire of Cuba as it faces corruption, economic pressure from the United States, and political instability. At the outset, the young republic, led by dictator Ricardo Monteblanco, is beset by money woes. A Mr. Stoneliver, president of the "Norlandic Bank of Coaybay," frowns upon unpaid external debt and a chaotic monetary system. While Coaybay's 1876 Liberal Revolution was glorious on the level of ideals, it left a financial mess in its wake: "[N]adie dejaba de advertir que desde aquella fecha la plata y el oro habían desaparecido, así como los precios razonables de las cosas, para dejar lugar a una invasión de papel moneda sin valor estable, y a un aumento incesante en el costo de la vida" [No one could avoid noticing that from that date onward silver and gold disappeared, as well as reasonable prices for things, leaving in their wake paper money of unstable worth and a steady increase in the cost of living] (72–73). Stoneliver wipes out the debt and begins new lines of credit, and—as was indeed the case for much of the region during the 1870–1914 period—such credit enables an export-led economy to flourish.[49] But when World War I breaks out, Coaybay stops exporting raw materials, which in turn brings imports to a halt, drastically lowering customs collections. Previously banks loaned money with little attention to real value; now "cuando esos bienes y mercancías volvieron a su precio natural, el dinero prestado quedó en el aire" [when those goods and merchandise returned to their natural price, the loans remained floating in the air] (76).

Coaybay's ghost is no longer Martí's spirit but the nation-state itself: *Coaybay* is allegedly the name for the land of the dead in the Taino, the language of an original Caribbean people. The nation's disappearance is further embodied in its main character, Washington, who symbolically kills himself off at the novel's end after emigrating to Norlandia and changing his name twice. Washington is the character modeled most closely on Ramos. He spends a few years in the United States, as did Ramos, and is a pragmatist, a bit of a socialist, and a "productivist": he abandons his old-fashioned father for a farm where he will raise chickens and pigs and crops—"A producir algo" [to produce something] (106). In the same year that Maeztu publishes his lectures collected as *El sentido reverencial del dinero*, Washington lectures others on "el sentido económico de la Historia" [the economic sense of

History] while another character is worried about "el origen y la verdadera naturaleza del dinero" [the origin and true nature of money] (134, 114).

Midway through the novel, Washington assumes the name Arturo Portales after assassinating Coaybay's dictator. The dictator's death allows Washington's father, Marcelo Peñalba de Mendoza, a well-meaning patriot and veteran of the fictitious 1876 Glorious Revolution, to assume the presidency during an interregnum. Despite his republican ideals, Peñalba de Mendoza quickly becomes a dictator himself in the name of efficiency and safety. Washington flees to Norlandia and changes his name again. His maternal *nombre de guerra*, Portales, becomes "Paul Tallies," an anglicized corruption:

> Arturo Portales, a la sazón, también había desaparecido. La torpeza de un capataz para escribir nombres latinos lo había aniquilado, escribiendo en una nómina Paul Tallies como el de aquel extranjero que hubo de decírselo a viva voz al recoger su chapa de simple peón: Mr. Portales. Paul Tallies, despierto a la vida intensa y complicada de Norlandia, dejó pronto su metálica chapa bautismal de simple peón para manejar—con enormes ventajas sobre sus infelices compañeros—una moderna invención, utilizadora del aire en la vieja ambición humana que empezó en Babel. (344)
>
> [Arturo Portales, by then, had also disappeared. Some boss's inability to write Latino names had annihilated him, writing on a list Paul Tallies like that stranger who had to tell him in person to get his simple peon's title: Mr. Portales. Paul Tallies, alive to the intense and complicated life in Norlandia, soon abandoned his humble metal baptismal plaque to manage—with great advantage over his hapless colleagues—a modern invention, which used air in the old human ambition that began in Babel.]

Portales begins his career in Norlandia with a simple printing press but shows a knack for succeeding in a world of "tallies" and media. Washington/Paul, in a letter to his father, scorns "the messianism, the fatal tendency cultivated for centuries in our minds," demanding in its place a scientific organization of politics, and dismisses all "candidates for Messiah" (131, 133). His brother, eventual minister of Coaybay in

Norlandia, advises their father to replace messianic dreams of national sovereignty with technology, cited above in the introduction: "Wake up, mon vieux, for the world is transforming before our eyes. That exalted independence of our delirious patrias . . . is no longer possible"; instead a host of new media are the elements of spiritual value: "What does it matter that we are losing day by day a little of the old values: that absolute and invulnerable independence for example?" (334).

The messianism of the independence era is gone, and a networked global market is the new horizon of historicity. An article from a 1926 issue of *Revista telefónica cubana*, a Cuban trade magazine oriented toward workers of the International Telephone and Telegraph Company, confirms this view, arguing that "inalterable, indivisible, eternal" time itself is now best embodied by planetwide technologies: now, the article declares, it is the telephone company, not "human misery," that is truly immortal. (See Figure 12.) The telephone "collects human voices from pole to pole . . . and transmits them to the farthest points of the planet. For it, distance is a myth . . . stronger than death, it rises above all the earth, challenging space and time."[50] Commonplaces about the abolition of time and space by media technologies become an argument for the transcendence of time, space, and humanity.

While male genealogies measure time in both *El traidor* and *Coaybay*, the object of male struggle changes in the decade between 1915 and 1926. In *Coaybay* the conflict between two generations of Cuban men takes on a different cast. (Washington's mother is dead before the story begins, allowing the struggle to unfold as one between fathers and sons.) In *El traidor* Juan García, *padre* of the Ten Years' War, accuses his son of being a traitor to Cuban independence from Spain; in *Coaybay* Don Marcelo, veteran of the Glorious Revolution, accuses Washington of being a bad son, a "bad patriot," and a "traitor" for moving to Norlandia (346). In the earlier play, the father kills his son; in *Coaybay* Washington/Arturo/Paul dispenses with his selves in a single generation. At the novel's end he admits to feeling "dominado por otro individuo, que me impide ser yo mismo" [dominated by another individual, which impedes me from being myself] (341).

I suggest we read these repetitions not as gratuitous redundancies but, like other works' retrocessions, repetitions, and descriptions of a time out of joint, as pointing to something important about what time felt like in 1920s Cuba. *Coaybay*'s creaky narrative, dependent on stock characters such as Washington and his patriarchal dictator father, allegorizes its own repetitiveness as a product of repeating

Figure 11. "Cualquiera puede 'filmar' con un Cine-Kodak." Kodak Cubana, Ltd. *Social*, May 1929, p. 60. General Research Division, The New York Public Library, Astor, Lenox, and Tilden Foundations.

boom-and-bust cycles. In a scene concerned with the consolidation (*refundir*) of the external debt, the director of the Norlandic Bank proposes a resolution to the economic crisis in the shape of a new loan "en el cual se refundiría . . . *el Refundido*, así como los intereses pendientes de éste. Todo dependía de la rápida pacificación del territorio nacional" [In which he would consolidate . . . *the Consolidated*, as well as all related interests. All depended upon the pacification of the national territory] (243). A debt restructured during brighter days becomes an unwanted tie to the foreign bank that now holds the nation's future in

Figure 12. Humanity contained in the telephone company. *Revista telefónica cubana*, 1926. Cuban Heritage Collection, University of Miami.

its hands—and demands the "pacification" of anyone that might resist its policies. The notion of the bank restructuring its restructured debt suggests the circular time often invoked in republican literature, as well as the way that capital controls the "national territory," which must be tamed to enable its advance. The repetitive doubling of hombres/war veterans/revolution as ghosts in *El traidor* ("qué hombre más extraño este hombre") becomes, in the wake of another failed revolution, a doubling of debt restructuring in which the future conditional modifies the past ("refundiría . . . el Refundido"), suggesting little escape from the cycle.

The book's final section begins with a citation from Thorstein Veblen's *Absentee Ownership*: "[P]atriotic sentiment and national ambitions are no longer of any material consequence, except as ways and means by which the statesmen are enabled to further the material interests of the substantial citizen. A 'substantial citizen' is an absentee owner of much property" (*Coaybay* 257). Patriotism and nationalism serve dubious ends. The romantic nationalism of the "spirit of Martí" has vanished, and Veblen is deployed to point out that nationalisms serve to hide transnational class interests. Martí's messianic belief in Cuba's world-historical role is deflated by Washington's brother Minón, who reflects "how tragically insignificant for civilization and for humanity it then seemed to him, the entire history of his *patria*" (75). The final words of *Coaybay*, in the form of a letter by Paul Tallies, sum up the situation:

> ¿Qué caso harían de mí mis compatriotas . . . aferrados a su concepto romántico de la historia—que constituye todavía la base de todos los medios educativos de la nación, desde la escuela hasta el periódico—abandonando al invasor, ciega e irremisiblemente, sus tierras, sus fábricas, sus bancos, empréstito tras empréstito, dentro del sistema económico de Norlandia, sin perjuicio de acusar de imperialismo a la mera entidad política de esta gran República, ni dejar de aprestarse cada día, con discursos y leyes a la defensa de la patria, de la religión, de la lengua, de la raza de no sé cuántas cosas más? . . . ¿A qué hacerme la ilusión de reducir lo porvenir a lo que me sugiere este fugaz día de hoy, residuo imperceptible de un pasado que apenas es mío? (357)
>
> [What will my compatriots make of me . . . clinging as they do to their romantic concept of history—which still constitutes the basis for all the nation's educational means, from schools to even the newspaper—abandoning to the invader, blindly and unforgivably, their lands, factories, banks, loan by loan, within the economic system of Northland, without the prejudice of accusing of imperialism the mere political entity of this great Republic, nor ending the borrowing

> each day, with discourses and laws in defense of the fatherland, religion, the tongue, the people, and who knows what else? . . . Why pretend to reduce the future to what this fleeting day suggests to me, imperceptible residuum of a past that is barely mine?]

The novel has been read as a critique of U.S. intervention and influence on the island. But we see that Ramos ends it with a critique also of nationalist, sentimental anti-imperialism.

The Cuban republic that was depicted in *Coaybay* details the conditions that gave urgency to the 1959 Cuban Revolution. And yet, in the developmentalist 1960s, the revolution's own obsession with production would likewise elevate to primacy the concrete, in what Duanel Díaz, borrowing from Badiou, calls the revolution's "passion for the real," now bereft of the subtlety of, say, Czech philosopher Karel Kosik's *Dialectics of the Concrete* (1963). Kosik's book was influential for Prague's 1968 movement and insisted on the dialectical nature of reality, according to which the concrete, far from a reified thing, is totality. (Kosik, who was published in Spanish in Mexico by Grijalbo in 1967 and in Portuguese in Brazil the same year by Editora Civilização Brasileira, hails cybernetics as a new science for "the development of humanism," pointing to the period connections between Marxian totality and new systems theorizing.)[51]

In Cuba, consumption was nationalized, and films and advertisements from the period register campaigns "dedicated to consumption of Cuban products: *Consumiendo Productos Cubanos*" (Pérez, *On Becoming Cuban* 483). This move was part of a continent-wide transition in the 1930s or 1940s from export-led economies to the midcentury heyday of import-substitution industrialization. But this nationalizing of products did not mean a real change in the symbolic role they played in collective imaginaries. Indeed they were folded into the millenarian discourse of the early years of the revolution.[52] In a 1959 revolutionary Christmas fair in Havana, for instance, Lillian Guerra finds demands for exclusively Cuban products a fusion of a "universal celebration of the birth of Christ with *cubanía*" (Guerra, *Visions* 97).

The Cuban revolution aimed to wrest what it understood as a true concrete totality from illusions. As early as 1961, Díaz has pointed out, José Antonio Portuondo announced at the First National Congress of Writers and Artists of Cuba that the nation required an art that "would discover the essential in the apparent and would reveal it in forms accessible to all, an essentially communicative, concrete art—though not in Mondrian's sense—that would manifest reality in its historical and social transcendence."[53] But two years earlier Sarduy had already warned, "Objective Art had to have happened earlier."[54]

Portuondo need not have looked to Mondrian to dismiss "bad" concretude. He could have found in the 1946 Argentine "Manifiesto Invencionista, Revista Arte Concreto-Invención" the affirmation that "concrete art will be the socialist art of the future."[55] Indeed, the Romanian-born Cuban concrete painter Sandu Darie had long been in contact with Gyula Kosice of the Grupo Madí in Argentina, in whose exhibitions Darie participated. Meanwhile, in Brazil, where concrete art and poetry found their greatest theorists in the late 1950s, concretism was poised to dissolve into a post-concrete processualism, the other part of a dialectics of the concrete, a move beyond thingliness toward the virtual, the digital, the immaterial, the speculative, even the incipiently postnational.

CHAPTER 6

Object, Non-object, Trans-object, Relational Object

From Concrete Poetry to A Nova Objetividade

A half century after Brazil's purported essence was deciphered on the rocks of Canudos, an advertisement in the magazine *Manchete* crowed that "modern man" no longer needed to "write on stones": the "modeníssima" Lincoln pen was within everyone's reach; literature's "civilizing mission" was vested in products.[1] These were years characterized by rapid modernization and industrial production that just preceded the 1964 right-wing military coup, which critics have variously granted the power of ending modernism, utopia, millenarianism, and twentieth-century poetry.[2] While some saw the authoritarian regime as the culmination and extension of the modernization process, vanguard literature and art pulled away from any coincidence with its values.

In the developmentalism of the 1950s, nineteenth-century millenarian battles over religion and alternative communities and teleologies were replaced by utopian visions of production and consumption. The art critic Ronaldo Brito called Brazil's constructivist tendencies, too, "a project that was, to a certain degree, messianic, implying a sequence of attempts to overcome underdevelopment" (47). But the decade of the 1960s saw grand narratives of development and messianic teleologies cede to an embrace of process over products. The constructivism of concretude that peaks as object-oriented production dissolves by the late 1960s into a more virtual and postmessianic art and literature of the immanent and the body, and a time of the act, not the future.

In this chapter I delineate the move from an art of the object to an art of the non-object, from concrete poetry to the late 1960s *poema/processo*. I do this through readings of theoretical and aesthetic works by concrete poets, process/poets, and "tropicalist" artists Hélio Oiticica and Lygia Clark. Through these readings I map a transition from developmentalism to postmessianism and from national populism to other politics and poetics. Gonzalo Aguilar has convincingly suggested that between 1967 and 1969 mass media helped destabilize concretism's modernism (149). The importance of media for emerging art is emphasized, too, in Oscar Masotta's 1968 *Conciencia y estructura*, which self-consciously periodizes Argentine art's transformation toward the more virtual and less "thingly" in cultural production. But in fact the line linking various concrete movements with subsequent ones from the later 1960s and 1970s, such as the neoconcretes and process/poets, was more continuous than discontinuous, and I see electronic media as having always been central to the concretes. Rather than describe a mathematical, overly rational concretism giving way to a soft, organic neoconcretism, as some period documents assert, I want to argue that at the heart of both concrete and neoconcrete poetics lies a void.

That voids are central to neoconcrete art, where boxes, folds, and environments were preferred forms, is not surprising: the neoconcrete artist Lygia Clark developed a practice that, over more than three decades, moved from 1950s geometric painting through objects fashioned around what she called a "full void" and to an anti-art practice that used "relational objects" to treat psychiatric problems by the 1980s. But the idea that voids—or an interest in negativity, absence, and an internal space for an Other—are a central concern for concrete poetry may be less obvious. After all, concrete poetry had declared its interest in making poems that were things and with responding to a tangible world of advertising and products. But I argue that even as concrete poetry coincided with a postwar explosion of consumer culture, it demonstrated a simultaneous interest in non-objects, reflecting the split nature of concretude that earlier vanguards had observed.

I do, however, see post-concrete celebrations of virtuality and non-objectivity as ushering in a renewed interest in subjectivity. To better understand these processes this chapter makes use of the psychoanalytic theories of Jacques Lacan and of his students or peers such as Pierre Fédida, Nicolas Abraham, and Maria Torok, all of whom influenced Clark's work, with which I conclude this chapter.[3] Indeed we might even think of Lacan's psychoanalytic theories, developed at the same time as concrete poetry, as not only an attempt to understand subjectivity and objectivity in philosophical and psychical terms but as themselves a response to contemporary debates about desire amid increasing consumer culture. To this end, for example, I read Lacan's Seminar "La relation d'objet et les structures freudiennes" (1956–57) in relation to concrete theories of the object and the "thing" that date from the same years, years of Brazil's first Exposição Nacional de Arte Concreta, held in 1956 in São Paulo and 1957 in Rio de Janeiro.

THE DEVELOPMENT OF CONCRETE POETRY

For many critics, Brazilian concrete poetry's midcentury aesthetics represent an unmediated and acritical expression of, or as having "somehow reflected," the euphoric national developmentalism characteristic of the era of President Juscelino Kubitschek, who famously oversaw the construction of Brasília, emblem of a utopian national developmentism (Perrone, *Seven Faces* 48). Others saw the innovative poetry as proof of Brazil's global vanguardism. Concretism's multiple global, regional, and local influences included the Swiss-Peruvian poet Eugen Gomringer and the Argentine artist, designer, and critic Tomás Maldonado (later director of the Hochschule für Gestaltung Ulm [Ulm School of Design]), who linked European concrete art movements with Latin American ones,[4] as well as earlier "nonobjective" visual art, and select poets such as Pound, Mallarmé, João Cabral de Melo Neto, and Oswald de Andrade.[5]

Brazil's poetic and plastic concretisms were much in dialogue. The art groups Grupo Frente and Ruptura were close to the São Paulo–based poets and critics Augusto de Campos, Haroldo de Campos, and Décio Pignatari, founders of the journal *Noigandres*. These authors were joined by the Rio-based poet and critic Ferreira Gullar, who, in turn, was influential for visual artists Clark, Oiticica, Cordeiro, and Amilcar de Castro. For both artistic and literary concretism, the Swiss architect Max Bill, artist and cofounder of the Ulm School, was a crucial influence, and his 1950 show and 1951 work for the first São Paulo Biennial were important touchstones for the developing movements.

Brazilian concrete poetry arrived at the end of a period of remarkable growth. Brazil's revolution of 1930 ushered in an authoritarian state along with economic expansion. Nationalization supplanted decades of foreign investment and was accompanied by import-substitution industrialization. This was the background for manifestos that, echoing the language of Argentina's Madí artists, Van Doesburg's manifesto on concrete art, and the aesthetic theories of the nineteenth-century philosopher Konrad Fiedler, presented concrete poems as "useful objects": not a representation of external reality but reality itself. The position constituted what the *Noigandres* group would call variously "ultimate" or "total" realism: a desire to make word equal thing; to eradicate mediation in the media itself and to turn lyric, originally an oral, immaterial form, into a concrete product.

The move from representation to instantiation was, as the concrete poets themselves insisted, also closely linked to the growing importance of print culture and television. McLuhan, whom Pignatari translated, emphasized the role of type and of visual media in splitting subject and object. At the same time Walter Ong argued that by emphasizing words' visual nature, print helped people conceive their "interior conscious and unconscious resources as more and more thing-like" (132). The idea that there was cross-pollination between postwar industrialization, mass media, and Brazilian concrete poetry is commonplace today. Here, however, I wish to go beyond this association to argue that concrete poetry was not uncritically adopting new media and that its investment in media's virtuality and immateriality is surprisingly central to three prominent debates with which the poetry engaged: (1) debates concerning the object and the "non-object," (2) debates concerning realism, and (3) debates about the relations between form and nationalism.

Discussions in the late 1950s and early 1960s about the object and non-object referred to earlier constructivisms and to longstanding philosophical debates; they also translated into the aesthetic realm questions about the nature of consumption and production.[6] In debates about what realism should look like in the twentieth century, concrete poetry's early, utopian desire to abolish the distance between word and thing, which could be translated into Lacanian notions of the symbolic and the real, does parallel developmentalism's quixotic desire to "leap" out of underdevelopment (itself echoing Maoist and Hegelian "leaps")—a leap perhaps summed up in the title of a 1964 concrete poetry article, "O salto ao objeto" [The leap to the object] (Lima Mendonça 211). Industrial production was the new utopia on which art should model itself: Cordeiro once claimed that standardization would turn artists into "the mythological 'art laborers' of one hundred years ago."[7]

This initial embrace of developmentalism was soon countered by economists of dependency theory. Dependency theorists argued that developmentalism ignored global capitalism's foreclosure of ecstatic circumventions of and voluntary leaps over centers and peripheries. As Josefina Saldaña-Portillo argues, however, dependency theory reinscribed a fatalism it saw in developmentalism: only wholesale change was possible, through leaps or revolution.[8] According to Heloisa Buarque de Hollanda, concrete poetry, like developmentalism, took underdevelopment to be a *stage*, not comprehending its structural nature. Buarque de Hollanda (who later revised many of her 1960s positions) saw concretism as integrated into "relations of production" such that concrete poems used the language of the developmentalist system "but proved incapable of dealing with it critically."[9] Yet neither is it true that concrete poetry was *mimetic* of developmentalism. Explicitly, anyway, it opposed linearity. An internal tension between the virtual and the thingly that was already explicit in the "plano-piloto" intensified, and concrete poetry increasingly separated itself from the reification associated with commodities.

OBJECT AND NON-OBJECT

The *Noigandres* group famously declared that a concrete poem was "an object in and for itself, not an interpretation of exterior objects and/or sensations more or less subjective" (de Campos, de Campos, and Pignatari, *Teoria* 216). They celebrated poetry, rather than prose, for the very reasons that Sartre decried it: it was the literary mode in which word is taken as a thing (de Campos, de Campos, and Pignatari, *Teoria* 46n4). But it was not enough simply to adopt a poetic mode. Leery of romantic proclivities in subjective lyric, the concrete poets called for the end of verse as it had been known and for a scientific objectivism.

And yet their first manifestos already evinced a certain ambiguity vis-à-vis the status of the term "object." On the one hand, an object was a thing, an autonomous creation with a material, formal quality: this was the "object" that appeared in essays such as Haroldo de Campos's "Kurt Schwitters ou o Jubilo do objeto" [Kurt Schwitters, or The Jubilee of the Object] (1956).[10] On the other hand, it was "object*ive*," which is to say, mathematical, scientific, and nonsubjective (de Campos, de Campos, and Pignatari, *Teoria* 70). Finally, and perhaps paradoxically, it was also *non*-objective—the 1930s term for nonrepresentational or abstract art—to the extent that the concrete poem was *objectal*: a thing in itself whose noumenal qualities meant that it was not representation but manifestation. (Cordeiro once attempted to distinguish between "objective and object-y artists" [*objetivos e objeterios*].)[11]

This ambiguity was, of course, nothing new. The equivocal nature of the terms had plagued the Russian Constructivists and Productivists who inspired the concrete poets.[12] But the debate was resignified in the Brazilian context. In the midst of its objectal jubilee, concrete poetry received an immanent critique from Reynaldo Jardim and Ferreira Gullar, the Rio de Janeiro–based poet and art critic who split from the São Paulo–based *Noigandres* poets to form the "neoconcretes" around 1957. In 1959 the first neoconcrete art exhibition was organized, and Jardim, Gullar, and several other artists published a manifesto critiquing the cold rationalism and scientific "objectivism" of concrete art and poetry, arguing for an art that was neither "machine" nor "object."[13] Brito observes that neoconcretism's early insight, like some Hegelian *Aufhebung*, preserved and canceled the reigning constructivism of concrete art in a single move: "This is the neoconcrete truth: to have been the vertex of Brazilian constructive consciousness . . . and simultaneously the agent of its crisis, opening the way to its overcoming" (9).

In a seminal essay one year after the "plano-piloto" titled "Teoria do não-objeto," or "Theory of the non-object" (1959), Gullar called for new attention to poetry's reception by readers and for the abandonment of the obsession with objecthood per se.[14] He argued for a new object that was *not an object*: "um novo objeto que se distingue dos objetos por se concluir em puro aparecimento: o não-objeto" [a new object distinguished from objects by ending in pure appearance: the non-object] (*Etapas da arte* 139). The definition was a bit vague, or at best capacious. In a follow-up article, Gullar acknowledged that non-objects could emerge from objects: "Quando nos subtraímos à ordem cultural do mundo, vemos os objetos *sem nome*—e nos defrontamos com a sua opacidade de coisa. Pode-se dizer que, nessas circunstâncias, o objeto torna-se próximo do que chamo de não-objeto" [When we withdraw from the cultural order of the world, we see objects *without their names*—and we come face to face with their opacity as thing. One could say that, in these circumstances, the object becomes close to what I call the non-object].[15] Gullar argued that if an object—existing, in Sartrean terms, in itself—lay at one end of a spectrum, the non-object lay at the other. Represented objects (such as a still life) lay somewhere in between (Gullar, "Diálogo" 4).

Gullar was aware of the multiple valences of the term "non-object." He recalls inventing the term while viewing a new work by Lygia Clark with his friend and the critic Mário Pedrosa. Pedrosa protested that "non-object" was an inappropriate term, since object meant "object of knowledge," and a "non-object-of-knowledge" would therefore be nothing. Gullar countered that:

> Do ponto de vista filosófico, sua objeção procedia, mas que usara o nome no sentido corrente, como na expressão "objetos de uso pessoal," como caneta, mesa, cadeira, livro. E expliquei como chegara ao nome não-objeto: como o trabalho da Lygia, que acabáramos de ver, não podia ser classificado como relevo nem escultura, pensei, "é um objeto"; mas, como os objetos têm uso e este não tem, posso chamá-lo de não-objeto. (*Experiência neoconcreta* 44)

> [He was quite right from a philosophical perspective, but that I was using the term in its modern sense, to mean "an object of personal use", like a pen, a table, a chair or a book. I explained how I had hit upon the term non-object: as the work Lygia had just shown us could not be classified as either relief or sculpture, it was, nevertheless, "an object", and yet, as objects have uses and this clearly did not, it must therefore be a non-object.] (*Experiência neoconcreta* 125)

With philosophical recourse once more to tables and chairs, Gullar describes Clark's works as nonuseful objects, reminding us of Reyes's *jitanjáfora*s and of Brull's playful daughters, a reprise of Kantian purposive purposelessness.

Drawing on phenomenology, the neoconcretes emphasized the *subjective* experience of encountering a poem. They cautioned that while their emphasis on the materiality of the page might lead some to think they intended "to transform the poem into something material . . . an object," in fact the page marked a temporal, *immaterial* experience, a silence and absence (Gullar, *Etapas da arte* 136). By highlighting this paradox—the materiality of absence—neoconcrete art magnified concrete poetry's ambivalence over the status of "object." The neoconcretes were interested in a nonrepresentational and organic art (Gullar, *Etapas da arte* 243). They detected in the *Noigandres* poets a naïve fidelity to a scientific objectivity that conflated antilyrical anti-expressionism with a fetishizing of objecthood.

But Gullar's critique had a touch of bad faith, or perhaps just polemics, about it. Although it was true that the objectal nature of the poem was paramount for the *Noigandres* poets, it was also true that these had called for an "open work" that, consonant with an era of mass media, would dialogue with a mass public. Concrete poetry wanted to be objectal—a closed, autonomous form—*and* to facilitate engagement and circulation. Without aping the commodity fetish, as its detractors sometimes intimated, the concrete poem thus operated a bit like a psychoanalytic fetish, reconciling presence and absence, avowed and disavowed beliefs. In Freud's masculinist definition, a fetish is "stable, visible, tangible; a real object and not a phantom . . . capable of symbolizing at the same time the penis and its lack."[16] Freud's emphasis on the fetish's tangibility and materiality is similar to early concrete poetry's emphasis on presence—which neoconcretism would reject in favor of absence.

Other artists acknowledged ways that neoconcretism was on a continuum with concretism. *Musique concrète* had inspired concretism, but electronic music also spilled over as an influence on neoconcretism. Cordeiro, for example, jotted in undated notes: "O NC [neoconcretism] trata as coisas como a música eletrônica trata os barulhos. . . . / A consumação do objeto como processo de signos. / Arte da contingência com meios contingentes. / Consumação artística do objeto" [NC (neoconcretism) treats things like electronic music treats sounds. . . . / The consummation of the object as a process of signs. / Art of contingency with contingent media. / Artistic consummation of the object].[17]

In the scant years between the launching of *Noigandres* (1952), the "pilot-plan for Brasília" (1957), the "pilot-plan for concrete poetry" (1958), and the "Theory of the non-object" (1959), concretude was theorized, entered into dialogue with nationalist architecture, and was critiqued, opened up, and passed through. We could view this as a progressive history in which, say, European constructivism is worked through in a Brazilian context, and moved beyond into a precocious relational aesthetics (to use a more recent term), but the linearity of this version would belie the idea of moving beyond teleology after all. I prefer to visualize the relation between the movements with recourse to a figure from the period, in which Cordeiro began to experiment with computer art: as a collection of punch cards each conveying different information but sharing the common logic of perforations or voids.

INTO THE VOID

What do these conflicting impulses between objecthood and non-objecthood, concreteness and openness, materiality and immateriality reveal about the charged historical moment? In concrete poems, words become objects whose hollowness seems to allude to the dreams that commodities both feed on and promise to satisfy.[18] Such an interest in hollowness organizes Augusto de Campos's 1960 poem "caracol" [snail], which plays on interrelated sounds, phonemes, and letters within the word for snail, including "máscara" [mask], "caracol" [spiral], "cola; colar" [glue; to glue], and "colocar" [place], with many others that can be created from the poem's crossword puzzle-like layout, such as "sacro" [sacred]. It is as if the snail shell, a carapace like the poem itself, "masked" a hollowness, both physical and metaphysical ("não valer um caracol," "not worth a snail," means insignificant), in which words reverberate, like a biblical shofar. This interest was not unique to Brazil, of course: Hal Foster has identified a similar operation in the later works of Marcel Broodthaers in which "shelled things like eggs" are used to "render [a] hardening at once literal and allegorical, in a word, reflexive—as if the best defense against reification were a preemptive embrace."[19]

Such a meditation on a form like a shell, a carapace, or a *caracol*, that contains multiple meanings within it, evokes the allegorical function of poetry (allegory being a form that *speaks otherwise*), the very function that concretude explored. As Haroldo de Campos put it in a 1957 essay, concrete language "Coloca, por uma súbita mudança de campo de operação, seu arsenal de virtualidades em função de uma nova empresa: criar uma forma, criar, com seus próprios materiais, um mundo paralelo ao mundo das coisas—o poema" [via a swift change of operative fields, places its arsenal of virtualities in the function of a new endeavor: the creation of a form, the creation, with its own materials, of a new world parallel to the world of things—the poem] (de Campos, de Campos, and Pignatari, *Teoria* 105). The arsenal of virtualities, like the hollowness within the shell or the poem, becomes the shell or form—the thing—itself. In other words, the thing is virtual. The void is the heart of the form.

Such a vacillation between thingliness/form and hollowness can be found already in Haroldo de Campos's poem "no â mago do ô mega" (1956), mentioned in this book's introduction (fig. 1). The heart of the O is a void, synonymous with the modern thing's *Ding*, per Lacan:

that which animates the power of thingliness but which, truly sublime, escapes it. The thing (the poem) contains "um osso": a hollow or a bone enclosing marrow. This nothingness may be the "nihilo" from which comes creation, as well as the limits of language: the "A" from "amago" is the ancient Greek alphabet's first letter and Omega its last.

Sarduy does not cite "no â mago do ô mega" in *Barroco*, his study of an Iberian baroque and neobaroque, though he was friends with Haroldo de Campos. But the poem illustrates nicely what Sarduy would later gloss as a baroque built around circles, loops, and voids, and which I suggested was anticipated by—or indebted to—Carpentier's cigarette sign blown to bits by a cyclone in *Ékue-yamba-ó*. Sarduy's description of the baroque reads: "Círculo-estructura primaria [. . .] Ojo. Boca. Anillo-aro-ano. Nada: gesto sin sujeto. Firma de la especie. Y luego cero, inicial del Otro" [Circle-primary structure (. . .) Eye. Mouth. Ring-hoop-anus. Nothing: gesture without a subject. Species' signature. And then *zero*, beginning of the Other] (218). This "nothing," hollowness, or void repeats in "no â mago do ô mega."[20] Constituting the literal interior of the poem's numerous "o"s and the marrow within the poem's bone, the void is furthermore that zero (0) that mathematical set theory and, after it, Lacanian psychoanalysis posit as necessary for any creation—an internal ex nihilo, as "no â mago do ô mega" anticipates.[21]

This creative "ex nihilo" can also be understood as the space at once outside of and internal to a poet who, according to the tenets of concretism, must conceive her artwork objectively, not subjectively—by drawing on the external world. Lacan once described the process of communication between subjects as a circuit between the voice and the ear cavity, a palpable void (akin, in what he calls its "snail-like shape," to the *caracol*). But in Lacan's view the voice resonates not so much in this *physiological* void but "in the void which is the void of the Other as such, *ex nihilo*." In other words, creation "out of nothing" can be understood as creation that emerges from others: "The voice comes back to us through the loop of the Other" (Dolar 160).

By placing the onus of creation outside of the lyric subject, the concrete poets sought to write for a broader, if never truly mass, audience, taking lessons from mass media. "Hollowness" at the heart of concrete poetry thus includes the internalized public (Other) space that they thought was necessary if modern poetry was to be a viable contemporary form with a sizable public (of course, it remained an elite form, outside of music). The ex nihilo at its most utopian would be not the summoning of poetry out of the ether by a lyric genius but opening up to the world the realm of poetry, hitherto conceived of as private and interior. This insistence on hollowness emerges as one reads the early poems: the poem just preceding "no â mago do ô mega" in *Noigandres* 3 plays again with circles and images of containers: "orelha" [ear]; "auréola" [aureole]; "cornu cópia" [corni copia/corni copy], again the shofar and the abundance of "mechanical reproduction."[22]

The void troped in "no â mago do ô mega" thus refers to poetic creation, to language, and to desire as premised on lack. At the time these ideas perhaps did not seem as abstruse or academic as they may today. Lack and desire are closely tied to the spectacular production and consumption of consumer goods: "a coisa da coisa da coisa." "[N] o â mago do ô mega" addresses, among other things, the lack that is the flip side of the objects produced during the height of developmentalism. It is the lack that fuels desire for commodities.

These tensions between the object and the non-object, the thing and *das Ding*, are also present in Gullar's 1959 *livro-poemas*, or poem-books, titled "osso" [bone] and "fruta" [fruit]. In these books the poem unfolds on different sheets, each one revealing a new word: as the reader opens the poem, she activates its emergence. Gullar's 1954 poem "o formigueiro" [the anthill] had already attempted to be a poem in which the word *formiga* [ant] "disintegrates into its elements (letters) and reintegrates in a new form" (Gullar, *Experiência neoconcreta* 75). The poem only comes into being in the act, anticipating neoconcretism.

Such tensions are present, too, in the 1962 three-dimensional versions of Wlademir Dias-Pino's 1956 poem "Sólida" [Solid], exhibited at the National Exhibition on Concrete Art: an envelope/box with a series of loose papers within that plays with versions of the words "solitude" and "solid" (*sólida, solidão, só lida, sol saído do lida do día*).[23] (See Figure 13.) As the reader rifles through the papers, "sólida" decomposes. As in "o formiguero," "As the letters gain autonomy and suddenly swallow the memory of the word . . . the word dissolves into the supporting page."[24] The more the *word* "sólida" dissolves, the Uruguayan poet Clemente Padín has observed, the more the *object*—a poem about the word—comes into being. The word and the object (the box) are connected, together constituting a non-object. As in "no â mago do ô mega," the *central* role of the letter "o" in the word *sólida* plays an important part as an organizing void. The "O" becomes an example of what Lacan called a "quilting point," a nexus about which the various transformations occur or which pins down the words'

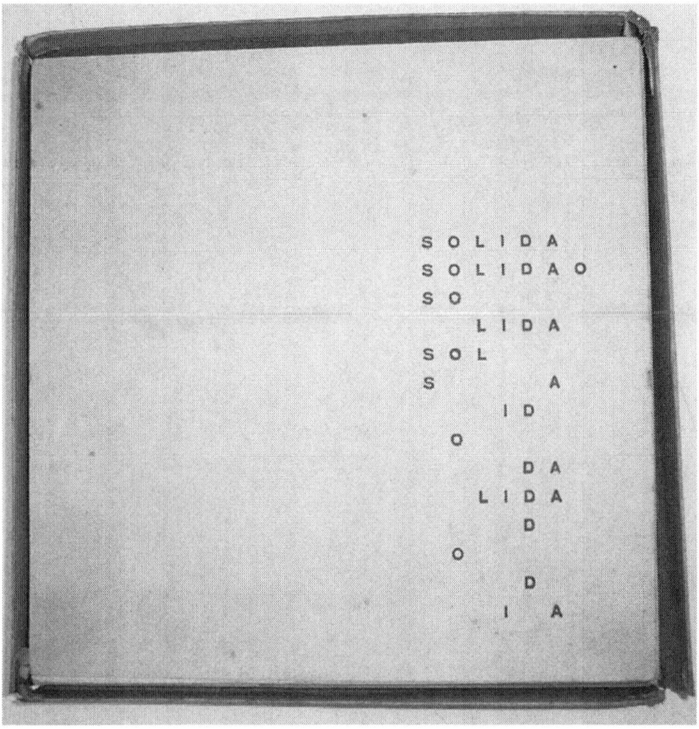

Figure 13. Wlademir Dias-Pino, "Sólida" (1956). Courtesy of Wlademir Dias-Pino.

changing meanings depending upon where the letters begin or end in relation to the "o."

Both the Dias-Pino and de Campos poems privilege negative space on the page. At the same time, typographical recombinations work to corral this lack, figured as "o"s and lodged in the heart (*âmago*) of other words and concepts. As Lacan noted in a rare passage on scansion and poetry in his Seminar IV, *La relation d'objet*, "the smallest surge in writing [graphie] makes emerge at the same time orthography [orthographie], that is to say, the possible control of a lack."[25]

The link between reflections on lack and absence and explorations of desire is crucial for understanding concretism's vexed relation to developmentalism. In Lacanian theory—particularly the 1956 seminar *La relation d'objet*, which dates to concrete poetry's "heroic" period—desire is defined as the difference between need and demand. For

Figure 14. Wlademir Dias-Pino, "Sólida" in a permutation (2009). Courtesy of Wlademir Dias-Pino.

instance, a baby needs milk, demands with a cry, but in fact is calling for something beyond mere milk or the arrival of the breast: it desires love. Beyond any concrete thing is a desire for an immaterial thing, according to period interpreters of Hegel (Kojève) and Freud (Lacan).[26] This absence beyond any language or symbol of love (like a breast), in Lacanian terms, is the Real: site of plenitude but a void that necessarily cannot be filled with this or that specific content. At the heart of a thing designed to placate a given desire lies the truth that such *things* cannot satisfy the desire for some deeper, more social Thing. Once a "real" object satisfying a real need becomes a symbolic object, Lacan writes in Seminar IV, any other object that satisfies the need—"which very well may be realized as the word"—may occupy its place.[27] Both words and objects of consumption can become Things charged with desire and psychoanalytic objecthood.

Haroldo de Campos's poem points to the lack inherent in things, as does Décio Pignatari's famous poem "beba coca cola" (1957), which, again turning on changes in the poem's "o"s and "a"s, tracks the conversion of the iconic consumer product into feces. (See Figure 15.) Nineteen

Figure 15. Décio Pignatari, "beba coca cola" (1957).

fifty-seven is also the year in which Gullar, Jardim, and Oliveira Bastos publish "Poesia Concreta: Experiência Intuitiva" [Concrete Poetry: Intuitive Experience], which declares "in the concrete poem, the reader is brought to an encounter with a durable object—and this places the poem in opposition to advertisement processes in general" (Gullar, *Experiência neoconcreta* 77–78). A simple anticorporate reading of Pignatari's poem might see in it the transformation of the product into so much shit. But a more psychoanalytically inflected one might note the way in which both "Coca-Cola" (paramount industrial product; replacement of real nutrition with empty calories) and excrement are *objet petit a*'s, partial objects imbued with desire. Decades later Sarduy would remind readers of the proximity between feces and other pieces of desire in his riff on "o"s: "Barroco va de la *a* a la *o*: sentido del oro, del lazo al círculo, de la elipse al círculo; o al revés: sentido de la excreción—reverso simbólico del oro—del círculo al lazo, del círculo a la elipse, de Galileo a Kepler" [Barroco goes from *a* to *o*: gold's direction (or sense), from the lasso to the circle, from the ellipse to the circle; or the reverse: the direction (or sense) of excretion—the symbolic inverse of gold—from the circle to the lasso (link), from the circle to the ellipse, from Galileo to Kepler].[28]

But perhaps then it is not that Lacan illuminates poetry but rather that concrete poetry's reflections on industrial production illuminate Lacan. The void is first apprehended by poets. As Sianne Ngai reminds us, Lacan's illustration of what *das Ding* is, as related in *The Ethics of Psychoanalysis*, is set during a visit to the house of Jacques Prévert, screenwriter and word-game poet.[29] In Prévert's house Lacan encounters not poetry but the void and *das Ding* in a series of empty matchboxes, recalling Dias-Pino's "Sólida," Celso Dias's 1967 "Caixa de fumaça sem soporte" [Box of smoke without frame], a "poem" that is just an image of a box made of smoke (Dias-Pino, *Processo* n.p.), or Neide de Sá's 1969 "transparência," nesting clear boxes covered with writing, whose meaning, as in "Sólida," changed when manipulated (Gullar once called the non-object transparent ["Diálogo" 4]). (See Figure 16.)

It was Prévert's *collection* of empty matchboxes, the *seriality* of the box-object, that provoked Lacan's quasi-absurd epiphany about daily life: a box of matches is not necessarily any old thing but, "in the form of *Erscheinung*, as it appeared in its truly imposing multiplicity, it may be a Thing" (Lacan, *Ethics* 114). Lacan thus ties Thingness to repetition (Ngai, *Ugly Feelings* 280). Thingness emerges out of the "wholly gratuitous, proliferating, superfluous" collection of matchboxes—or, we might say, in the repetitions of "o"s in concrete poetry (Lacan, *Ethics* 114). Cordeiro wrote in 1965 that a new realism approached "direct presentation of the things of industrial mass production . . . there arises the new idea of thinginess, which coincides with semiotics" (Cordeiro, *Waldemar Cordeiro: Uma aventura* 132). Concretism would fix upon Benjaminian reproducibility, while the process/poets of the 1970s would write: "the twentieth century animated reproduction" (Dias-Pino, *Processo* n.p.).

Lacan uses the anecdote about matchboxes to illustrate the concept of sublimation, the elevation "of an object to the dignity of the Thing" (Lacan, *Ethics* 112). Ordinary objects—here, an object forged around a central emptiness ("less the matchbox than the Thing that subsists in a matchbox" [114])—become transcendental. The seriality of voids underscores not thingness but Thingness. But what does this crucial act

Figure 16. Neide Dias de Sá, *transparência* (1969). Courtesy of Neide Dias de Sá.

of sublimation of things into Things mean? What is a thing and what a Thing? *Das Ding* for Lacan is that part of "being" which remains in some kind of beyond as a result of the purported castration that comes with using language. It is desire, but not desire for any one thing. An object or a thing, on the other hand, which exists in the here-and-now, may be what remains of *das Ding* after language enters the picture (Lacan, *Ethics* 63).

Concretism operates through a similar kind of dualism. Although the concrete poets explicitly wanted their poems to be objects, they were also, I believe, interested in making "Things"—non-objects of their own. In a moment of mass production, they both engaged with the commodity fetish and critiqued it, wrapping both strategies in a metacommentary on language. "No â mago do ô mega," "Sólida," and "beba coca cola" are all about "solid" things but nonetheless summon absence, "o"s, zeros, and cores. Haroldo de Campos wrote that only Mallarmé dared "contemplate that hollowness and convert such a contemplation of the void into the material of his poetry" (*O arco-íris branco* 264). This hollowness would become the raw material for Haroldo de Campos's poetry as well. Lacan claimed that "creation *ex nihilo* is coextensive with the exact situation of the Thing as such" (Lacan, *Ethics* 122). Hollowness *is* the material of poetry, as a potter creates a vase around emptiness, "ex nihilo, starting with a hole" (Lacan, *Ethics* 121).

Haroldo de Campos's allusion to Mallarmé reminds us that 1960s concretism responded not only to products but to the onset of a *post*industrial age of the virtual. This vacillation was anticipated by 1920s Russian constructivist thought, which understood that the creation of useful objects was desirable even as the "integral, discrete object" was being disaggregated by electricity, quantum physics, and mass production (Gough 145). Paradoxically, "the more technologically advanced the process of the object's production, the less corporeal, tangible, and objectlike" the object became (Gough 147).

A similar attention to the intangible four decades later aligns the concretes with the neoconcretes. The neoconcrete, non-objective emphasis on negativity—Gullar's poem "Não" (1959) was a flat box in which "the reader pulls back a white plaque and below surges a red surface, violent, on which is written the word "NO"—is like the central absence in the concretism it sought to move beyond.[30] And if the ultimate goal of the neoconcretes was to overcome the division between subject and object, this annihilation of the subject/object divide had been intimated to some extent by the concretes. Indeed, the abolition of the divide underlay their theories of realism.

MODERN CRATYLUS, OR THE REAL OBJECT OF CONCRETE POETRY

"The concrete poem . . . checks the structural logic of traditional discursive language, because it encounters in [the latter] a barrier to accessing the world of objects," wrote Haroldo de Campos (de Campos, de Campos, and Pignatari, *Teoria* 69). Overcoming this barrier would be one of the original aims of early concrete poetics. The "ultimate" or "total" realism that concrete poetry professed was to be identity, not representation. Not only were concrete poems things themselves, but they often played with anagrams and permutations of a word such that the word seemed to carry within it the beginnings and ends of its possibilities for meaning.

A total realism that would remove the bar between life and art is an old dream of the historical avant-gardes, reactivated in the 1960s in movements such as *nouveau réalisme*, which Sarduy linked to Kandinsky's claim that art would either become totally abstract or tend toward a "total realism," an attempt to reproduce rather than represent the object (Sarduy, *Obra completa* 2:1190). For Kandinsky, the fetishistic example of the real was not the mystical void of a matchbox but the cigarette butt that would sing its "internal sound" free from meddling representation (Sarduy, *Obra completa* 2:1190). In the case of the concrete poets, an object's inner sound—like that inside "caracol"—was best approached through finding an isomorphism, as they called it in gestalt vocabulary, between the thing and the poem "about" it. Thus even as the concrete poets disparaged early twentieth-century calligrams for their naïve fusion of form and content, their own anagrammic approach still depended upon the "isomorphism" between the meaning of the poem and the meaning of the words involved. So Augusto de Campos's "quadrado" (1959) (containing the word "quadra," quadrant) is a poem of four squares of the words "quarto" [fourth, room], "quadro" [painting], "quadrado" [square, squared].[31] "Terremoto" [earthquake] is a block or interconnected words whose permutations likewise yield "temor" [fear], "morte" [death], "termo" [limit], "metro" [metro, meter], "morto" [dead], "motor," and "torto" [tort] (*Poesia* 105). (See Figure 17.)

Part of the pleasure of these poems lies in the emergence, as if out of a magic box, of endless unexpected surprises, all of which are nonetheless vaguely familiar, because versions of each other. But another part of the pleasure comes from the notion that it is *not* mere coincidence that the words that so seem to interact with one another are simply one letter apart. What is in the magic box—*quadro*—appears preordained. The painting within its square frame encompasses all related concepts. The earthquake discloses through the poem's broken surface all the subterranean connections between death, fear, life at the limit, crevasses, the rumble of a motorcycle, and so forth.

In some sense these poems reveal their production in the form of etymology, of words that could well have been chosen for the title, and were not. But in another sense the neatness of the connections denies arbitrariness and chance. The poems instead perform an absolute realism that paradoxically represses the production process because its basic philosophy is one of identity: signifier is connected to signified.[32] This kind of relationship is difficult to avoid in poems that place a premium on concision: meaning is forced between ever-fewer elements, which take on proportionately greater importance.

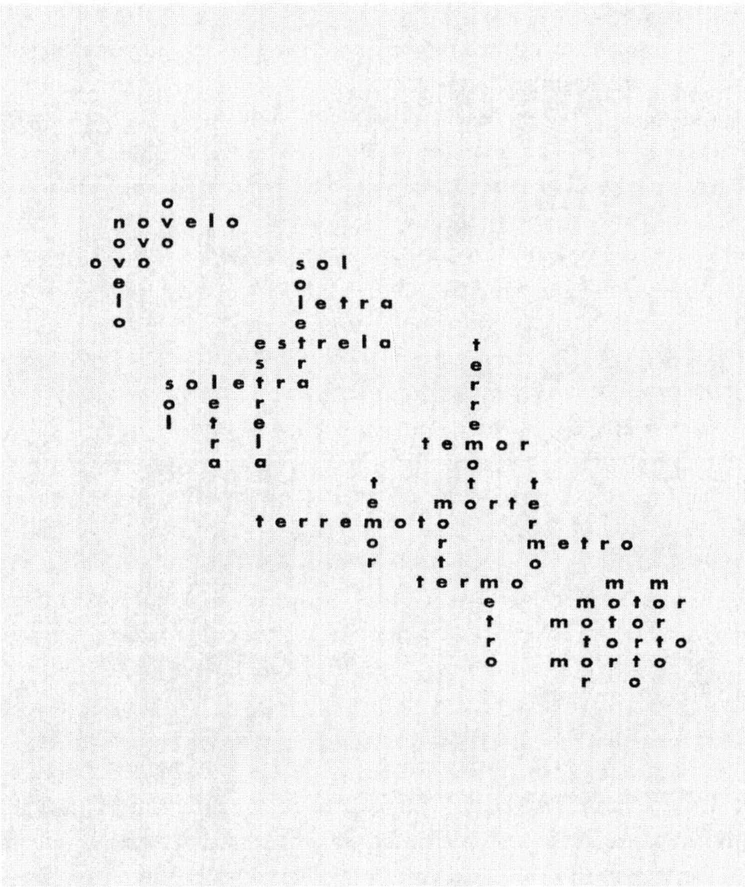

Figure 17. Augusto de Campos, "terremoto" (1956). Courtesy of Augusto de Campos.

As critics, the *Noigandres* group praised the 1920s realism of the modernist poet Oswald de Andrade in contradistinction to nineteenth-century realism. While the latter depends upon metonymy to produce psychological portraits of typical characters and situations, Haroldo de Campos wrote, Andrade's realism was of a different, "special" nature: it employed "metonymy in itself."[33] Of interest was Andrade's

> processo metonímico pelo qual os dados de uma realidade trivial . . . são reelaborados, rearticulados, reordenados para adquirir condição estética. Trata-se aqui de um

> realismo especial, quase etimológico, fundado na realidade do texto como coisa de palavras, cuja coerência se mede pelos seus próprios materiais (palavras numa determinada ordem de contigüidade) . . . a nítida propensão da prosa miramarina no sentido de conquistar a emancipação de seu mundo de signos e de fundar na realidade do texto a sua própria realidade (a absolutização da metonímia).[34]
>
> [metonymic process by which the facts of a trivial reality . . . are re-elaborated, rearticulated, reordered to acquire an aesthetic condition. It is a special realism, almost etymological, founded in the reality of the text as a thing of words, whose coherence is measured by its own materials (words in a determinate order of contiguity) . . . the piercing propensity of *miramarine* prose in the sense of conquering the emancipation of its world of signs and founding its own reality within the reality of its text (the absolutization of metonymy).]

This "special" realism held that the reality—or truth—of the poem inhered in the words themselves. The fact that this special realism is "almost etymological" is important for understanding the concrete poets' relation of word and world. Poems such as Augusto de Campos's "V" (1957), "tensão" (1956), and "terremoto" (1956) uncover a reality of (albeit limited) possibility within the given word chosen to be the seed of the poem, suggesting a meaningful relation between the iterations of barely differentiated words. Thus it is no coincidence that the Saussure often cited by the concrete poets is not the author of *Course in General Linguistics* but the Saussure that Jean Starobinsky recovered in *Words upon Words*.[35] In this posthumous book—Saussure himself never published the fanciful research—Starobinsky revealed that Saussure hoped to find a secret code of hypograms (encoded proper names) buried in Latin poems. It was precisely this "attempt to individuate an occult poetic law" that the *Noigandres* poets believed allowed Saussure to break with the "'linearity of the signifier'" "in favor of an 'amalgam outside of time,' a 'medium of acoustic impressions outside of any linear time'" (H. de Campos, *Ideograma* 66).

A preference for the anagrammic and extralineal repeat in *Noigandres* literary criticism: Sousândrade's use of the anagram of "titular" to parody the purchase of titles of nobility, for instance, is of interest to them: "(Egipcíaca ESFINGE do deserto:) / —(Pessoal, não res publica, / Titular . . . lar-titu: / Só em vos crendo o povo: / Deste ovo / Que fazeis? . . . Hu! Hu! Hu!" [(Egyptian SPHINX of the desert:) / —(People, not *res publica*, / Titular . . . *titu*-home: / The people believing only in you / From this egg / What do you do? . . . Hu! Hu! Hu!] (de Campos and de Campos, *ReVisão* 264). Titles of nobility represent a naïve trust in form—the visible coat of arms, the paper decreeing purity of blood—to ensure continuity of an alleged essence through the ages, a continuity that can be bought. The anagram similarly preserves a secret in its form, a secret not of genealogy—*o ovo*—but recombination. The external form changes, yet the anagram retains a (quasi-genetic) reshuffling of elements.

While the de Campos brothers endorse Sousândrade's *satirizing* of such logic, they themselves use the anagrammic reduction of content to form when it allows them to break with theories of Progress. The anagrammic "break" provided them with an avenue outside of teleological thought. But it also reinforces the movement's earlier, naïve goal of breaching the barrier between words and things; of finding a syntax in which signifier and signified would be one and the same, à la Pound's selective uptake of Chinese ideograms.[36]

One could read the concretes' desire for ultimate meaning in utopian terms—an overcoming of that alienation of subject and object. But dreams of closure just as easily can lead to totalizing regimes of meaning. The *Noigandres* poets were sharp critics of the authoritarian regime of the 1960s and 1970s. But for their critics, their desire for a total realism, by which a "trivial reality" might be escaped through the "emancipation of [the] world of signs" into formalist autonomy, bore some similarities to some of the midcentury's utopian developmentalisms. For the critics of *Noigandres*, the problem, to borrow from Haroldo de Campos's own analysis of Andrade, was that the early work risked converting a "trivial" everyday reality ("development" and "underdevelopment") into an aesthetic problem to be resolved by an appeal to immediacy.

Moreover, concrete poetics had come to appear suspicious to some in part because their interest in production, technology, and advertising was shared by the modernizing authoritarian regime. Analyzing a nefarious economy in which Brazilians allegedly traded democracy for consumption in the years 1954–64, Ana Cristina Camargo Moraes Figueiredo unearths efforts by big business to connect consumerism with nationalism, preparing the middle class to embrace the coup when a 1963 offensive was organized against Goulart's populist government (1961–64) (138). Anticommunist campaigns attempted to dissuade students from criticism, while advertising campaigns represented communism as the "negation of consumption" and described a national industrial sublime in which Brazil's very integrity as a nation owed to industrialization production (Camargo Moraes Figueiredo 152, 44). They linked the future of Brazil's sovereignty to its industrial and economic autonomy, paradoxically one secured through international capital (49).

The left responded to this anticommunist industrial sublime with its own retrenchment into a nationalism that accused concrete poetry of participating in the technological developmentalism that was the mandate of the new regime. In essays such as *Cultura posta em questão* (1965) and *Vanguarda e subdesenvolvimento: Ensaios sobre arte* (1969), Gullar critiqued concrete poetry for employing an "international" form to express a "national" essence.[37] Gullar's insights were keen. But in a populist turn he opposed "realism"—understood as "committed" and appropriate to a nationalist project—to "formalism," which he claimed turned its back on "Brazilian reality" and sought an irresponsible universalism (Gullar, *Vanguarda e subdesenvolvimento* 194). Concrete art, echoed Ronaldo Brito a decade later, was apolitical; for him there remained something "colonized" about its mimesis of European Constructivism (50). Yet these early writings by Gullar and Brito missed the extent to which form *was* a theme of 1960s Brazil, as Aguilar has argued persuasively, noting Brasília's airplane-shaped urban planning that promised a future instantiated. The reification of the real, however, soon was put aside for transient action.

POEMA/PROCESSO AND *A NOVA OBJETIVIDADE*

In December 1967 the *poema/processo* movement was launched in Rio de Janeiro and Rio Grande do Norte as an alternative to concrete poetry, although in many ways it continued and amplified a proto-digital side of concretism.[38] Shunning what they saw as the academic cosmopolitanism of the *Noigandres* poets, process/poems' theorists emphasized not "the intranslatabl[ity] . . . of other languages" but the universality of *processes*. They took to an extreme the concrete poets' emphasis on visuality: they dispensed with words altogether to assert an absolute internationalism, a "universal language, even if Brazilian in origin" (Dias-Pino, *Processo* n.p.). In this, too, the movement echoed earlier constructivisms, such as El Lissitzky's claim that "the hieroglyph-book is international (at least in its potentiality)" ("Our Book" 357). But it also announced a new era: one document included in Wlademir Dias-Pino's edited collection of documents *Processo: Linguagem e communicação* (1971) announces that poems without words signal the "end of modernism" (n.p.). While proposing poems without words, Dias-Pino's classic anthology of the movement also evinces the rise of information theory and incipient computation as influences. It hails "series: degree of information," emphasizing reproduction, seriality, and information rather than objecthood (n.p.). Contributing manifestos stress the inclusion of the "most recent scientific advances" including "laser, electronic channels, cinema, computer" (n.p.). What was lauded as an internationalism in the era can now be read as an early moment in globalization.

Álvaro de Sá and Neide Dias de Sá hosted the movement in their home in Rio's leafy Jardim Botânico neighborhood. Álvaro's work favored series of process/poems inspired by cartoons but whose bubbles contained mere symbols, not words. Neide focused on poem-books, performances, and sculptural works. But the 1968 hardening of the dictatorship brought increased police vigilance of the movement's meetings and by 1972 forced the movement's end, announced in a manifesto *Parada—Opção Tática* [Stop—Tactical Option] (many of the associated happenings used humorous signage to protest the dictatorship).

Within the small group Dias-Pino, son of an anarchist typographer, was the foremost exponent of the process/poem; his 1956 poem-object "A ave" [The bird] had influenced poem-books by Lygia Pape and others. (See Figure 18.) Indeed, revisiting postwar Brazilian experimental poetics, Dias-Pino emerges as one of the most compelling and innovative figures, consistently locating poetry in relation to historical change and addressing both aesthetic and political questions. The combinatorial poem "A ave" emerged out of his interest in creating a mathematical poetry, explored in earlier books, but it was also a poem that "consumed itself" (Cirne 37). In a 1958 interview Dias-Pino already discusses the importance of process and declares he is against "personality" (he also declares his hatred of Pound): "Minha 'arte' é contra a personalidade (veja a publicidade Americana) e o heroísmo. Uma arte anônima (ou quase) como a do carpinteiro" [My art is against personality (see American advertising) and heroism. An anonymous (or almost anonymous) art, like that of a carpenter] (Dias-Pino, *Processo*

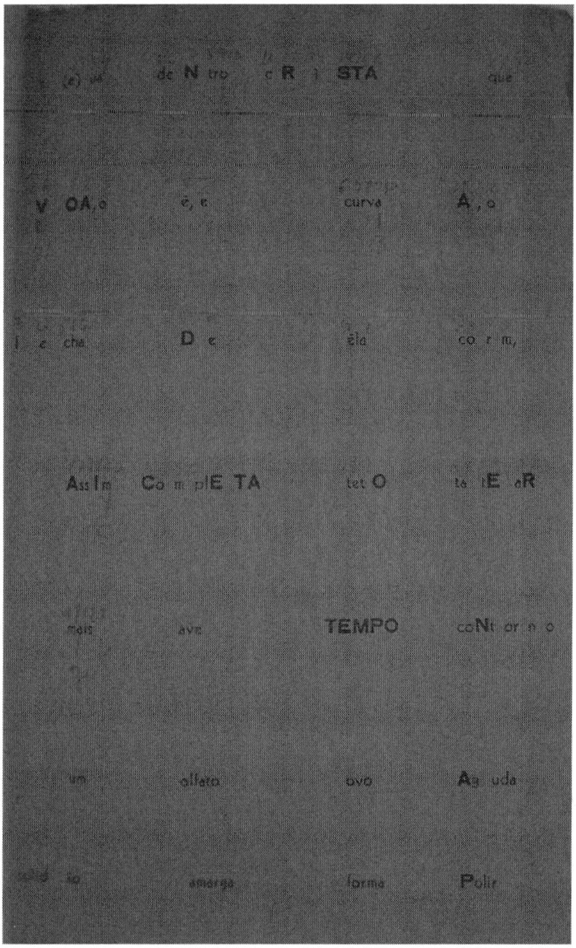

Figure 18. Wlademir Dias-Pino, "A ave" (1956). Courtesy of Wlademir Dias-Pino.

n.p.). Again carpentry is as an ultimate materiality, a bare craft against personality, but here also in the name of process.

Process/poems stressed the possibilities latent in a given material and involved the reader (Cirne 44). They also demanded a person accustomed to consumption (Lima Mendonça 116). But this notion of consumption, in name alluding to consumer culture, in fact understood the consumption of art as *in opposition* to its reification.[39] The process/poem resolved the problem of reification or the division between subject and object not through a "leap" to the object but through the object's consumption, literalized in "poemas comestíveis" [edible poems], such as the 1970 performance at the Recife Art Fair, where a loaf of bread two meters long was baked and then consumed by five thousand people (a plaque accompanying it announced, "This artwork was boycotted by the glorious São Paulo Biennial Foundation," an allusion to the contested São Paulo Biennial under the dictatorship).[40]

The eating of the poem, recalling Revelations' image of eating a book, echoes earlier concretism's privileging of immediacy over interpretation. *Poemas comestíveis*, coincident with movements such as Daniel Spoerri's Eat Art, particularly summon connections to early modern emblem poetry. Emblemata—images with mottos and poems to illustrate them—evolved from sixteenth-century Milanese jurist Andrea Alciati's *apophoreta*, party favors of motto-engraved, consumable sweets. Consumable poetry, emblemata were veritable precipitates of meaning poured into calcareous sugar molds and mottos: words made into things.

The process/poem, however, aspired to a post-*letrado* moment, proclaiming in a 1968 exposition at the Museum of Modern Art in Bahia, "immediate consumption as anti-nobility. end of (individualist) artesanal civilization" (Dias-Pino, *Processo* n.p.). The direct consumption of the book linked the "object" and "non-object" tendencies in concretism as the everyday, material aspects of the objects—what could be more quotidian than daily bread?—disappear through consumption, turning them effectively into performance pieces or non-objects. Dias-Pino once criticized pop art as folkloric and argued that true mass culture meant not enlarging a Coca-Cola insignia but producing massively consumed poems.[41]

By emphasizing performance, the process/poem joined a spate of antidogmatic and antimessianic projects from the late 1960s. Since the process/poem's unfolding depended upon its "consumption" by the reader/consumer/audience, its temporality was contingent. Time was controlled not by subjects or national plans but by the process of consuming the poem (Dias-Pino, *Processo* n.p.). In this process/poems echoed art of the non-object, which Hélio Oiticica declared was an art "of time."[42]

Emphasis on the object's undoing intensified in the art of Oiticica and Clark. Gullar had been central to neoconcrete poetry, but it is perhaps more surprising that the sometimes dogmatic poet-critic was such an important influence on Oiticica and other neoconcrete visual artists associated with Tropicalism, which shunned left moralisms as much as right-wing censure. Yet Gullar documents in his "Teoria do não-objeto" and *Experiência neoconcreta* how neoconcretism emerged from mutually constitutive exchanges between painters, sculptors, and poets.

Gullar's "Teoria do não-objeto" spawned multiple reinventions of "the object," reincarnated, variously, in Willys de Castro's constructivist "objetos ativos" [active objects] and in Oiticica's work as "entre-objetos," "trans-objetos," and "probjetos," designed to foster collective, participatory art (Basualdo 20).[43] Clark's work underwent a similar evolution. She moved from painting to sculpture and then to "propositions" in which the spectator was supposed to be "participated" by others.[44]

Oiticica was the brilliant center of a group of artists he gathered in a show and associated movement he called Nova Objetividade Brasileira, exhibited in 1967 at Rio's Museum of Modern Art.[45] His statement for the show, "Esquema Geral da Objetividade" [General plan of objectivity], outlined attributes of a late 1960s Brazilian vanguard, including "constructivist will" and spectator participation, engagement with political issues, and production of collective projects. He called for a national art in a way many of his Tropicalist peers might have eschewed—"Here, social underdevelopment signifies, culturally, the search for national characterization, a weapon against 'cultural colonialism'" (85).

Oiticica and Clark, like Gullar before them, borrowed from phenomenology to propose an art-making process that would not reinscribe a strict subject-object division or produce an object to be appropriated by a subject. Maria Alice Milliet believes Clark took from Maurice Merleau-Ponty the stance that "The world is not an object such that I have in my possession the law of its making."[46] In another passage that seems a source for Clark's ruminations on temporality Merleau-Ponty wrote: "The ideal of objective thought is both based upon and ruined by temporality. The world, in the full sense of the word, is not an object, for though it has an envelope of objective and determinative attributes, it has also fissures and gaps into which subjectivities slip and lodge themselves, or rather which are those subjectivities themselves" (389). The passage from concrete to neoconcrete thus also mirrors phenomenology's passage from Husserl, a touchstone for object-oriented modernists, to the body-oriented Merleau-Ponty.

With the turn to *nova objetividade* in the mid-1960s, Clark and other artists, rejecting an acquisitive relationship to the world, returned to the anthropophagist metaphors of the 1920s modernists, reinterpreting them in ways concordant with their own projects: sometimes not consuming but being consumed. Oiticica's *penetráveis*, for instance, gave him "the powerful sensation of being devoured"; he claimed they were "the most anthropophagic work in Brazilian art."[47] After 1966, Clark began to create what she called "objetos á-corps," pieces that worked with bodies.[48] She began to discuss her work in terms of the "full void" (*o cheio-vazio* and *o vazio-pleno*). The concretes' void is conserved, but it has been transformed.

If concrete poetry was concerned with establishing the objective at the expensive of subjectivity, neoconcrete art aspired to move beyond (or outside) these binaries altogether. In addition to anthropophagist motifs, the Möbius strip returned. Max Bill had installed a sculpture of a Möbius strip at a 1950 solo exhibition in Brazil and again at the 1951 São Paulo Biennial; now the strip returned in Clark's work as a figure for the indissociability of inside and out, beginning and end. At roughly the same time that Lacan proposed the Möbius strip as iconic of the relation between unconscious and conscious (in his 1963 seminar on anxiety, in which he also claimed that the neurological envelope "has no interior, as it is a single surface"),[49] Clark saw the Möbius strip as a symbol of overcoming subject and object in art-making and in life.[50] Now, perhaps, we might also see this moment as the beginning of postfordist globalization, the empire that Michael Hardt and Antonio Negri have characterized as an era in which "there is progressively less distinction between inside and outside," especially as concerns questions of sovereignty.[51]

Clark had moved progressively toward a destruction of barriers between subjects and objects since the early 1960s. After her 1964 proposition *Caminhando*, for which participants cut a single Möbius strip into multiple new ones, her works, now termed "proposições" [propositions], were designed to be "participated" by others through acts that "turned the virtual into a concrete undertaking" [*a transformação de uma virtualidade em um empreendimento concreto*].[52] (See Figure 19.) The act trumped the art object. Clark's 1965 text "A propósito da magia do objeto" [On the magic of the object] argued that artists who reframed "readymades" believed they invested found objects with "poetic power"; *Caminhando*, she proposed, derived its power from another source: it was not the object but the act that gave rise to its "poetry."[53]

A short text, "O ato" (1965), takes the importance of the act further still. Now the act is presented as uniting subject and object across

Figure 19. Lygia Clark, *Caminhando/Walking* (1964). Photograph by Beto Feliciano. Courtesy of The World of Lygia Clark Cultural Association.

the planet in a "global rhythm" that spans Mozart and beach soccer (Gullar, *Lygia Clark* 23; Clark, Diary 1963). Spatially comprehending the entire globe, the time of the act unfolds in play: the play of music, the play of sport. The resolutely *presentist* time of the act inured it against capture by a futurist horizon. In "A propósito do instante" [On the instant] (1965), Clark spelled out an antimessianic philosophy behind her art. Gone was a belief in utopian futures. It was only in the *instant* of the act that "future being is inscribed" (Gullar, *Lygia Clark* 27; Clark, *Lygia Clark: Fundació Antoni Tàpies* 155). Clark even attempted to imagine how such "act-ual" art might look in the realm of literature, asking, "How could literature express itself in this new concept of 'Art-without-art' and 'act-gesture'"? Clark suggests a kind of hypertext in which an author lets her readers complete the text, depersonalized but not without expression:

> Isto aparentemente seria despersonalizar-se e toda uma coletividade pois ele terá que abdicar da sua própria personalidade e deixar de jogar com dados singulares. A história é qualquer história, o herói não existe pois deve ter uma abertura para que todos possam vir a ser este herói. É apresentar uma amálgama de possibilidades onde cada indivíduo que a lê, possa se encontrar dentro do contexto.[54]
>
> [This would apparently be to depersonalize oneself and a whole collectivity because the author would have to abdicate his or her own personality and stop playing with singular data. The story is any story, the hero doesn't exist because there should be an openness allowing all to become this hero. It would present an amalgam of possibilities in which each individual that reads it can find herself within the context.]

Such work was emblematic of a 1968-era art and politics that abandoned modernist, nationalist, individual, and heroic paradigms. In a 1971 letter to a friend Clark describes contemporary youth movements as beyond all ideologies, and she includes in her letter a parodic—though serious—"note to the censor" (the Big Other of the dictatorship potentially reading her mail) in which she avows her opposition to all dictatorships right and left. She describes having seen a program on television about Latin America and observes that youth no longer identify with communism or any authority that substitutes for religion, or any other myth; they simply want to *be*, against all ideologies.[55]

Finally, just as time and historicity were crucial for Martí's poetics of the concrete, and lay at the heart of the struggles over Canudos and the Atlantic vision of Sousândrade, as Maeztu sought to vest a Catholic time in goods, and just as the postimperial temporality of the Cuban republic was rendered untimely and recursive in its literature, so, again, time was at the center of the neoconcrete and *novaobjetivista* move away from an earlier concretude, as Oiticica insisted on more than one occasion. In "Da arte concreta à arte neoconcreta," Gullar likewise asserted that the concrete and neoconcrete projects differed precisely in their imagination of an object's time.[56]

LYGIA CLARK AND THE END OF EVERYTHING

Clark developed these questions further than any other Brazilian artist of her generation, proposing an "end of everything" that would also be a new beginning. Her *Bichos*, metal sculptures made of recombinant parts (which, although they were made of intersecting planes, Clark imagined as turning about a void), were premised on infinite transformations of one thing into its alleged opposite, designed to break down the fixity of any single category of being.[57] They were, she wrote, living organisms. She specified in a diary entry that they bore similarities to crabs or conch shells: "Cada 'Bicho' é uma entidade orgânica que se revela totalmente dentro de seu tempo interior de expressão. Ele tem afinidade com o caramujo e a concha," an echo of both Haroldo de Campos's belief in the "ex nihilo" and Augusto's "Caracol" [every *Bicho* is an organic entity that reveals itself completely within its interior time of expression. It has affinities with the snail and the conch] (Clark, Diary 1960 n.p.).

Clark called this space within the *Bichos*, and within other works, a "full-void" of infinite possibilities whose totality—indeed its meaning as an artwork—was revealed in a singular act of art- and meaning-making. The notion of the full-void, which Clark related to a feminine ontology, became the core of her subsequent work. It also coincided with her deepening, idiosyncratic interest in psychoanalysis. In her diary entries Clark writes repeatedly of vaginas, uteruses, and pregnancy—material voids that become full—and a fullness that leads to voids.[58]

Clark suffered from periodic depressions and had a minor breakdown in 1964, the year the authoritarian regime came to power. Her therapeutic working-through of the crisis led her to explore, in a surprising echo of Lacan's theory of sublime Things, the void in a series titled "estruturas em caixas de fósforo" [matchbox structures]. (See Figure 20.) In a letter Clark describes her self-administered therapy:

> Ontem estive pensando que a minha crise em Paris abrangeu uma série de problemas com uma certa lógica

> interna . . . o problema dos nomes me veio com uma acuidade enorme . . . me sinto absolutamente sem pai—De uma tal maneira que percebe ser a minha brincadeira o chamar de nosso pai, várias pessoas autoritárias e generosas. . . . Durante a minha doença, comecei a brincar com caixas de fósforos, pensando em "bolar" uma casa toda feita de caixotes. Disto saiu um mausoléu aliás dois, que são bem a continuação do problema da metafísica da fase preta de linhas brancas. . . . Começo a me restituir o sentido da poética do objeto e das coisas simples . . . é fundamental para mim neste momento me reencontrar com esta metafísica das caixas e por conseguinte do mundo.[59]
>
> [Yesterday I was thinking that my crisis in Paris involved a series of problems with a certain internal logic . . . the problem of names came to me with an enormous acuity. . . . I feel totally without a father—To such an extent that I perceive that my joke is to call several authoritarian and generous people "father." . . . During my illness I began to play with matchboxes, devising a whole house made up of boxes. Out of this came the mausoleum, or rather two, which are the continuation of the problem of the metaphysics of the black phase of white lines. . . . I am beginning to restore my sense of the poetics of the object and the simple things . . . it is fundamental for me at this moment to find myself again with this metaphysics of the boxes and therefore of the world.][60]

Lacan's circa 1960 narration of his encounter with matchboxes had served as his example of how an object is elevated to the "dignity of the Thing"; Clark's encounter with matchboxes four years later echoes this experience. Clark's crisis had to do with a "problem of names," as she put it, which left her feeling fatherless and caused her to grant undue power to authoritarian figures, like the military men of the post-coup era, who extolled the values of church, property, and family. Her crisis questioned a veritable Lacanian "Name of the Father," that power that inheres in authoritarian patriarchal figures and in the order of things.

Recovery came in the form of matchboxes, dedicated to Oiticica. In the matchboxes she found a "poética do objeto" just as Lacan had in his elevation of the object to a Thing. Like her contemporaneous artwork *A casa do poeta* [house of the poet], the matchboxes contain a

Figure 20. Lygia Clark, *Estruturas em caixas de fósforo/Matchbox structures* (1964). Courtesy of The World of Lygia Clark Cultural Association.

full-void. (See Figure 21.) In a diary entry, she described it as a uterus in which her *trepantes* and *Bichos* were incubated, "box-cubes whose interior space . . . is a full-void for in them are implied possibilities for the Bichos's birth."[61]

Clark continued to introduce overtly psychoanalytic elements into works that highlighted bodily functions, consumption, and orifices, such as *Canibalismo* and *Baba antropofágica* (Clark, *Lygia Clark: Fundació Antoni Tàpies* 49). While 1920s modernism's interest in antropofagia was a clear inspiration for this work, so too, Paulo Herkenhoff has suggested, was a piece of writing by the French analyst Pierre Fédida, "Destins du cannibalisme."[62] Clark underwent analysis with Fédida while in Paris. She began incorporating psychoanalysis into her work on the body. In *Fantasmática do corpo* Clark staged a series of

Figure 21. Lygia Clark, *A casa do poeta/House of the Poet* (1964). Courtesy of The World of Lygia Clark Cultural Association.

encounters with students in which she attempted to convey to them her own trajectory of passing through objects and into performance, writing about the encounters, "I transfer to them the first experiences that I lived in the transit from the object to the collective body. Passing through the virtual experience of cannibalism, of anthropophagy."[63]

Clark found psychoanalytic confirmation of her own work with bodies and of her interest in introjection, consumption, and the blurring of subject and object, well under way already in the 1950s, in the writings of analysts Nicolas Abraham and Maria Torok, whom she read in a 1972 issue of the *Nouvelle revue de psychanalyse*. (Two years prior, Fédida published on relics in an issue dedicated to "objets du fétichisme".) In a diary entry Clark noted, beneath quotations from Abraham and Torok, a series of observations about the relationship between subject and object, ending in musings on cannibalism:

1) O sujeito relaciona-se c/ o objeto
2) O objeto está em processo de ser encontrado ao invez [sic] de ser colocado pelo sujeito no mundo
3) O sujeito destroi o objeto

4) O sujeito pode usar o objeto
sobre o canibalismo[64]

[1) The subject relates to the object
2) The subject is in the process of being found as opposed to being placed in the world by the subject
3) The subject destroys the object
4) The subject can use the object
On cannibalism]

It appears, then, that Clark read Abraham and Torok and used their ideas about introjection for her own thoughts on *canibalismo*, in the anthropophagist tradition.

Once Clark had broken down objects and bodies into what she called "pieces" she was ready to create her last works: the "relational objects" that shared a concept with the eponymous one advanced by the British psychoanalyst D. W. Winnicott and that bear some relation to her Abraham- and Torok-inspired musings about how subjects use objects to establish connections to the exterior world. Clark's relational objects from the 1970s and 1980s included materials such as stones, pillows, bags of water, and shells, which she employed in treating patients in a home studio. Participants manipulated the materials to dislodge their rigid sense of identity. In the process, by creating relationships between "fullness and voids," calcified, psychotic identity was supposed to dissolve into a "processual" identity (Gullar, *Lygia Clark* 49).

Clark's discrete, scattered objects, important for their relational aspects rather than their singular integrity, seem consistent with a 1965 piece she wrote, asking, "Estaremos tão próximos assim do fim?" [are we really so close to the end of everything?].[65] She affirms her own question with little sentimentality:

> We should then accept this end as it is, because it announces a new beginning. . . . [I]f the last century brought an awareness of the death of God, we feel in our epoch, in man, the death of individuality that gave meaning to his life . . . to the extent that participation makes the separation between subject and object disappear, we must absorb in ourselves this subject-object relation in order to check the spiritual void, lacking apparent meaning, that surrounds us. (Clark, *Diary* 1963–65)

Clark's relational objects were designed to enact this process of consumption and renewal. They were made to be destroyed but to simultaneously negate destruction, just as Winnicott's transitional objects were designed to suffer a child's aggression and survive it (Gullar, *Lygia Clark* 50). For Winnicott, a transitional object is a child's first "not-me" object. It is the first object in relation to whose alterity a child begins to shape her subjectivity. When one recalls that Oswald de Andrade's 1922 *Manifesto antropófago* had declared "only what is not mine interests me," Clark's relational objects, like the process/poem, close a modernist era and open toward a more contemporary era, beyond the subject/object divide, beyond individual art and for collectivities.

Epilogue

Hacia *Post-Concretude*

Just as there is no evidence that Martí and Sousândrade met in 1880s Manhattan, it is unclear whether Clark and Sarduy met, despite their having orbited in similar circles in 1960s Paris.[1] Clark was prominent in the Parisian art world and underwent analysis with Fédida; Sarduy was a well-known author and, later, painter in contact with analysts Jacques-Alain Miller and Lacan. Both wrote about art's materiality. And both were interested in interiority's flip into exteriority, the Möbius strip's undoing of the categories. A few years after Clark produced her sculpture titled *o adentro é o fora* (the inside is the outside), Sarduy wrote a poem in which he concluded, "el afuera es un adentro / y el adentro es un afuera" [the outside is the inside / and the inside is an outside] (*Obra completa* 2:1194). And in his 1966 article "De la pintura de objetos a los objetos que pintan" [From the painting of objects to objects that paint], he absorbed poststructuralism to arrive at an almost object-oriented ontology: Sarduy traces a dialectics of subject and object in twentieth-century art to argue that whereas we once thought we painted objects, we now are ourselves the objects for other objects (*Obra completa* 1:235).

In his essays on concretude Sarduy celebrated the excess that mocks use value; Clark wrote of "the magic of the functionless object. Might function be a way of impeding one from feeling the poetic reality of the object?" (Clark, *Diary* 1963–65). Like Clark's neoconcretism, Sarduy's concretude splits into fixity and mobility, thingliness and immateriality, the thing itself and a metaphor pointing elsewhere. If the first intimations of what "concretude" might be for Sarduy had indicated a "condensation" of language, concretude soon appears more metaphoric insofar as it provokes a dislocation of "verbal bodies: planets out of orbit that abandon their ellipses to move into others" ("Rumo à concretude" 121). (The roots of *metaphor* mean a carrying over from one realm into another.)[2]

Sarduy's image of the ellipses of orbiting planets is a visual analog for the great ellipsis zero, the empty placeholder that recurs in his writings on concretude and on a Latin American neobaroque. Sarduy was acquainted with Miller's influential 1966 essay "Suture," which described how set theory's understanding of zero might be applied to psychoanalytic thought. For Miller, following the mathematician Gottlob Frege, zero represents the space of something not-identical-to-itself, the concept of the inconceivable, the positive idea of absence.

This positive absence—like Clark's *cheio-vazio/vazio pleno*—was central to Sarduy's work as well. In an essay titled "Cómo no he escrito mis libros," Sarduy claimed that the void was the most important element of his writing process (*Antología* 15). Voids structure his art criticism as well. He admired *Fiberglass Sleeves* (1967) by the U.S. artist Robert Morris, a collection of hollow rectangular fiberglass pieces resembling *luminarias*, because of the hollowness *within* each shape. The sleeves contained voids whose "scansion" of presence and absence was infinitely replicable.[3]

According to Sarduy, the sleeves are objects that call attention to the intervals *between* ostensibly "identical" items. They coincide with art's widespread move from the thingly to the processual in the late 1960s, a movement that also coincides, interestingly, with visual art's turn to concrete *poetics*. In the United States, the supposed dematerialization of the art object was accompanied by a rematerialization of language. But in the Brazilian context the causality was somewhat reversed.

If New York conceptualism withdrew "from visuality or objecthood in favor of a work of art constituted by series of linguistic propositions" (Kotz 8), the neoconcrete tradition in Brazil entailed the opposite: Gullar's theory of the "non-object"—elaborated in response to Clark's visual art, to be sure—went on to influence Clark and Oiticica. Gullar recalls how his architectural plan for a "poema enterrado," an underground poem-room, was realized by Oiticica, who went on to develop other such environments. In Brazil, taking poetry to its limit led to processual art.

Meanwhile, the process/poem abandoned language for sheer image. Its theorists reflected: "Just as the sphinx (immoveable and monumental) marks well the civilization of one epoch, so, dialectically, electric apparata (versatile and increasingly small) mark ours," highlighting the circulation of electronic consumer goods and dematerialized forms as the mark of a post-1968 period (Dias-Pino, *Processo* n.p.). Another contributor to Dias-Pino's anthology claimed that "if yesterday Poetry described objects, today it is the functionality of the object that opens onto the Poem" (Dias-Pino, *Processo* n.p.).

Let us return to our point of departure for the "epoch" that these writers self-consciously felt themselves to close. A century earlier, in 1868, Cuban antislavery and independence wars and the first attempt at a Spanish republic, as well as Brazilian abolitionist and pro-republican movements, marked a moment characterized by the language of sovereignty in the Iberian Atlantic. By the 1890s, Brazil congealed a new nation-state by expelling alternative notions of community and temporality, while in Cuba, dreams of equality were set aside upon the close of its long wars. The years 1868–98 gave rise to many ideas about politics that did not necessarily assume the shape of existing nation-states—visions that bloomed and then were pushed aside or imperfectly assimilated to twentieth-century republics. At the dawn of the twentieth century, literature turned its attention to the new forms—material and immaterial—of a new moment.

Brazilian process/poets of the 1960s allude to the link between poetics and these histories when they link "modern" nationalism with literary modernism through a reference to Canudos and go on to mark their own position as being beyond such logics. A late 1960s document titled "Process/Poem: Reading of Products (of Positions)" first asserts the typical vanguard motto "New situations require new processes," then clarifies

> Modernism began, surreptitiously, in 1893, with the first symbolist book (*Broquéis:* Cruz e Sousa). Canudos (1896) inaugurated the nationalist thinking that crested in the centennial of independence . . . modernist poetry turned on the word and its semantic implications. . . . And so poems made with words in a dictionary state and even those made up of atomized letters close, definitively, modernism. . . . The poem without words or the process/poem inaugurates, without a doubt, the new era. (Dias-Pino, *Processo* n.p.)

The new period was postmodernist and postnationalist, even postverbal, with the earlier forms seen as limited and intolerant. The closure of objectivism and nationalism had ceded to the processual and, in the work of Cordeiro, to the digital.

The year 1968, however, brought with it not only slogans of liberation but also, of course, repressive measures that had provoked and followed them: the massacre at Mexico City's Tlatelolco; the Padilla affair and Fidel Castro's endorsement of the Soviet crushing of the Prague spring; Brazil's AI-5 measures. Media were part of the changing nature of the political, for better and for worse. When, in 1968, the student Edson Luís was killed in Rio de Janeiro by military police, a student of concrete poet Décio Pignatari scrawled the graffiti "luto luta" [mourning fights on].[4]

Precisely in this moment of repression, artists embraced a postobjective, performance- and process-oriented art. While many Latin American nation-states grew increasingly authoritarian, the poetic and art object was consumed, and the discourse of subjects and objects itself was called into question. One side of concretude that Martí had celebrated in new media technologies returned: not reification but virtuality, not an aping of economic processes but their critique, not solely a masculinist aesthetic but a mobile and feminist one—consumption and production, noumenon and phenomenon. Clark's notion of an inaugural end concludes the arc that began with romantic concerns with sovereignty and the subject and moved through and beyond the object.

Notes

INTRODUCTION

1. José Martí, *Obras completas*, vols. 1–22, 2nd ed. (Havana: Editorial de Ciencias Sociales, 1975), 22:156. Unless otherwise indicated, all translations are mine. When citing literary works, I have generally opted to include both original languages and English translations; when citing more historical prose I have sometimes included only the English translation for the reader's ease.

2. Augusto de Campos, Haroldo de Campos, and Décio Pignatari, "Plano-piloto para Poesia Concreta," *Noigandres* 4 (1958), in Augusto de Campos, Haroldo de Campos, and Décio Pignatari, eds., *Teoria da poesia concreta: Textos críticos e manifestos, 1950–1960* (1965), 4th ed. (São Paulo: Ateliê, 2006), 216.

3. Haroldo de Campos, "Olho por olho a olho nu (manifesto)," first published in *Ad-arquitetura e decoração*, no. 20 (November/December 1956), in de Campos, de Campos, and Pignatari, *Teoria*, 73–76.

4. Bill Brown discusses this trend in the introduction to his edited volume *Things* (Chicago: University of Chicago Press, 2004). The introduction to Fiona Candlin and Raiford Guins's *Object Reader* (New York: Routledge, 2009) lists a spate of similar developments: "in 2001, Reaktion Books launched its 'Objeckt' series. . . . The final volume of MIT Press's Anyone Corporation architectural series was dedicated to 'things'"; to this list the editors add the 2003 Spanish art magazine *Exit*'s issue titled "Objetos Cotidianos" ("Ordinary Things"); a 2004 Pennsylvania State University conference, "Objects in/and of Visual Culture"; a 2005 University of California Humanities Research Institute group titled "Object of Media Studies"; and a 2005 Bruno Latour and Peter Weibel curated book *Making Things Public: Atmospheres of Democracy* (2005). Recent additions to the trend include a summer

2012 conference in Brazil, "The Secret Life of Objects" and, in science studies, Bruno Latour's *Reassembling the Social: An Introduction to Actor-Network-Theory* (New York: Oxford University Press, 2005) and Lorraine Daston and Peter Galison's *Objectivity* (Boston: Zone Books, 2007). Object-oriented philosophy titles include Jane Bennett's *Vibrant Matter: A Political Ecology of Things* (Durham, DC: Duke University Press, 2009), Ian Bogost's *Alien Phenomenology: Or What's It Like to Be a Thing* (Minneapolis: University of Minnesota Press, 2012), Levi Bryant's *The Democracy of Objects* (Ann Arbor: Open Humanities Press, 2011), and Graham Harman's *Tool-Being: Heidegger and the Metaphysics of Objects* (Chicago: Open Court, 2002). Anglophone literary studies on the theme include Elaine Freedgood, *The Ideas in Things: Fugitive Meaning in the Victorian Novel* (Chicago: University of Chicago Press, 2006), Bill Brown, *A Sense for Things: The Object Matter of American Literature* (Chicago: University of Chicago Press, 2004), and the rather earlier Douglas Mao, *Solid Objects: Modernism and the Test of Production* (Princeton: Princeton University Press, 1998). In Latin American studies, Anke Birkenmaier's *Alejo Carpentier y la cultura del surrealismo en América Latina* (Madrid: Iberoamericana Vervuert, 2006) discusses surrealist objects. Art history likewise boasts a number of recent volumes, including Christina Kiaer's *Imagine No Possessions: The Socialist Objects of Russian Constructivism* (Cambridge, MA: MIT Press, 2005).

5. Fred Moten, *In the Break: The Aesthetics of the Black Radical Tradition* (Minneapolis: University of Minnesota Press, 2003).

6. Tony Ballentyne and Antoinette Burton, "Empires and the Reach of the Global," in *A World Connecting, 1870–1945*, ed. Emily Rosenberg (Cambridge, MA: Belknap, 2012), 285–431. Ballentyne and Burton argue that the decades between 1870 to 1945 "accelerated transnational economic connections and sutured them to a variety of globalizing capitalist work regimes, forms of accumulation, and mechanisms of delivery and consumption" long before twenty-first-century globalizing forces (338).

7. William Glade, "Latin America and the International Economy," in *The Cambridge History of Latin America*, vol. 4, *1870 to 1930*, ed. Leslie Bethell (New York: Cambridge University Press, 1986), 21, 46.

8. Werner Hamacher, "*Lingua Amissa*: The Messianism of Commodity Language and Derrida's *Specters of Marx*," in *Ghostly Demarcations: A Symposium on Jacques Derrida's "Specters of Marx*," ed. Michael Spinker (London: Verso, 1999). See also Carl Schmitt, *Political Theology: Four Chapters on the Concept of Sovereignty*, trans. George Schwab (Chicago: University of Chicago Press, 2006), 36.

9. Severo Sarduy, "Hacia la concretud," *Blanco* (Fall 1979): 12–19.

10. Severo Sarduy, "Sabe Usted lo que es 'concretud'?" in *Antología*, ed. Gustavo Guerrero (Mexico City: Fondo de Cultura Económica, 2000), 240–42. This article was originally written in French, discovered posthumously, likely delivered in conferences or on the radio, and translated for Guerrero's *Antología* (Guerrero, email to the author, February 17, 2013).

11. Fredric Jameson, *Representing Capital: A Reading of Volume I* (New York: Verso, 2011), 131.

12. Friedrich Kittler, *Gramophone, Film, Typewriter*, trans. Geoffrey Winthrop-Young and Michael Wutz (Stanford, CA: Stanford University Press, 1999).

13. Sergiusz Michalski, "Neue Sachlichkeit: A Style and a Name," trans. Michael Claridge, in *New Objectivity: Painting, Graphic Art and Photography in Weimar Germany, 1919–1933* (Los Angeles: Taschen, 2003); Ronaldo Brito, *Neoconcretismo: Vértice e ruptura do projeto construtivo brasileiro* (1985; São Paulo: Cosac & Naify Edições, 1999), 19, 25. Roh coined the term "magic realism" to describe the movement, against which Alejo Carpentier would later differentiate his "real maravilloso." Franz Roh, *German Art in the Twentieth Century*, trans. Catherine Hutter (Greenwich, CT: New York Graphic Society, 1968), 112–13. Roberto González Echevarría discusses the Spanish translation of Roh in *Alejo Carpentier: The Pilgrim at Home* (Ithaca: Cornell University Press, 1977), 114–16.

14. Gwen Kirkpatrick, *The Dissonant Legacy of Modernismo: Lugones, Herrera y Reissig, and the Voices of Modern Spanish American Poetry* (Berkeley: University of California Press, 1989), 4.

15. Noé Jitrik, *Las contradicciones del modernismo: Productividad poética y situación sociológica* (Mexico City: Colegio de México, 1978).

16. Roberto González Echevarría, "Modernidad, modernismo y nueva narrativa: El recurso del método," *Revista Interamericana de Bibliografía* 30 (1980), 159.

17. Ericka Beckman, *Capital Fictions: The Literature of Latin America's Export Age* (Minneapolis: University of Minnesota Press, 2013), 53. Beckman does see the *form* of "decadent" literature to gesture toward relations between Europe and Latin America (131).

18. Nicholas Brown, *Utopian Generations: The Political Horizon of Twentieth-Century Literature* (Princeton: Princeton University Press, 2005), 19.

19. José Antonio Ramos, *Coaybay* (Havana: Impr. "El siglo XX," 1926), 331.

20. This theory is best known through Giovanni Arrighi's *The Long Twentieth Century: Money, Power and the Origins of Our Times* (New York: Verso, 1994). In Atlantic studies it has been used productively by Ian Baucom to theorize a long twentieth century that recapitulates the British eighteenth century in which slaving, insurance, and the emergence of finance capital are mutually imbricated. Ian Baucom, *Specters of the Atlantic: Slavery, Finance Capital and the Philosophy of History* (Durham, NC: Duke University Press, 2005). See also Saskia Sassen, *Territory, Authority, Rights from Medieval to Global Assemblages* (Princeton: Princeton University Press, 2006), 133.

21. Juan Pan-Montojo also comments on a global "1898" in *Más se perdió en Cuba: España, 1898 y la crisis de fin de siglo*, ed. Juan Pan-Montojo (Madrid: Alianza Editorial, 1998), 9–30.

22. Carl Schmitt, *The Nomos of the Earth in the International Law of the Jus Publicum Europaeum*, trans. G. L. Ulmen (New York: Telos Press, 2003), 252.

23. James Beniger, *The Control Revolution: Technological and Economic Origins of the Information Society* (Cambridge, MA: Harvard University Press, 1986), 31.

24. John Kraniauskas, "Difference Against Development: Spiritual Accumulation and the Politics of Freedom," *Boundary 2* 32 *(2)* (Summer 2005): 54.

25. Nilo María Fabra, *Presente y futuro: Nuevos cuentos* (Barcelona: Gili, 1897). My attention was first drawn to this work thanks to José-Carlos Mainer's *La doma de la quimera: Ensayos sobre nacionalismo y cultura en España* (Madrid: Iberoamericana, 2004).

26. Friedrich Kittler argues that the war between Spain, Cuba, and the United States was a "zero-sum game" in which "islands such as Cuba and the Philippines changed from old to modern colonial power simply because the telegraphically most advanced country had no trouble winning what its general staff surnamed 'the war of coal and cables.' For at the same time coal gave ships their kinetic energy, cables carried the information as to where this energy had to be freighted. Since the United States had intercepted all transatlantic cables, the Spanish fleet perished without a shot, simply by lack of energetic resources. The formal identity between Boltzmann's entropic formula and Shannon's informational one had been proved." Friedrich Kittler, *Literature Media Information Systems*, ed. John Johnson (Amsterdam: G & B Arts International, 1995), 121.

27. Vladimir Il'ich Lenin, *Imperialism, the Highest Stage of Capitalism* (Moscow: Foreign Languages Publishing House, 1947), 27.

28. Gilles Deleuze, "Postscript on the Societies of Control," *October* 59 (Winter 1992): 3–7.

29. See, for instance, Ballentyne and Burton, "Empires and the Reach of the Global"; Beckman, *Capital Fictions*; and Immanuel Wallerstein, "States? Sovereignty? The Dilemmas of Capitalists in an Age of Transition," in *States and Sovereignty in the Global Economy*, ed. David A. Smith, Dorothy J. Solinger, and Steven C. Topik (New York: Routledge, 1999), 20–33.

30. Manuel Moreno Fraginals, *El ingenio*, vol. 3 (Havana: Editorial Ciencias Sociales, 1978), 13.

31. Severo Sarduy, "Rumo à concretude," in Haroldo de Campos, *Signantia quasi coelum = Signância quase céu* (São Paulo: Editorial Perspectiva, 1979), 120–21.

32. Maria Gough, *The Artist as Producer: Russian Constructivism in Revolution* (Berkeley: University of California Press, 2005).

33. El Lissitzky, Lazar Markovitch, "Our Book," in *El Lissitzky: Life, Letters, Texts*, ed. Sophie Lissitzky-Küppers (Greenwich, CT: New York Graphic Society, 1967), 356.

34. See Oscar Masotta's essay "Después del Pop: Nosotros desmaterializamos," in *Conciencia y estructura* (Buenos Aires: Editorial Jorge Álvarez, 1968), 218–44, in which Masotta describes a new kind of art characterized as "art of mass media communications" and which he connects to artist Roberto Jacoby's work: "'communication works' also define the area of their own 'materiality.' The 'material' ('immaterial,' 'invisible') with which informational works of such a type are constructed is nothing other than the processes, results, deeds and/or the phenomena of the information unleashed by mass media" (226). Eduardo Kac notes that the 1960s' "dematerialization" of the art object into process was first commented upon by Masotta in

"Después," presented as a talk at Buenos Aires' Instituto Di Tella on July 21, 1967. Since U.S. critic Lucy Lippard met with Masotta in Buenos Aires in the fall of 1968 and had published, with John Chandler, an article in *Art International* in February 1968 on the dematerialization of the art object, and since Lippard's book "mentions several events and works in Argentina," Kac suggests Lippard may have been informed by meeting with Masotta but neglected to credit him. Her article from February 1968, however, precedes the autumn 1968 meeting, though it follows Masotta's 1967 lecture. Eduardo Kac, *Telepresence and Bio Art: Networking Humans, Rabbits and Robots* (Ann Arbor: University of Michigan Press, 2005), 57n52. In any case, Masotta traces his interest in Lissitzky's concept of dematerialization to several *New Left Review* pieces from 1967 that reproduced Lissitzky's "Future of the Book" on how dematerialization accompanies new media (Masotta, "Después," 227; see also Lissitzky-Küppers), which Lippard could well have read. In search of a Latin American dematerialist forebear, Kac might better have noted that the Brazilian poet and critic Ferreira Gullar had discussed Lissitzky's relevance for neoconcretism in 1959–60. Ferreira Gullar, *Etapas da arte contemporânea: Do cubismo ao neoconcretismo* (São Paulo: Livraria Nobel, 1985), 132.

35. Charles Maier, "Leviathan 2.0: Inventing Modern Statehood," in *A World Connecting, 1870–1945*, ed. Emily Rosenberg (Cambridge, MA: Belknap, 2012), 34.

36. In both Cuba and Brazil forty years of elite defense of slavery eroded in the 1860s. Márcia Berbel, Rafael Marquese, and Tâmis Parron, *Escravidão e política Brasil e Cuba, c. 1790–1850* (São Paulo: FAPESP, 2010).

37. Roberto Schwarz signaled in a seminal essay on the period how the very flourishing of culture despite the 1964 coup led to the repressive clamp down in 1968. Roberto Schwarz, "Cultura e política, 1964–1969: Alguns esquemas," in *O Pai de Família e outros estudos* (Rio de Janeiro: Paz e Terra, 1978), 61–92.

38. Fredric Jameson noted that "the 60s, often imagined as a period in which capital and first world power are in retreat all over the globe, can just as easily be conceptualized as a period in which capital is in full dynamic and innovative expansion, equipped with a whole armature of fresh production techniques and new 'means of production.'" Fredric Jameson, "Periodizing the 60s," *Social Text*, no. 9/10, The 60's Without Apology (Spring–Summer 1984): 186.

39. Manuel Castells, *The Rise of the Network Society*, 2nd ed., vol. 1 of *The Information Age: Economy, Society and Culture* (Malden, MA: Wiley Blackwell, 2000); Augusto de Campos, "Informação e redundância na música popular," in *Balanço da bossa: Antología crítica da moderna música popular brasileira* (São Paulo: Editora Perspectiva, 1968), 179–89.

40. Humberto Maturana, introduction to Humberto Maturana and Francisco Varela, *Autopoesis and Cognition: The Realization of the Living* (Boston: D. Reidel Publishing, 1980), xvi. This historical anecdote is not included in the Spanish version of the book.

41. Waldemar Cordeiro, "Letter to Božo Bek, August 5, 1968," in *A Little-Known Story About a Movement, a Magazine, and the Computer's Arrival*

in Art: New Tendencies and Bit International, 1961–1973, ed. Margit Rosen (Cambridge, MA: MIT Press, 2011), 241; see also Rachel Price, "Early Brazilian Digital Culture; or, The Woman Who Was Not B.B.," *Grey Room*, no. 47 (Spring 2012): 65.

42. See, among many other studies, José Lezama Lima, *La expresión americana* (Havana: Editorial Letras Cubanas, 2010); and Irlemar Chiampi, *Barroco e modernidade: Ensaios sobre literatura latino-americana* (Petrópolis: Editorial Perspectiva, 1998). See also the exchanges between Octavio Paz and Haroldo de Campos, published as *Transblanco: Em torno a Blanco de Octavio Paz*, 2nd ed. (São Paulo: Editora Siciliano, 1994).

1. *ESPIRAL NEGRA*: CONCRETUDE IN THE ATLANTIC

1. Angus Maddison states that the United States "overtook" the United Kingdom in terms of productivity in the 1890s. Angus Maddison, *Contours of the World Economy* (New York: New York University Press, 2007), 73. Victor Bulmer-Thomas notes that "the principal investor [in Latin America] in the nineteenth century, Great Britain, had been replaced in most countries by the United States by 1930." Victor Bulmer-Thomas, *The Economic History of Latin America Since Independence*, 2nd ed. (New York: Cambridge University Press, 1994), 11.

2. Avihu Zakai, *Exile and Kingdom: History and Apocalypse in the Puritan Migration to America* (New York: Cambridge University Press, 1992), 80.

3. Jacques Le Goff, *Medieval Civilization, 400–1500*, trans. Julia Barrow (Cambridge, MA: Basil Blackwell, 1990), 171–72.

4. See Djelal Kadir, *Columbus and the Ends of the Earth: Europe's Prophetic Rhetoric as Conquering Ideology* (Berkeley: University of California Press, 1992) and Nicolás Wey Gómez, *Tropics of Empire: Why Columbus Sailed South to the Indies* (Cambridge, MA: MIT Press, 2008).

5. Brooks Adams, *America's Economic Supremacy* (London: Macmillan, 1900), 51.

6. Sophus Reinert, *Translating Empire: Emulation and the Origins of Political Economy* (Cambridge, MA: Harvard University Press, 2011), 4.

7. Pedro Henríquez Ureña, "Ariel," in *Ensayos críticos* (Havana: Imprenta de Esteban Fernández, 1905). My thanks to Arcadio Díaz-Quiñones for this reference.

8. Of course, British capital in the nineteenth century had already exercised significant influence in Latin America. For a discussion of its representation in Latin American literature, see Jennifer French, *Nature, Neo-colonialism, and the Spanish American Regional Writers* (Hanover, NH: University Press of New England, 2005).

9. Focused on economic power and allegedly unstoppable historical development, his comments may, however, have been a response to Theodore Roosevelt's 1904 corollary to the Monroe Doctrine, which struck a more classically (territorial) imperial stance by asserting a U.S. right to intervene in Latin America. Euclides da Cunha, "Temores vãos," in *Obra completa*, ed. Afrânio Coutinho, 2nd ed., vol. 1 (Rio de Janeiro: Editora Nova Aguilar,

1995), 197. For more on period economics, see Robert Levine, *The History of Brazil* (Westport, CT: Greenwood Press, 1999), 84.

10. Nicolau Sevcenko, *Literatura como missão: Tensões sociais e criação cultural na Primeira República* (São Paulo: Brasiliense, 1983), 207.

11. Vicente Huidobro, *Finis Britannia: Une redoutable société secrète s'est dressée contre l'imperialisme anglais* (Paris: J Budry & cie, 1923), 83–84.

12. Jesús Pabón, "El 98, acontecimiento internacional," in *Días de Ayer* (Barcelona: Aleph, 1963), 139–95. This essay is cited and discussed in its context in Manuel Espadas Burgos, "Las lecturas históricas del 98," in *La nación soñada: Cuba, Puerto Rico y Filipinas ante el 98*, ed. Consuelo Naranjo Orovio, Miguel Angel Puig-Samper, and Luis Miguel García Mora Aranjuez (Madrid: Doce Calles, 1996), 697–712.

13. In the 1930s Schmitt drew on Latin American politicians' critique of the Monroe Doctrine to defend Hitlerian ambitions. Carl Schmitt, "Grossraum Versus Universalism: The International Legal Struggle over the Monroe Doctrine," trans. Matthew Hannah, in *Spatiality, Sovereignty and Carl Schmitt: Geographies of the Nomos*, ed. Stephen Legg (New York: Routledge, 2011), 46–54.

14. In this Schmitt anticipated by three years a series of debates about "informal" versus formal empire ensuing from John Gallagher and Ronald Robinson's 1953 essay "The Imperialism of Free Trade," which argued that Britain had long extended its actual mercantile empire beyond jurisdiction to create a de facto "informal" economic empire, in Latin America among other places. John Gallagher and Ronald Robinson, "The Imperialism of Free Trade," *Economic History Review*, 2nd ser., 6, no. 1 (1953): 1–15.

15. Gareth Williams, "Imagined Secularization: The Nomos of the Earth and the Challenge of the Western Hemispheric Interstate System," *South Atlantic Quarterly* 104, no. 2 (2005): 331.

16. Emily Rosenberg, *Financial Missionaries to the World: The Politics and Culture of Dollar Diplomacy, 1900–1930* (Cambridge, MA: Harvard University Press, 1999), 52.

17. Jeremy Adelman notes that the eighteenth-century Spanish economist Pedro Rodríguez Campomanes distinguished between "empires of conquest . . . and empires of commerce," though Rodríguez Campomanes associated "conquest" with access to physical resources and not necessarily territorial control and settlement. Jeremy Adelman, *Sovereignty and Revolution in the Iberian Atlantic* (Princeton: Princeton University Press, 2006), 25.

18. John Elliott, *Empires of the Atlantic World: British and Spanish in America, 1492–1830* (New Haven: Yale University Press, 2006); Jorge Cañizares-Esguerra, *Puritan Conquistadors: Iberianizing the Atlantic, 1550–1700* (Stanford, CA: Stanford University Press, 2006).

19. Lauren Benton, *A Search for Sovereignty: Law and Geography in European Empires, 1400–1900* (New York: Cambridge University Press, 2009), 280.

20. Gopal Balakrishnan, *The Enemy: An Intellectual Portrait of Carl Schmitt* (New York: Verso, 2000), 244.

21. Bernard Stiegler, *Technics and Time, II: Disorientation*, trans. Stephen Barker (Stanford, CA: Stanford University Press, 2009), 113.

22. C.L.R. James, *The Black Jacobins* (New York: Vintage, 1963); Paul Gilroy, *The Black Atlantic: Modernity and Double Consciousness* (Cambridge, MA: Harvard University Press, 1993); Antonio Benítez Rojo, *The Repeating Island: The Caribbean and the Postmodern Perspective*, 2nd ed., trans. James Maraniss (Durham, NC: Duke University Press, 1996); Stephan Palmié, *Wizards and Scientists: Explorations in Afro-Cuban Modernity and Tradition* (Durham, NC: Duke University Press, 2002); Édouard Glissant, *Caribbean Discourse*, trans. Michael Dash (Charlottesville: University of Virginia Press, 1999).

23. Jorge Cañizares-Esguerra, "Some Caveats About the 'Atlantic' Paradigm," *History Compass* 1 (2003): NA 004, 1–4.

24. Alejandro Mejías-López, *The Inverted Conquest: The Myth of Modernity and the Transatlantic Onset of Modernism* (Nashville: Vanderbilt University Press, 2009).

25. Arrighi's title was itself an allusion to Karl Polanyi's famous book *The Great Transformation: The Political and Economic Origins of Our Time* (Boston: Beacon Press, 1944).

26. Giovanni Arrighi, *Adam Smith in Beijing: Lineages of the Twenty-First Century* (New York: Verso, 2007).

27. Andre Gunder Frank, *ReOrient: Global Economy in the Asian Age* (Berkeley: University of California Press, 1998).

28. See also Dennis O. Flynn and Arturo Giráldez, *China and the Birth of Globalization in the 16th Century* (Burlington: Ashgate, 2010).

29. Kenneth Pomeranz, *The Great Divergence: China, Europe and the Making of the World Economy* (Princeton: Princeton University Press, 2000), 24, 161.

30. For recent scholarship on the relevance of this relationship, see Manel Ollé, *La empresa de China: De la Armada Invencible al Galeón de Manila* (Barcelona: Acantilado, 2002).

31. Sarduy, "Rumo à concretude," 117–25; "Vers la concretude," *Barcelona: América Latina, Cahiers Confrontations*, no. 5 (1981): 53–60; "Towards Concreteness," trans. Amelia Simpson, *Latin American Literary Review* 14, no. 27, Brazilian Literature (January–June 1986): 61–69.

32. Alfonso Reyes, "Las jitanjáforas," in *La experiencia literaria* (Buenos Aires: Editorial Losada, 1942), 178–218; Reyes, "Las jitanjáforas," *Libra* (Buenos Aires, Winter 1929), in *El libro de las jitanjáforas y otros papeles seguidos de retruécanos, sonetórpidos y porras deportivas*, ed. Adolfo Castañón (Madrid: Iberoamericana Verveurt, 2011), 21–59; Reyes, "Alcance a las jitanjáforas," *Revista de avance* 4, no. 46 (May 1930): 133–34, 136–40.

33. "Por el mundo de las 'jitanjáforas': Mariano Brull, gran poeta cubano, sugirió al escritor mexicano Alfonso Reyes sus curiosas teorías recientes," *Excélsior-El País* (October 1, 1929), reprinted in Alfonso Reyes, *El libro de las jitanjáforas*, 140.

34. Francisco Ichaso, "Las 'jitanjáforas' o el Cheer Lírico," *Excélsior-El País* (October 3, 1929), reprinted in Reyes, *El libro de las jitanjáforas*, 145.

35. One study speculates that the poem references Brull's childhood in Ceuta, Morocco, and in Andalusia (identified as a land of "gitanas" [gypsies]). Ricardo Larraga, *Mariano Brull y la poesía pura en Cuba* (Miami: Ediciones Universales, 1994), 83. In a letter to Reyes dated May 7, 1929, Brull wrote, "En verdad, no necesitaba usted consultarme el cambio de la g por j de gitanjáfora (ahora jitanjáfora). Bastaba que usted lo creyera mejor. La sugestión ortográfica de gitano me llevó a conservar la g, sin otra razón, en la palabra inventada" [In truth, you need not have consulted me about changing the g for a j of gitanjáfora (now jitanjáfora). It was enough that you thought it better. The orthographic suggestion of gypsy led me to keep the g, with no other reason, in an invented word], lending some credence to Larraga's speculations. In Reyes, *El libro de las jitanjáforas,* 122.

36. The mixture of mystifying and pseudo-philological attributions of *jitanjáforas* to African languages has a long history. Ortiz imagined *jitanjáforas* as a quasi-magical language: "la forma poética del lenguaje mágico . . . que todavía se mantienen vivas y pegadas a ciertos oídos por la arrebatadora fuerza hipnótica y emotiva de sus ritmos" [the poetic form of magic language . . . that still remains alive and fresh to certain ears for its powerful, hypnotic and emotive force of its rhythms]. Fernando Ortiz, "Los últimos versos mulatos," *Revista Bimestre Cubana* 35, no. 3 (1935): 321–36, reprinted in *Las vanguardias en el Caribe: Cuba, Puerto Rico y República Dominicana*, ed. William Luis (Orlando, FL: Iberoamericana Vervuert, 2010), 553. Luis Alberto Sánchez alleged in 1935 that while the *jitanjáfora* exists in all languages, "en Cuba, por natural consecuencia del abolengo africano, es común" [in Cuba, as a natural consequence of its African heritage, it is common] (quoted in Ortiz, "Los últimos," 554). González Echevarría has also argued that words in Nicolás Guillén's *Motivos de Son* have a direct link to African vocabularies. Roberto González Echevarría, "Guillén as Baroque: Meaning in *Motivos de Son*," reproduced in *Las vanguardias en el Caribe*, ed. Luis, 459–76.

37. Fernando Ortiz, "Más acerca de la poesía mulata: Escorzos para su estudio," *Revista Bimestre Cubana* 37, no. 1 (January–June 1936): 23.

38. Sianne Ngai, "A Foul Lump Started Making Promises in My Voice: Race, Affect, and the Animated Subject," *American Literature* 74, no. 3 (2002): 572–73.

39. Enrico Mario Santí discovers an allusion to Heidegger's 1950 lecture on "The Thing" in Sarduy. Enrico Mario Santí, "Textual Politics: Severo Sarduy," *Latin American Literary Review* 8, no. 16, Hispanic Caribbean Literature (Spring 1980): 152–60; González Echevarría links this Heideggerian allusion to a Kongo cosmogram in *La ruta de Severo Sarduy* (Hanover: Ediciones del norte, 1987), 130.

40. Harryette Mullen, "African Signs and Spirit Writing," *Callaloo* 19, no. 3 (1996): 672; Robert Ferris Thompson, *Flash of the Spirit: African and Afro-American Art and Philosophy* (New York: Vintage, 1984), 113. For the concrete, visual writing of Cuban Abakuá symbols, see Lydia Cabrera, *La sociedad secreta Abakuá* (Miami: Ediciones C. R., 1970), and Todd Ramón Ochoa, *Society of the Dead Quita Manaquita and Palo Praise in Cuba*

(Berkeley: University of California Press, 2010). I am indebted to Sonya Posmentier for this reference to Mullen.

41. Alejo Carpentier, *Écue-yamba-ó novela afrocubana* (Havana: Editorial Arte y Literatura, 1977), 120, 162, 165. Anke Birkenmaier reads Carpentier's attention to objects in this novel as proof of a surrealist, museological, ethnographic gaze (60); she points out that in the introduction to his second edition Carpentier reflects that while he had thought he knew his characters, in fact "they had hidden from me in recondite impulses of rebellion: in ancestral beliefs and practices that signified, in reality, a resistance to the dissolving power of external factors" (quoted in Birkenmaier, *Alejo Carpentier*, 26).

42. I owe this attention to "hieroglyphic" writing to conversations with Sonya Posmentier (October 2012). Nicolás Guillén, in his introduction to *Sóngoro Cosongo*, defined his verses as "versos mulatos" [mulatto verses], clarifying, "La inyección africana en esta tierra es tan profunda, y se cruzan y entrecruzan en nuestra bien regada hidrografía social tantas corrientes capilares, que sería trabajo de miniaturista desenredar el jeroglífico" [the African injection in this land is so deep, and so many capillary currents cross and crisscross in our well-watered social hydrography, that it would be a miniaturist's work to unravel the hieroglyph]. "Prólogo, *Sóngoro Cosongo*," in Nicolás Guillén, *Obra Poética Tomo I, 1922–1958*, ed. Ángel Augier (Havana: Letras Cubanas, 2004), 92.

43. An "olor dulzón" of tropical fruit and the sound of Cuban music (updated to the 1970s) repeats in Sarduy's 1992 "Exiliado de si mismo," a reflection on what is missed when in "exile," suggesting an identification with Brull or with Reyes. Severo Sarduy, "Exiliado de si mismo," *El País* (April 4, 1992): 9.

44. Severo Sarduy, *Anamorphosis* (Caracas: Monte Ávila, 1982). In 1968 Sarduy published an article titled "Anamorphoses" about Julio Cortázar's collection *Gites*, in which Sarduy lauded the Argentine's "renversement du réalisme" and literary anamorphoses by which the designs in Cortázar's novels change according to the varying points of view adapted by the reader. Severo Sarduy, "Anamorphoses," *Quinzaine litteraire*, no. 50 (May 1, 1968).

45. Rubén Gallo, "Severo Sarduy, Jacques Lacan y el psicoanálisis: Entrevista con François Wahl," *Revista Hispánica moderna*, nos. 1–2 (June–December 2006): 51–60.

46. Severo Sarduy, *Obra completa*, vols. 1–2, ed. Gustavo Guerrero and François Wahl (Paris: Colección Archivos, 1999), 2:1272.

47. The *jitanjáfora*, as a part of Antillean experimental lineage, also draws on the transatlantic practice of *decimar*, improvising *décimas*, which combines a legacy of European and Afro-diasporic poetic traditions that both place a premium on versical formalism and ingenuity. This tradition of Atlantic formalism could well include the forgotten "literary curiosity" titled "Amar hasta fracasar" [Love Unto Failure] by Rubén Darío, who attributed it to an author, "quizá antillano" [perhaps Antillean]. "Amar hasta fracasar" is a Georges Perec–like sketch, *avant la lettre,* about Ana and Blas of La Habana in which the only vowel to appear is "a"—by chance that letter Sarduy loved for its neobaroque sensual hollows and for its double identity as the sign for the

Lacanian objet a, a partial object for a necessarily frustrated [*fracasada*!] desire (Sarduy, *Obra completa*, 2:1250–51). Rubén Darío, "Amar hasta fracasar," *Mundial Magazine* 5, no. 27 (July 1913): 284–85, reprinted in *Rubén Darío Cuentos Completos*, ed. Ernesto Mejía Sánchez (Managua: Nueva Nicaragua, 1993), 432–36.

48. Severo Sarduy, "Mood Indigo," in *Obra completa*, ed. Gustavo Guerrero and François Wahl (Paris: Colección Archivos, 1999), 1:158–59.

49. The poem was similar to paintings Sarduy was undertaking at the time and which he claimed were a kind of self-portrait. François Wahl, "Severo de la rue Jacob" (*Obra completa*, 2:1506).

50. Haroldo de Campos, whose friendship with Sarduy dated to 1966, also translated Lezama Lima's "La prueba del jade" in 1971. Gênese Andrade, "Afinidades eletivas: Haroldo de Campos traduz os hispano-americanos" (São Paulo: Caracol Revista do Programa de Pós-graduação em Língua Espanhola e Literaturas Espanhola e Hispano Americana Universidade de São Paulo No. 1, 2010), http://www.revistas.usp.br/caracol/article/view/57637.

51. See Frederic Jameson's analysis of Tel Quel's own critique of reification in *Valences of the Dialectic* (New York: Verso, 2009), 264.

52. Gilbert Simondon, *Du mode d'existence des objets techniques* (Paris: Éditions Montaigne, 1958), 1.

53. At the time exteriorization was being theorized and articulated in many areas of thought. The French ethnographer Andre Leroi-Gourhan was busy depicting all of human history as a long and rather Hegelian narrative of increasing "exteriorization" of consciousness manifest in scratchings, marks, and other forms of inscription—expanding Mondrian's claim that all modern art was concerned with exteriorization. Andre Leroi-Gourhan, *Gesture and Speech*, trans. Anna Bostock Berger (Cambridge, MA: MIT Press, 1993); Waldemar Cordeiro, "O neo-plasticismo e a construtivismo, do ponto-da-vista de pura visualidade," in *Waldemar Cordeiro*, ed. Analívia Cordeiro (São Paulo: Caboverde Design Digital, Galeria Brito Cimino, 2001), n.p., CD-ROM.

54. Marshall McLuhan, *Understanding Media* (New York: McGraw-Hill, 1964), 222.

2. JOSÉ MARTÍ'S MATERIAL TRACES

1. Fina García Marruz, "El tiempo en la crónica norteamericana de Martí," in *En torno a José Martí: Coloquio Internacional* (Bordeaux: Biere, 1974), 394–95. Julio Ramos follows García Marruz in discussing concretion in Martí, even coining the term "poetics of concretion" in his discussion of Martí's U.S. chronicles. Ramos sees these "imagénes-objetos" (García Marruz's concept) and a "poética de la concreción" as an attempt to put together the destabilizing fragmentary nation of the modern city. Julio Ramos, *Desencuentros de la modernidad: Literatura y Política en el Siglo XIX* (Mexico City: Fondo Económico de la Cultura, 1989), 180, 196.

2. Michelle Clayton sees César Vallejo as an example of a more general modern poetics, crafted especially by writers operating in two or more cultural zones, that was characterized by "bodies attempting to articulate themselves

in a shattered context." Michelle Clayton, *Poetry in Pieces: César Vallejo and Lyric Modernity* (Berkeley: University of California Press, 2012), 2.

3. Juan Marinello, *Obras martianas* (Caracas: Fundación Biblioteca Ayacucho, 1987), 46.

4. Jacques Rancière, "The Aesthetic Revolution and Its Outcomes: Emplotments of Autonomy and Heteronomy," *New Left Review* 14 (March/April 2002): 143. Similar ideas are discussed in Jacques Rancière, "The Politics of Literature," *SubStance: A Review of Theory and Literary Criticism* 33, no. 1 (2004): 10–24.

5. See Julio de Riverand's essay "El historicismo martiano en la idea del equilibrio del mundo," *Anuario del Centro de Estudios Martianos* 2 (1979): 111–34. Riverand notes that Martí's notion of a "world equilibrium" was conceived during the conference and that a chronicle written while Martí was attending it (November 2, 1889) includes a description of participants affirming "the independence of Spanish America, where lies the equilibrium of the world" [la independencia de la América española, donde está el equilibrio del mundo] (115). Fina García Marruz coins the term "crucial" to describe this notion of equilibrium in her essay "El tiempo en la crónica norteamericana de Martí" (397) and returns to this theme in *El amor como energía revolucionaria en José Martí* (Havana: Centro de Estudios Martianos, 2003), 98.

6. Peter Sloterdijk, *Esferas II (Globos)*, trans. Isidoro Reguera (Madrid: Ediciones Siruela, 2004), 748.

7. See Wey Gómez, *Tropics of Empire* and Kadir, *Columbus and the Ends of the Earth*.

8. See Susan Fernández, *Encumbered Cuba: Capital Markets and Revolt, 1878–1895* (Gainesville: University of Florida Press, 2002), 40.

9. Antonio Santamaría García and Alejando García Álvarez write that planters were forced to modernize their *ingenios* and expand the scale of production for a larger U.S. market. When tariffs prevented such trade and labor grew scarcer in the postslavery period, Spanish trade policies crippled the Cuban economy. Antonio Santamaría García and Alejandro García Álvarez, *Economía y colonia la economía cubana y la relación con España, 1765–1902* (Madrid: Consejo Superior de Investigaciones Científicas Instituto de Historia, 2004), 348–49.

10. Oscar Zanetti, *La República: Notas sobre economía y sociedad* (Havana: Editorial de Ciencias Sociales, 2006), 16.

11. Susan Stewart finds this generic comparison of temporalities in Benedetto Croce. Susan Stewart, *Poetry and the Fate of the Senses* (Chicago: University of Chicago Press, 2001), 247.

12. Ian Balfour, *The Rhetoric of Romantic Prophecy* (Stanford, CA: Stanford University Press, 2002), 249.

13. José Martí, *Obras completas: Edición crítica*, vol. 2 (Havana: Centro de Estudios Martianos, 2000), 33.

14. Louis Pérez Jr., *On Becoming Cuban: Identity, Nationality and Culture* (Chapel Hill: University of North Carolina Press, 1999), 18; Moreno Fraginals, *El ingenio*, 24; Moreno Fraginals, "Plantation Economies and Societies in the Spanish Caribbean, 1860–1930," in *The Cambridge History of*

Latin America, vol. 4, ed. Leslie Bethell (New York: Cambridge University Press, 1986), 201. Julio Ramos sees the pressure to convey mere information provoking a reactive overwriting in Martí's chronicles. *Divergent Modernities: Culture and Politics in 19th Century Latin America*, trans. John Blanco (Durham, NC: Duke University Press, 2001), 106–7.

15. José Lezama Lima and Cintio Vitier, *Martí en Lezama* (Havana: Centro de Estudios Martianos, 2000), 53; Ada María Teja, *La poesía de José Martí entre naturaleza e historia: Estudios sobre la antítesis y la síntesis* (Cosenza: Marra, 1990), 249.

16. Arcadio Díaz-Quiñones points out that Martí's appeal to messianic traditions of the exiled prophet demanded forswearing sexuality. Arcadio Díaz-Quiñones, *El arte de bregar: Ensayos* (San Juan: Ediciones Callejón, 2000), 266–68.

17. José Martí, *Poesía completa, edición crítica* (Mexico City: Universidad Nacional Autónoma de México, 1998), 98.

18. Compare the dismemberment with Petrarch's Canzione 15, "come posson queste membra / da lo spirito lor vivir lontane?" [how can all these parts of me / survive so far away from their own soul?].

19. José Martí, *José Martí: Selected Writings*, trans. Esther Allen, ed. Roberto González Echevarría (New York: Penguin Books, 2002), 63.

20. Martí compiled an anthology of "Poets of 1868." *Los poetas de la guerra* (New York: "America" Editiorial, S. Figueroa, 1968 [1893]).

21. Rafael Rojas, *José Martí: La invención de Cuba* (Madrid: Editorial Colibrí, 2000).

22. Dragan Klaic, *The Plot of the Future: Utopia and Dystopia in Modern Drama* (Ann Arbor: University of Michigan Press, 1991), 20.

23. Theodore Olson, *Millennialism, Utopianism, and Progress* (Toronto: University of Toronto Press, 1982), 15.

24. Friedrich Hölderlin, *Friedrich Hölderlin: Essays and Letters on Theory*, trans. Thomas Pfau (Albany: State University of New York Press, 1988), 102.

25. Gilles Deleuze, *Difference and Repetition*, trans. Paul Patton (New York: Columbia University Press, 1994), 89.

26. Although he does not cite Hölderlin, Eduardo Cadava sees photography functioning similarly in Walter Benjamin. Eduardo Cadava, *Words of Light: Theses on the Photography of History* (Princeton: Princeton University Press, 1997), 59.

27. Ivan Schulman, "Historia colectiva e individual en la obra de José Martí," in *En torno a José Martí: Coloquio Internacional* (Bordeaux: Biere, 1974), 96.

28. Lacan would turn to the "quantification of communication" enacted by the Bell Telephone Company to prove that "language, which is the instrument of speech, is something material." Jacques Lacan, *The Ego in Freud's Theory and in the Technique of Psychoanalysis, 1954–1955*, trans. Sylvana Tomaselli (New York: Norton, 1978), 82. For Lacan, the phonograph allows the first "separation between the real and the symbolic, between phonetics and phonology, which is to say the possibility of structural linguistics itself." Kittler, *Literature Media Information*, 140.

29. Beatriz González-Stephan reads Martí's interest in this invention as related to its speed. "Invenciones tecnológicas. Mirada postcolonial y nuevas pedagogías: José Martí en las exposiciones universales," in *Galerías del progreso: Museos, exposiciones, y cultura visual en América Latina*, ed. Jens Andermann and Beatriz González-Stephan (Rosario: Beatriz Viterbo, 2006), 221–53.

30. Mladen Dolar, *The Voice and Nothing More* (Cambridge, MA: MIT Press, 2006), 55.

31. Walter Benjamin, *The Arcades Project*, trans. Howard Eiland and Kevin McLaughlin (Cambridge, MA: Harvard University Press, 1999).

32. This quotation is also discussed in García Marruz, "El tiempo," 389.

33. Martí alludes to Schelling's "system" in one of his notes: "En lo más pequeño, el todo, y en el todo lo más pequeño. Así el sistema" [In the smallest part, the whole, and in the whole the smallest part] (*Obras completas*, 21:56).

34. Aris Fioretos, *The Solid Letter: Readings of Friedrich Hölderlin* (Stanford, CA: Stanford University Press, 1999), 52; Giorgio Agamben, *Stanzas: Word and Phantom in Western Culture*, trans. Ronald L. Martinez (Minneapolis: University of Minnesota Press, 1993), xvii; Theodor Adorno, *Notes to Literature, Volume I*, trans. Sherry Weber Nicholson (New York: Columbia University Press, 1991), 43; Paul De Man, *The Resistance to Theory* (Minneapolis: University of Minnesota Press, 1986), 47.

35. An anecdote about the making of his poetry book *Ismaelillo* was turned into a poem allegorizing this aesthetic: "Musa traviesa" details the final acts of writing *Ismaelillo*. Martí's son entered the room where the manuscript was pinned under an onyx paperweight and yanked the tablecloth from the desk, scattering the poems and sending the paperweight crashing to the floor. Rubén Pérez Nápoles, *José Martí: El poeta armado* (Madrid: Algaba Ediciones, 2004), 189.

36. In a talk peppered with racist allusions about African-descended Cubans, Jorge Mañach emphasized Martí's "Spanishness." Jorge Mañach, *El espíritu de Martí: Curso de 1951* (Havana: Cooperativa estudiantil E. J. Varona, 1952), 200. Marinello identified Golden Age authors as Martí's strongest literary influence. Federico de Onís discerned traces of Santa Teresa, Gracián, and Quevedo. Federico de Onís, "Martí y el modernismo," *Antología crítica de José Martí, recopilación introducción y notas de Manuel Pedro González* (Mexico: Publicaciones de la Editorial Cultura, 1960), 155–66.

37. Rafael Almanza Alonso argues that Martí wavers between advocate of free trade and protectionist in *En torno al pensamiento económico de José Martí* (Havana: Editorial Ciencias Sociales, 1990).

38. The 1975 edition of the *Obras completas* notes that while it is impossible to date the fragments precisely, one can deduce that they were "written mainly in New York, between 1885 and 1895" (*Obras completas*, 22:9).

39. Fredric Jameson, "Time and the Concept of Modernity," in *Anytime*, ed. Cynthia Davidson (Cambridge, MA: MIT Press, 1999), 217.

40. Martí's attitude toward architecture changes markedly from the opinion he held in his youth, when he wrote in 1875, "Yo no amo a París. Ha creado tantos edificios, ha acumulado tanta piedra, ha dorado todo esto con

prisa tal de profusión, que a la par que las calles se realzan, los corazones se petrifican y se doran" [I don't love Paris. It has created so many buildings, it has accumulated so much stone, it has gilded all this with such speedy profusion, that as the streets come into their own, hearts petrify and are gilded] (Martí, *Obras completas: Edición crítica*, 3:19).

3. THE WRITING ON THE WALLS: BABYLON, WALL STREET, CANUDOS

1. Thanks to Laura Ziarko, archivist for Manhattanville College, for locating Maria de Souza Andrade's records testifying to Sousândrade's address at least part of the time of his New York residence. I take these dates from Frederick Williams, "Sousândrade: A Study of His Life and Work" (Ph.D. diss., University of Wisconsin, 1971), later published in Portuguese as *Sousândrade: Vida e obra* (São Luis: Edições Sioge, 1976), and Luiza Lobo, *Tradição e ruptura: "O Guesa" de Sousândrade* (São Luis: Edições Sioge, 1979).

2. Joaquim de Sousândrade, *O Guesa errante* (London: Cooke and Halsted, the Moorfields Press, 1884[?]), 254. *O Guesa* was printed individually in 1876 and 1877, but in an incomplete form, without the full number of thirteen cantos. A London edition of the book from 1884 included "Wall Street Inferno" as Canto X. Posthumous books included *Harpa de Ouro*, *Liras perdidas*, and *Novo Eden* (Williams, "Sousândrade: A Study," 55). Luiza Lobo guesses that the full version of the epic was published in 1884, correcting Williams's earlier suggestion of 1888. Joaquim de Sousandrade (Sousândrade), *O Guesa errante*, ed. Luiza Lobo (São Luis: Academia Maranhense de Letras, 2012), 29.

3. See Luiz Costa Lima, "O campo visual de uma experiência antecipadora: Sousândrade," in *ReVisão de Sousândrade*, 2nd ed., ed. Augusto de Campos and Haroldo de Campos (São Paulo: Edições Invenção, 1964), 395–424.

4. Romano de Sant'Anna's poem begins, "O poeta pede ao seu guia que o conduz ao tôpo do edifício passando pelo inferno de Wall Street" [The poet asks his guide to take him to the top of the building passing through the Wall Street Inferno]. Affonso Romano de Sant'Anna, "Empire State Building," *Revista Civilização Brasileira* 17 (January/February 1968): 117. Frederico Coelho describes Oiticica's engagement with Sousândrade in *Livro ou livro-me os escritos babilônicos de Hélio Oiticica (1971–1978)* (Rio de Janeiro: EdUERJ, 2010).

5. Marília Librandi Rocha questions the trajectory of Sousândradine "anticipation" as a retrospective gaze from the concretes. Marília Librandi Rocha, *Maranhão-Manhattan* (Rio de Janeiro: 7Letras, 2009), 220.

6. Friedrich Kittler, *Discourse Networks, 1800/1900*, trans. Michael Metteer with Chris Cullens (Stanford, CA: Stanford University Press, 1990).

7. Augusto de Campos and Haroldo de Campos, *Os Sertões dos Campos: Duas vezes Euclides* (Rio de Janeiro: Editora 7Letras, 1997). The third contributor to the 1964 *ReVisão de Sousândrade*, Luiz Costa Lima, also published a study of da Cunha's writing of *Os Sertões* in the centennial year of 1997, *Terra Ignota: A construção de Os Sertões* (Rio de Janeiro: Civilização Brasileira, 1997).

8. Haroldo de Campos, *A arte no horizonte do provável e outros ensaios* (São Paulo: Editora Perspectiva, 1969), 150.

9. Adriana Campos Johnson, *Sentencing Canudos: Subalternity in the Backlands of Brazil* (Pittsburgh: University of Pittsburgh Press, 2010), 70.

10. Frederick Williams cites José Carlos Rodrigues, the Brazilian publisher of the New York–based newspaper *O Novo Mundo* housed in the New York Times building (and for which Sousândrade wrote), to establish Sousândrade's home as a room in a private residence with views onto Sacred Heart (Williams, *Sousândrade: Vida e obra*, 10–11). Yet a ledger from Sacred Heart lists his address as the Hamilton Hotel, 125th Street and 8th Avenue.

11. Luiza Lobo writes, "Sousândrade já foi considerado romântico, parnasiano, simbolista, e por que não pré-modernista?" (*Épica e modernidade em Sousândrade* [Rio de Janeiro: Presença, 1986], 11). Frederick Williams argues that "to think of Sousândrade in something other than a romantic context is not to know him" ("Sousândrade: A Study," 71), while Sebastião Moreira Duarte confirms that *O Guesa* oscillates between romanticism and postromanticism. Sebastião Moreira Duarte, *A épica e a época de Sousândrade: Pequena introdução à leitura d'O Guesa* (São Luis: Edições AML, 2002).

12. David Quint, *Epic and Empire: Politics and Generic Form from Virgil to Milton* (Princeton: Princeton University Press, 1993), 33. On the Guesa's relation to epic, see Idelber Avelar, "A Arqui-Textura de Sousândrade: Poética e Política," in *Limites: Anais do 30 Congresso da Associação Brasileira de Literatura Comparada* (São Paulo: Edusp, 1995), 685–90.

13. Rio de Janeiro's bubble known as "o Encilhamento" was a wave of speculation set off indirectly as a result of abolition, as the Brazilian government floated bonds to offset the losses of former slave owners, unleashing a credit bonanza. It was immortalized in Alfredo de Taunay's novel *O encilhamento: Scenas contemporâneas da bôlsa em 1890, 1891 e 1892*. Alfredo d'Escragnolle Taunay, *O encilhamento: Scenas contemporâneas da bôlsa em 1890, 1891 e 1892* (Rio de Janeiro: Domingos de Magalhães, 1894–95).

14. Sevcenko, *Literatura como missão*, 40; Emília Viotti da Costa, "Brazil: The Age of Reform, 1870–1889," in *The Cambridge History of Latin America*, vol. 6, ca. 1870 to 1930 (New York: Cambridge University Press: 1995), 748; Flora Süssekind, *Cinematograph of Words: Literature, Technique and Modernization in Brazil*, trans. Paulo Henriques Britto (Stanford, CA: Stanford University Press, 1997).

15. Frederick Williams also cites this line, though he does not connect it to the Haitian Revolution (Williams, "Sousândrade: A Study," 146).

16. Sibylle Fischer, *Modernity Disavowed: Haiti and the Cultures of Slavery in the Atlantic* (Durham, NC: Duke University Press, 2004).

17. In Canto VII the Guesa visits Senegambia and speaks out against slavery. In an article titled "A Emancipação e o Imperador," published in *O Novo Mundo* on November 24, 1871, and in response to an article in the *New York Herald* attributing to Dom Pedro II leadership in abolitionism, Sousândrade argues that in fact the general populace is the base of antislavery activism (Williams, "Sousândrade: A Study," 59).

18. Berbel, Marquese, and Parron, *Escravidão e política Brasil e Cuba*, 94–104; Luiz Mott, *Escravidão, homossexualidade e demonologia* (São Paulo: Ícone, 1988), 13; Carlos Eugênio Soares and Flávio Gomes, "Sedições, Haitianismo e conexões no Brasil escravista: Outras margens do Atlântico negro," *Novos estudos*, CEBRAP, no. 63 (July 2002): 137.

19. Joaquim de Sousândrade, "From O Guesa Errante: The Wall Street Inferno," trans. Robert Brown, *Poems for the Millennium: The University of California Press Book of Romantic & Postromantic Poetry*, vol. 3, ed. Jerome Rothenberg and Jeffrey C. Robinson (Berkeley: University of California Press, 2009), 655.

20. Sven Beckert writes that the years after the U.S. Civil War "saw a shift of economic power away from merchants and toward manufacturers and financiers." Sven Beckert, *The Monied Metropolis: New York City and the Consolidation of the American Bourgeoisie, 1850–1896* (Cambridge: Cambridge University Press, 2001), 151.

21. Steven C. Topik and Allen Wells, "Commodity Chains in a Global Economy," in *A World Connecting, 1870–1945*, ed. Emily Rosenberg (Cambridge, MA: Belknap Press, 2012), 593–813.

22. Luiza Lobo notes that Sousândrade's constant rewriting of the epic meant that he eventually inserted figures from the "Wall Street Inferno" episode back into Canto II (Sousandrade, *O Guesa errante*, 13).

23. Earlier in Canto X Sousândrade had signaled the "trinidade negra" [black trinity] of "escravos, a religião e os reis" [slaves, religion, and kings] (Sousandrade, *O Guesa errante*, 305).

24. See Ricardo Araújo's account of concrete poetry's intersection with cybernetics in *Poesia visual, vídeo poesia* (São Paulo: Editora Perspectiva, 1999).

25. Joaquim de Sousândrade, *Harpa de Ouro, 1889–1899*, ed. Jomar Moraes (São Luis: Edições Sioge, 1969), 23; also noted in Williams, "Sousândrade: A Study," 109.

26. Haroldo de Campos, *Ideograma: Logica, poesia, linguagem*, trans. Heloysa de Lima Dantas (São Paulo: Editora Cultrix, 1977), 95.

27. Décio Pignatari, "Vanguarda como antiliteratura," *Revista Convivium* 4, no. 4/6 (July/August/September 1965), reprinted in *Contracomunicação* (Cotia: Ateliê editorial, 2004), 121–26, quoted in Helba Carvalho, "Da poesia concreta ao poema-processo um passeio pelo fio da navalha" (Master's thesis, University of São Paulo, 2002), 66.

28. Wlademir Dias-Pino, *Processo: Linguagem e comunicação* (Petrópolis: Editora Vozes, 1971).

29. Moacy Cirne, *Vanguarda: Um projeto semiológico* (Petrópolis: Editora Vozes, 1975), 18.

30. Ramón Gómez de la Serna, *Mi tía Carolina Coronado* (Buenos Aires: Emecé, 1942), 11.

31. W.J.T. Mitchell, "Romanticism and the Life of Things: Fossils, Totems, and Images," in *Things*, ed. Brown, 243.

32. Victor Bulmer-Thomas, John Coatsworth, and Roberto Cortés Conde, eds., *The Cambridge Economic History of Latin America*, 1st ed., vol. 2

(Cambridge: Cambridge University Press, 2006), *Cambridge Histories Online*, March 17, 2014, http://dx.doi.org/10.1017/CHOL9780521812900, 50.

33. See José Antonio Aguilar and Rafael Rojas, *El Republicanismo en Hispanoamérica* (Mexico City: CIDE, 2002).

34. Matheus Gato de Jesús reads this critique in the lines from *Harpa de Ouro*, a book written to remind its readers of the republic's challenges: "Armas com que fiz a república / Pontas voltara contra mim" [arms with which I made the Republic / turned into tips against me]. Matheus Gato de Jesús, "'Tempo e melancholia': República, modernidade e cidadania negra nos contos de Astolfo Marques (1876–1918)," *Lua Nova* 85 (2012): 162.

35. Robert Levine, *Vale of Tears: Revisiting the Canudos Massacre in Northeastern Brazil, 1893–1897* (Berkeley: University of California Press, 1992).

36. Levine has estimated the height of the population at thirty-five thousand (*History of Brazil*, 82), but Campos Johnson cites skeptics who place it a something closer to five thousand (*Sentencing Canudos*, xxx).

37. Antônio Conselheiro, *Breviário de Antônio Conselheiro*, ed. Walnice Nogueira Galvão and Fernando da Rocha Peres (Salvador: Universidade Federal da Bahia, Centro de Estudos Baianos Odebrecht, 2002).

38. Michael Walzer, *Exodus and Revolution* (New York: Basic Books, 1985), 15–16.

39. Nogueira Galvão has emphasized the hierarchical nature of Conselheiro's world (Conselheiro, *Breviário*, 15–17). Campos Johnson has contested such depictions of Canudos, convincingly arguing for its "everydayness" (*Sentencing Canudos*, 100).

40. A contemporary official maintained that only roughly 14 percent of Brazilians were literate in 1890 (Sevcenko, *Literatura como missão*, 110).

41. Sara Castro-Klarén, "Santos and *Cangaceiros*: Inscription Without Discourse in *Os Sertões* and *La Guerra del fin del mundo*," *Modern Language Notes* 101, no. 2 (1986): 374.

42. José Calasans reprints an undated poem by João Melchiades Ferreira da Silva, "A Guerra de Canudos," which emphasizes the use of telegraphy, reiterating that the military, the officials, and the soldier-narrator all telegraphed back to Rio de Janeiro: "I also telegraphed / my dear family / to say / I made it out / Of that Canudos alive" [*Eu também telegrafei / A minha família querida / Dizendo atravessei / O tal Canudos com vida*]. José Calasans, *Canudos na literatura de cordel* (São Paulo: Atica, 1984), 40.

43. Jacques-Alain Miller, "Extimity," http://www.lacan.com/symptom/?p=36.

44. Geoffrey Batchen, "Electricity Made Visible," in *New Media, Old Media: A History and Theory Reader*, ed. Wendy Chun and Thomas Keenan (New York: Routledge, 2006), 34.

45. Bernard Stiegler, *Technics and Time, I: The Fault of Epimetheus*, trans. Stephen Barker (Stanford, CA: Stanford University Press, 1998), 212.

46. Olavo Bilac, *Vossa Insôlencia Crónicas*, ed. Antonio Dimas (1899; São Luis: Edições AML, 2002).

47. Bilac's contemporary Rilke proposed that the coronal suture of the skull's interior be played with a phonographic needle, a logic by which

"technology and physiology are responsible for material inscription" (Kittler, *Discourse Networks*, 316).

48. Slavoj Žižek, *The Parallax View* (Cambridge, MA: MIT Press, 2006).

49. Glauber Rocha, *Deus e o diabo na terra do sol* (Rio de Janeiro: Copacabana Filmes, 1964).

4. RAMIRO DE MAEZTU'S PRIMACY OF THINGS

1. José Luís Villacañas, *Ramiro de Maeztu y el ideal de la burguesía en España* (Madrid: Espasa-Calpe, 2000); Pedro Carlos González Cuevas, *Maeztu: Biografía de un nacionalista español* (Madrid: Marcial Pons, 2003); see also Alistair Hennessy, "Ramiro de Maeztu: *Hispanidad* and the Search for a Surrogate Imperialism," in *Spain's 1898 Crisis: Regenerationism, Modernism, Post-colonialism*, ed. Joseph Harrison and Alan Hoyle (New York: Manchester University Press, 2000), 105–17.

2. Vicente Marrero, *Maeztu* (Madrid: Rialp, 1955), 51.

3. Ramiro de Maeztu, *Autobiografía* (Madrid: Editora Nacional, 1962), 11.

4. Fredric Jameson, *Marxism and Form* (Princeton: Princeton University Press, 1974), 217–18.

5. Ramiro de Maeztu, *Don Quijote, Don Juan y la Celestina Ensayos en simpatía* (Madrid: Visor Libros, 2004), 40.

6. Maeztu saw Franco's policies as the continuation of the "obra milenaria" [millenarian work] of Columbus, Vasco de Gama, and nineteenth-century European explorers of Africa, the latest episode in the colonial epic epitomized by Camões. Ramiro de Maeztu, *Con el directorio militar* (Madrid: Editora Nacional, 1957), 198.

7. Ramiro de Maeztu, *El sentido reverencial del dinero* (Madrid: Editora Nacional, 1957), 200.

8. Ramiro de Maeztu, *Un ideal sindicalista* (Madrid: Editorial Nacional, 1960), 188–89.

9. See Susan Buck-Morss's article on the influence of the Haitian Revolution on Hegel's theories of subjectivity, in particular the Lord and Bondsman passage. Susan Buck-Morss, "Hegel and Haiti," *Critical Inquiry* 26, no. 4 (Summer 2000): 821–65.

10. In suggesting a rather Spenglerian global 1898 Maeztu anticipated José María Jover's *1898: Teoría y práctica de la redistribución colonial* (Madrid: Fundación Universitaria Española, 1979) and Pabón's "El 98, acontecimiento internacional." Maeztu wrote, "Remember that we received the painful lesson of defeat at the hands of the United States, in 1898, when all the Latin countries seemed to find themselves convinced of their irremediable decline" and he goes on to list Italian, French, and Portuguese volumes about the European nations' respective African colonial wars in the 1890s (*Con el directorio militar*, 334).

11. See Christopher Britt-Arredondo, *Quixotism: The Imaginative Denial of Spain's Loss of Empire* (Albany: State University of New York Press, 2005).

12. Maeztu argues already in the 1899 "La meseta castellana": "For such an undertaking, what is needed are not political parties, nor literary

sentimentalisms, nor democratic ideals, nor traditions of order, nor constitutive states, nor glorious epics, nor marches in Cádiz, nor humanities professors, neither brilliant nor upright men, but agricultural banks, capitalist unions, tough competition, brutal struggle." Ramiro de Maeztu, *Hacia otra España* (Bilbao: Cardenal, 1899), 18. The 1882 "ley de cabotaje" between Spain and its ultramarine possessions effectively secured Cuba as a privileged market for Spanish goods, while denying Cuban merchants the same privileges. Juan Bosco Amores Carradeño, *Cuba y España, 1868–1898: El final de un sueño* (Pamplona: Astrolabio, 1998), 179.

13. Juan Pan-Montojo argues that "el Desastre de 1898" was no economic disaster but instead facilitated the modernization of some Spanish financial institutions. "El atraso económico y la regeneración," in *Más se perdió en Cuba: España, 1898 y la crisis de fin de siglo*, ed. Juan Pan-Montojo (Madrid: Alianza Editorial, 1998), 290.

14. José Piqueras, *Cuba, emporio y colonia: La disputa de un mercado interferido (1878–1895)* (Madrid: Fondo de Cultura Económica de España, 2003), 221n12.

15. Francisco Márquez Villanueva, introduction to Benito Pérez Galdós, *Aita Tettauen* (Madrid: Ediciones AKAL, 2004), 17. Juan Pro Ruiz similarly argues that the Spanish discourse surrounding 1893 Melilla "vergüenza" already sounded calls for regeneration. Juan Pro Ruiz, "La política en tiempos del Desastre," in *Más se perdió en Cuba*, 233.

16. Ángel Ganivet, *Los trabajos del infatigable creador Pío Cid* (Madrid: V. Suárez, 1911).

17. Maria Teresa Pinto Coelho, *Apocalipse e regeneração: O ultimatum e a mitologia da pátria na literatura finissecular* (Lisbon: Edições Cosmos, 1996), 44.

18. Xavier Casals Meseguer, "Franco 'El Africano,'" *Journal of Spanish Cultural Studies* 7, no. 3 (2006): 207.

19. Gustau Nerín, *La guerra que vino de África* (Barcelona: Crítica, 2005). Under Franco, July 17, "Africa Day," was celebrated to commemorate the Moroccan insurrection that brought Franco to power (115).

20. See Pío Baroja's recollections of pitching the novel to an *El País* editor (*Obra completa* 7:741–42, cited in Ramiro de Maeztu, *La guerra del Transvaal y los misterios de la Banca de Londres*, ed. E. Inman Fox (Madrid: Taurus, 1974), 10. The novel was allegedly written by "Van Poel Krupp." It appeared just weeks after a text published under the title "Nuestro folletín," calculated to establish the veracity of Van Poel Krupp's identity (introduction to *La guerra del Transvaal y los misterios de la Banca de Londres*, ed. E. Inman Fox [Madrid: Taurus, 1974], 11).

21. Inman Fox notes that Maeztu "translated" passages from two contemporary histories, Gabriel Telhail's *Le Transvaal et la Chartered (La revolution de Johannesburg et les mines d'or)* (Paris: Paul Allendorf, 1897) and Victor Bérard's *L'Angleterre et l'Imperialisme* (Paris, 1900) (introduction to *La guerra del Transvaal*, 19).

22. Susan Martin-Márquez notes that Spain's colonial interests had never been restricted to simply North Africa but also included what would later be

Guinea: "Already in the fourteenth century, the Castilian king had asserted to the Pope that 'the Kingdoms of Africa are of our conquest.'" Susan Martin-Márquez, *Disorientations: Spanish Colonialism in Africa and the Performance of Identity* (New Haven: Yale University Press, 2008), 53.

23. For more on this kind of positioning, see María de Guzmán, *Spain's Long Shadow: The Black Legend, Off-Whiteness and Anglo-American Empire* (Minneapolis: University of Minnesota Press, 2005).

24. Villacañas has identified in *El sentido* entire paraphrases from *The Protestant Ethic and the Spirit of Capitalism.*

25. Zine Magubane, *Bringing the Empire Home: Race, Class, and Gender in Britain and Colonial South Africa* (Chicago: University of Chicago Press, 2004), 64.

26. See, for instance, Ramiro de Maeztu, "On the Primacy of Things," *The New Age* 17, no. 26 (October 28, 1915): 616–19.

27. John Guillory, *Cultural Capital: The Problem of Literary Canon Formation* (Chicago: University of Chicago Press, 1993), 300.

28. Guillory cites Jean Baudrillard's note that "exchange value is thus the condition for the retroactive construction of the use of an object as an expression of its value" (*Cultural Capital*, 301); see also Slavoj Žižek's discussion of value in *The Parallax View*, 52–55.

29. In 1927 Maeztu sought to explain his concept of the "reverential sense of money" to Princeton philosophy professor Walter Fite, linking economics, religious convictions, and, once again, 1898: "The idea came upon me reflecting on a passage of your Benjamin Franklin. . . . There are two ways of considering a piece of five shilling. The sensual one; and the reverential. . . . Money is to [*sic*] good to be wasted. It belongs to the infinite. This is, in short, the idea that I am trying to instill in my countrymen and also among the South-Americans. It began to adumbrate in me in 1898, during the Spanish-American war. I began then to see in money something more than I did before. . . . It is my hope that my idea of the 'reverential sense of money,' which is beginning to spread, notwithstanding our traditions, will help to create a better understanding among our countries, and specially between North and South America. The South-Americans are now too improvident and careless in matters of money. The result is that an absentee capitalism is developping [*sic*] in South-America. It is the worst and the weakest form of capitalism, as it attracts against it both the fury of socialism and that of nationalism. And in America that of colour race, too." Ramiro de Maeztu to Mr. Warner Fite, Madrid, January 9, 1927, Warner Fite collection, 1906–1928, Rare Books: Manuscripts Collection (MSS), Princeton University, Princeton Serrano 112, sides 1 and 2.

30. Sarah Porciau, personal communication with the author, November 2010.

31. Villacañas observes that in calling for objectivity, Maeztu was close to Ortega y Gasset (*Ramiro de Maeztu*, 132).

32. Lazar Markovich Lissitzky, "The Film of El's Life," in *El Lissitzky: Life, Letters, Texts*, ed. Sophie Lissitzky-Küppers (Greenwich, CT: New York Graphic Society, 1967), 325.

33. Guillory, *Cultural Capital*; Mary Poovey, *Genres of the Credit Economy: Mediating Value in Eighteenth- and Nineteenth-Century Britain* (Chicago: University of Chicago Press, 2008).

34. Michael Iarroci, *Properties of Modernity: Romantic Spain, Modern Europe, and the Legacies of Empire* (Nashville: Vanderbilt University Press, 2006).

35. Ricardo Landeira has found that Maeztu's recourse to novels is a "belletristic" solution to convince the working class of ideals such as "Truth, Justice, Love and the existence of God are indispensable to life." Ricardo Landeira, *Ramiro de Maeztu* (Boston: Twayne, 1978), 82.

36. Ramiro de Maeztu, *Authority, Liberty and Function in the Light of the War; A Critique of Authority and Liberty as the Foundations of the Modern State and an Attempt to Base Societies on the Principle of Function* (London: G. Allen & Unwin, 1916).

37. Ramiro de Maeztu, "On the Primacy of Things," *The New Age* 18, no. 22 (March 30, 1916): 515.

38. Maeztu acknowledged his debt to T. E. Hulme in the epigraph to *Authority*, and similarities between his "The End of Romanticism" and Hulme's coeval "Romanticism and Classicism" suggest the common aims of *The New Age* writers. Ramiro de Maeztu, "The End of Romanticism," *The New Age* 17, no. 22 (September 30, 1915): 521.

39. Karl Marx, *The Grundrisse*, ed. and trans. David McLellan (New York: Harper and Row, 1971), 70.

40. George Lukács, *History and Class Consciousness: Studies in Marxist Dialectics*, trans. Rodney Livingstone (Cambridge, MA: MIT Press, 1968), 89.

41. Michael Levenson, *A Genealogy of Modernism: A Study of English Literary Doctrine, 1908–1922* (New York: Cambridge University Press, 1984), 82.

42. Jacqueline Stevens, *Reproducing the State* (Princeton: Princeton University Press, 1999), 67.

43. An 1874 Spanish law book holds that "personalidad colectiva" [collective personality] emerges from "personalidad individual" [individual personality] and that sovereignty is "the distinct, rational, independent, and free manifestation of a general association, to realize general ends as well" (519–20). Thus for three principles generating law—personality, sociability, and property—"sovereignty is distinguished by liberty and independence, is ruled rationally, and therefore, is autonomous." D. Clemente Fernandez Elías, *Novísimo tratado completo de filosofía del derecho o derecho natural con arreglo á los adelantos y estado actual de esta ciencia exponiendo las doctrinas de Ahrens, Taparelli, Krause, Kant, Hegel, Savigni, Almetyer y otros notables autores con su estudio histórico sobre el desenvolvimiento de la ciencia del derecho* (Madrid: Leocadio López, 1874), 522.

44. Antony Anghie, *Imperialism, Sovereignty and the Making of International Law* (Cambridge: Cambridge University Press, 2005), 103–4.

45. Daniel Lee, "Civil Law and Civil Sovereignty: Popular Sovereignty, Roman Law and the Civilian Foundations of the Constitutional State in Early Modern Political Thought" (Ph.D. diss., Princeton University, 2010), 5.

46. Arnold Sio, "Interpretations of Slavery: The Slave Status in the Americas," *Comparative Studies in Society and History* 7, no. 3 (April 1965): 293. I am grateful to Alejandro de la Fuente for directing me to this article. De la Fuente argues that Frank Tannenbaum's much-critiqued argument that slaves under Spanish law enjoyed a "moral and juridical personality" not available in Anglophone nations, where the slave was by contrast mere "property," is on the whole correct. (Tannenbaum claimed that "the element of human personality was not lost in the transition to slavery from Africa to the Spanish or Portuguese dominions. He remained a person even while he was a slave . . . [he] had both juridical and moral personality.") Frank Tannenbaum, *Slave and Citizen* (1946; Boston: Beacon Press, 1992), 97–98. Alejandro de la Fuente, "Slave Law and Claims-Making in Cuba: The Tannenbaum Debate Revisited," *Law and History Review* 22, no. 2 (2004): 350.

47. Fernando Ortiz, *Los Negros Esclavos* (Havana: Editorial de Ciencias Sociales, 1975), 309.

48. Inés Roldán de Montaud, *La Restauración en Cuba el fracaso de un proceso reformista* (Madrid: Consejo Superior de Investigaciones Científicas Centro de Humanidades Instituto de Historia, 2000), 82–83. Lauren Benton notes that early theories of sovereignty, notably Bodin's, address territorial control as an "element of imperial rule, not a property firmly associated with sovereign jurisdiction," though by the nineteenth century, she admits, an isomorphism emerged between sovereignty and territory (*A Search for Sovereignty*, 288).

49. "Con motivo de cumplirse los 25 años de vida republicana se hace un balance: A corruptelas coloniales hemos añadido lacras de nuevo cuño," *Revista de avance* 1, no. 5 (May 15, 1927): 97–98.

50. Andrew Thacker, "A Language of Concrete Things," in *T. E. Hulme and the Question of Modernism*, ed. Edward P. Comentale and Andrzej Gasiorek (Abingdon: Ashgate, 2006), 39–55. Levenson dates Hulme's essay to 1911 or 1912; Levenson, *A Genealogy of Modernism*, 87–88. See also Thomas Ernest Hulme and Karen Csengeri, *The Collected Writings of T. E. Hulme* (Oxford: Clarendon Press, 1994).

51. Hulme's biographer Robert Ferguson writes that while Hulme and Maeztu were close, "there is no documentary evidence of their friendship." Robert Ferguson, *The Short Sharp Life of T. E. Hulme* (London: Allen Lane, 2002), 285n19.

52. Lynn Mary Festa, *Sentimental Figures of Empire in Eighteenth-Century Britain and France* (Baltimore: Johns Hopkins University Press, 2006), 55.

53. Here Maeztu echoes Josiah Strong: "There are no more new worlds. The unoccupied arable lands of the earth are limited, and will soon be taken. . . . Then will the world enter upon a new stage of its history—the final competition of races" (qtd. in Mejías-López, *The Inverted Conquest*, 131).

54. Nicholas Brown discusses a similarly paradoxical "nonracist racism" in Wyndham Lewis (*Utopian Generations*, 130).

55. Frank Tamayo, "Universalismo español," *Revista de avance* 1, no. 3 (April 15, 1927): 46.

5. THE SPIRIT OF MARTÍ IN THE LAND OF COAYBAY

1. Slavoj Žižek, *Enjoy Your Symptom* (1992; New York: Routledge, 2008), xxvi.

2. Luis Aguilar notes that high prices for sugar in 1920 gave way to a "devastating economic crisis which affected every segment of the population," the collapse of the domestic banking system, and the transference of "more than 76 per cent of the total deposits" to foreign banks by 1923. Luis Aguilar, *Cuba 1933: Prologue to Revolution* (Ithaca: Cornell University Press, 1972), 43.

3. "Bajo el signo de Martí," *Revista de avance* 5, no. 46 (May 15, 1930): 144.

4. *Historia de la literatura cubana* follows Jan O. Fischer's periodization: a single epoch (1899–1958) divided into two periods (1899–1922 and 1923–58). José Antonio Portuondo and Cira Romer, coords., *Historia de la literatura cubana*, vol. 2 (Havana: Editorial Letras Cubanas, 2002), 3, 129.

5. Alejandro de la Fuente, *A Nation for All: Race, Inequality and Politics in Twentieth-Century Cuba* (Chapel Hill: University of North Carolina Press, 2001), 12.

6. Miguel de Carrión, *Las impuras* (Havana: Editorial Letras Cubanas, 1984), 194.

7. Carlos Ripoll suggested that the very "ideological base" of *Revista de avance* (1927–30) lay in a reevaluation of Martí's thought. Carlos Ripoll, *Índice de la "Revista de avance," 1927–1930* (New York: Las Américas Pub., 1969), 5.

8. Raúl Roa, "Martí poeta nuevo," *Revista de avance* 1, no. 10 (August 30, 1927): 254–55.

9. Victoria de Grazia, *Irresistible Empire: America's Advance Through Twentieth Century Europe* (Cambridge, MA: Harvard University Press, 2005). Louis Pérez Jr. describes the early republican period in Cuba as characterized by "the tide of US consumer imports" (*On Becoming Cuban*, 327).

10. Emma Álvarez-Tabío Albo, *La invención de la Habana* (Barcelona: Editorial Casiopea, 2000), 146. Louis Pérez Jr. cites a period critique that U.S. sugar centrals acted like "'a foreign State on Cuban soil'" (*On Becoming Cuban*, 237), suggesting a corporate quasi-sovereignty.

11. João Felipe Gonçalves, "The 'Apostle' in Stone: Nationalism and Monuments in Honor of José Martí," *The Cuban Republic and José Martí: Reception and Use of a Symbol*, ed. Mauricio Font and Alfonso Quiroz (Lanham, MD: Lexington Books, 2006), 22–23; Pérez Nápoles, *José Martí*, 388; Enrico Mario Santí, "Thinking Through Martí," *in Re-Reading José Martí (1853–1895): One Hundred Years Later*, ed. Julio Rodríguez-Luís (Albany: State University of New York Press, 1999), 73.

12. Alfred López cites Felix Lizaso, a prominent Martí scholar under Batista: "Martí hasn't died, because like salt dissolved in water, he is dissolved in and flourishes in the most recondite and intimate places of spirituality, the greatest monument will be that in which Martí's spirituality which comes to us from all parts can be incarnated." Alfred López, *José Martí and the Future of Cuban Nationalisms* (Gainesville: University of Florida Press, 2006), 48.

13. Lillian Guerra, *The Myth of José Martí: Conflicting Nationalisms in Early Twentieth-Century Cuba* (Chapel Hill: University of North Carolina Press, 2005), 252.

14. Pierre Fédida, "La relique et le travail du deuil," *Nouvelle revue de psychanalyse 2 (objets du fétichisme)*, no. 2 (1970): 249–54.

15. The body of the war hero General Antonio Maceo was likewise made into relics. Racist ideologies, however, ensured that the treatment of his body, like that of Antônio Conselheiro, was closer to physiognomy than to hagiography. Marial Iglesias Utset, *Las metáforas del cambio en la vida cotidiana: Cuba, 1898–1902* (Havana: Ediciones UNIÓN, 2003), 211–14.

16. Only fragments of the play remain, reproduced in Martínez Carmenate's biography of Byrne (Martínez Carmenate, telephone conversation with the author, November 2007).

17. Jacques Derrida, *Specters of Marx: The State of Debt, the Work of Mourning and the New International*, trans. Peggy Kamuf (New York: Routledge, 1994), 7.

18. In 1941 *El traidor* was reprinted and dedicated to veterans of the independence wars.

19. Marc Redfield, "Imagi-Nation: The Imagined Community and the Aesthetics of Mourning," in *Grounds for Comparison: Around the Work of Benedict Anderson*, ed. Pheng Cheah and Jonathan Culler (New York: Routledge, 2003), 86.

20. Melina Pappademos finds in the postindependence constitution that "[s]ince Africans were not included in naturalization provisions granted to other foreigners such as recognition of loyalty to the anticolonial insurgency against Spain or continuous residency on the island since at least 1899, they were neither foreign nor Cuban." Melina Pappademos, *Black Political Activism and the Cuban Republic* (Chapel Hill: University of North Carolina Press, 2011), 102.

21. This feeling of a living dead lends credence to Pheng Cheah's claim that some postcolonial nations hover between life and death "like a ghost that cannot be contained within the organismic ontology informing our thinking of freedom." Pheng Cheah, *Spectral Nationality: Passages of Freedom from Kant to Postcolonial Literatures of Liberation* (New York: Columbia University Press, 2004), 209.

22. José Antonio Portuondo, "El pragmatismo y las purezas de la realidad," in José Antonio Ramos, *Coaybay* (Havana: Editorial Arte y Literatura, 1975), 379.

23. Jorge Ibarra, *Prologue to Revolution*, trans. Marjorie Moore (Boulder, CO: Lynne Rienner, 1998), 9–11.

24. Letter signed by José Antonio Ramos to José de la Luz León en Ginebra, Barcelona y la Habana, Archivo Nacional de Cuba, Donativos y remisiones, 1931–1937, Legajo 524, número de orden 55.

25. José Antonio Ramos, "Cubanidad y mestizaje," *Estudios afrocubanos* 1 (1937): 92–113.

26. Piqueras finds that between 1868 and 1895 Cuba was second among Latin American nations only to Uruguay in terms of per capita exports, eclipsing Uruguay by 1890 (*Cuba, emporio y colonia*, 64). He does not find an

economy in crisis, still less an economy hampered by external players, though he does suggest that the United States won a *trade war* against Spain in Cuba just before the official War of Independence began (136).

27. This was the result of the Movimiento Económico and subsequent Foster-Cánovas treaty of reciprocity between Cuba and the United States, extant from 1890 to 1894.

28. "Protesta contra la 'negrificacion' de Cuba al importarse negros de Haití y Jamaica por compañías azucareras que quieran pagar jornales bajos," *Revista de avance* 4, no. 39 (October 15, 1929): 287, 288. See also Francine Masiello's discussion of these tensions in "Rethinking Neocolonial Esthetics: Literature, Politics, and Intellectual Community in Cuba's Revista de Avance," *Latin American Research Review* 28, no. 2 (1993): 3–31.

29. "Uprising in Cuba," *Philadelphia Tribune*, May 25, 1912, p. 4. I owe this reference to Ashley Evelyn, "The Formation of Transnational Black Identity Among African-Descendants in Early Twentieth Century Cuba" (senior thesis, Princeton University, 2013), 52.

30. For a sustained reading of how Carpentier appropriates black Cuban culture to critique U.S. hegemony in the region, see Paul Miller, *Elusive Origins: The Enlightenment in the Modern Caribbean Historical Imagination* (Charlottesville: University of Virginia Press, 2010).

31. Alejo Carpentier, *Concierto barroco* (Mexico, D.F.: Siglo XXI, 1974), 9; Carpentier, *Baroque Concerto*, trans. Asa Zatz (London: A. Deutsch, 1991), 23. The things of the Hotel Americano also anticipate an attention to things as evidenced in the translation of Virginia Woolf's short story "Solid Objects," published in *Orígenes*. Virginia Woolf, "Objetos sólidos," trans. José Rodríguez Feo, *Orígenes* 6, no. 23 (1949): 6–10.

32. Birkenmaier, by contrast, reads this same scene as primarily a surrealist meditation on chance (*Alejo Carpentier*, 78).

33. Bonifacio Byrne, "Los muebles," in *La poesía moderna en Cuba (1882–1925): Antología crítica*, ed. Felix Lizaso and José Antonio Fernandez de Castro (Madrid: Casa Editorial Hernando S.A., 1926), 127–30.

34. Pedroso's "Dos poemas chinos" to his Chinese grandfather sought, amid Cuba's 1933 revolution, not to revive unmet promises from the late nineteenth century but to leave them behind. The narrator scorns his grandfather's riches, the result of coolie labor, and adds, "En los ópalos de tus pupilas moribundas / . . . / crepusculiza un pasado lleno de encanto exótico y gracias genuflexiva" [In the whites of your moribund eyes, / . . . / dies a past filled with exotic enchantment and kowtowing grace]. Regino Pedroso, *Regino Pedroso*, ed. Osvaldo Navarro (Havana: UNEAC, 1975), 93–95.

35. Miguel de Carrión, "El Doctor Risco," in *La última voluntad y otros relatos* (Alexandria, VA: Alexander Street Press, 2007), 51, also quoted in Pérez, *On Becoming Cuban*, 146.

36. Theodor Adorno, *Aesthetic Theory*, trans. Robert Hullot-Kentor (Minneapolis: University of Minnesota Press, 1997), 128.

37. Rubén Darío, "Los Anglosajones," in *Peregrinaciones*, http://www.cervantesvirtual.com/obra-visor/peregrinaciones—0/html/ff0811ae-82b1–11df-acc7–002185ce6064_1.htm#9.

38. César Vallejo, "XLIX," in *Trilce*, ed. Julio Ortega (Madrid: Cátedra, 1991), 230.

39. Alejo Carpentier, *Cuentos* (Havana: Letras Cubanas, 1979).

40. Alfonso Hernández Catá, "Los muebles," in *Alfonso Hernández Catá: Sus mejores cuentos*, ed. Eduardo Barrios (Santiago: Nascimento, 1936).

41. "La saleta o 'Living Room,'" *Social* (May 1922): 45.

42. Susan Buck-Morss, *Dreamworld and Catastrophe: The Passing of Mass Utopia in East and West* (Cambridge, MA: MIT Press, 2002), 200. In 1927 a new tariff law caused Cuba to begin an import-substitution program that included furniture. Louis Pérez Jr., "Cuba c. 1939–1950," in *The Cambridge History of Latin America*, vol. 7, ed. Leslie Bethell (New York: Cambridge University Press, 1990), 425.

43. Karl Marx and Friedrich Engels, *Das Kapital: A Critique of Political Economy*, ed. Serge Levitsky (Chicago: H. Regnery, 1959), 50. This use of furniture as a shorthand for both the most material and most immaterial continues to haunt philosophy, reappearing in the work of object-oriented philosophers such as Graham Harman. Graham Harman, "The Third Table," *Documenta Notebook* 85 (2012): 6–7.

44. The use of a piano to stand in for the concrete was echoed as recently as 2012 by U.S. artist Richard Artschwager's wooden piece "Piano/Malevitch."

45. Alfonso Hernández Catá, *Manicomio* (Madrid: Compañia Ibero-Americana de Publicaciones, 1931).

46. Quoted in Givaldo Medeiros, *Artepaisagem a partir de Waldemar Cordeiro* (São Paulo: Fauusp, 2004), 145–46.

47. Liz Kotz, *Words to Be Looked at: Language in 1960s Art* (Cambridge, MA: MIT Press, 2010), 182.

48. The positing of furniture as the most immanent and material is reflected in a statement by Cuban contemporary artists Los Carpinteros that since Cuban art of the 1980s "did politics," they had to try something different: "we make furniture." Rachel Weiss, *To and From Utopia in the New Cuban Art* (Minneapolis: University of Minnesota Press, 2011), 215.

49. For a study of Latin American literary responses to "the export age" see Beckman, *Capital Fictions*.

50. Ramón de Armas, "Año nuevo," *Revista telefónica cubana* (April–May 1926): 17–18.

51. Karel Kosik, *Dialectics of the Concrete: A Study on Problems of Man and World*, trans. Karel Kovanda with James Schmidt (Boston: D. Riedel, 1976), 20.

52. Lillian Guerra, *Visions of Power in Cuba: Revolution, Redemption, and Resistance, 1959–1971* (Chapel Hill: University of North Carolina Press, 2012).

53. José Antonio Portuondo, "En busca de la expresión estética de una nación para sí," *Lunes de Revolución*, August 1961, cited in Duanel Díaz, "Hasta sus últimas consecuencias: Dialécticas de la Revolución Cubana" (Ph.D. diss., Princeton University, 2012), 210.

54. Severo Sarduy, "Pintura y revolución," *Revolución*, January 31, 1959, 14, cited in Roberto González Echevarría, "Son de la Habana: La ruta de

Severo Sarduy," *Revista Iberoamericana* 37, no. 76–77 (July–December 1971): 728.

55. Tomás Maldonado, *Escritos Preulmianos,* ed. Carlos A. Méndez Mosquera y Nelly Perazzo (Buenos Aires: Ediciones Infinito, 1997), 50.

6. OBJECT, NON-OBJECT, TRANS-OBJECT, RELATIONAL OBJECT

1. Ana Cristina Camargo Moraes Figueiredo, *Liberdade é uma calça velha, azul e desbotada: Publicidade, cultura de consumo e comportamento político no Brasil (1954–1964)* (São Paulo: Editora Hucitec, História Social, USP, 1998), 31.

2. Antônio Sérgio Lima Mendonça writes: "if the modernist revolution begins with verse, it ends in concrete poetry, which with its end closes the cycle of modernism." Antônio Sérgio Lima Mendonça, *Poesia de vanguarda no Brasil de Oswald de Andrade ao poema visual* (Petrópolis: Editora Voces, 1970), 133. Haroldo de Campos claims that the 1964 coup and hardening authoritarianism in 1968 meant that "poetry was emptied of its utopian charge." Haroldo de Campos, "Poesia e modernidade: Da morte da arte à constelação. O poema pos-utópico," in *O arco-íris branco: Ensaios de literatura e cultura* (Rio de Janeiro: Imago, 1997), 268. Nicholas Brown argues that "the Brazilian case is a particularly dramatic instance of a global phenomenon of the end of a political modernism grounded in great utopian projects . . . [its] ultimate horizon . . . the turning of the cold war toward the consolidation of a US-led market hegemony, globalization as it is currently understood. What followed the coup was the complete collapse of development populism, along with economic nationalism and the aesthetic ideology that went along with it" (*Utopian Generations*, 188). While echoing the notion of a passage from modernism to postmodernism, Gonzalo Aguilar sees the 1964 coup as a continuation of modernizing dreams. *Poesía concreta brasileña: Las vanguardias en la encrucijada modernista* (Rosario: Beatriz Viterbo, 2003), 290. In "The Imperative of Invention: Brazilian Concrete Poetry and Intersemiotic Creation," Charles Perrone writes of the *poema/processo* (a final outgrowth of concrete poetry): "Processo, with the last of a series of group manifestos, represents the complete exhaustion of the poem as a literary construct in Brazil" (http://www.ubu.com/papers/perrone.html#foot19).

3. An important 1945 exhibition of concrete art that led to the Madí group took place in the Buenos Aires home of Enrique Pichon-Riviere, one of the leaders of the Asociación Psicoanalítica Argentina (APA). Gabriel Pérez-Barreiro, "The Negation of All Melancholy Arte Madí/Concreto-Invencion, 1944–1950," in *Art from Argentina, 1920–1944*, ed. David Elliott (Oxford: Museum of Modern Art Oxford, 1994), 56.

4. Maldonado's 1950 catalog for a Buenos Aires Instituto de Arte Moderno Concrete Art Exhibition clarifies in neoconstructivist terms that concrete art is "la exaltación de los elementos objetivos del arte. . . . Quiere ser mirado como un hecho o un objeto. Exactamente con el mismo fervor y beligerancia subjetiva con que todo hombre normal mira un hecho o un objeto" [the exaltation of

the objective elements of the art. . . . It wants to be seen like a fact or an object. Exactly with the same fervor and subjective belligerence with which every normal man looks at a fact or an object] (*Escritos Preulmianos*, 69). In 1948 the Argentine Asociación Arte Concreto Invención organized a show titled "Salón Nuevas Realidades, Arte abstracto, concreto, no-figurativo" (Maldonado, *Escritos Preulmianos*, 26). The Madí Manifesto (1946) defined drawing as points and lines on a surface; painting as color and two-dimensionality, sculpture as solid total form, architecture as the inscription of sound in space, poetry as invented propositions, "purely conceptual happening" [*suceder conceptual puro*], and so on (Maldonado, *Escritos Preulmianos*, 25).

5. See the concrete poets' *Teoria da Poesia Concreta*; Aguilar, *Poesía concreta brasileña*; Iumna Maria Simon and Vinicius Dantas, *Poesia Concreta: Seleção estudos biográfico, histórico e critico e exercícios* (São Paulo: Abril Educação, 1982); and Charles Perrone, *Seven Faces: Brazilian Poetry Since Modernism* (Durham, NC: Duke University Press, 1995).

6. The concretes drew on prior attempts to conceive an appropriate relation between subject and object, citizen and consumer. Russian Constructivism, for instance, had considered the notion of nonpossession from the vantage of an achieved socialist revolution that acknowledged subjects' desires (Kiaer, *Imagine No Possessions*, 26).

7. Waldemar Cordeiro, *Waldemar Cordeiro: Uma aventura da Razão*, ed. Aracy Amaral (São Paulo: Museu de Arte Contemporânea da Universidade de São Paulo, 1986), 117.

8. María Josefina Saldaña-Portillo, *The Revolutionary Imagination in the Americas and the Age of Development* (Durham, NC: Duke University Press, 2003), 59.

9. Heloisa Buarque de Hollanda, *Impressões de viagem: CPC, vanguarda e desbunde, 1960–1970* (São Paulo: Brasiliense, 1981), 42.

10. Haroldo de Campos, "Kurt Schwitters ou o Jubilo do objeto," *Suplemento dominical, Jornal do Brasil*, November 28, 1956, in Haroldo de Campos, *A arte no horizonte do provável*, 35.

11. Waldemar Cordeiro, "A fisica da arte," in *Waldemar Cordeiro*, ed. Analívia Cordeiro (São Paulo: Caboverde Design Digital, Galeria Brito Cimino, 2001), CD-ROM.

12. As Kiaer notes: "'objectivism' (*obzhektivizm*), though related to the term 'objective,' (*ob'ektivnyi*) from the title of the Working Group for Objective Analysis, was here more closely related to the foreign cognate word *ob"eckt* or *obzhekt*, meaning 'object', often used as a synonym for the Russian word *veshch'*, meaning object or thing. The group's goal, like that of the Constructivists, was the creation of a new kind of object . . . : 'Objectivism [*obzhektivizm*]—from the word object [*veshch'*]—materiality [*veshchestvennost'*]—derives from the negation of the representational, figurative, illustrative, etc. world'" (*Imagine No Possessions*, 13). Soviet Productivists had been ridiculed by their Constructivist peers as upholders of a "banal, bourgeois realism" for insisting that a useful material thing (object) might preserve dialectical materialism beyond the "bourgeois" split between the *philosophical positions* of subject and object, matter and spirit, etc. (70).

13. "Manifesto neoconcreto," *Suplemento Dominical, Jornal do Brasil* (March 22, 1959): 4–5.

14. Ferreira Gullar, *Experiência neoconcreta: Momento-limite da arte* (São Paulo: Cosac Naify, 2007); "Teoria do não-objeto," *Suplemento Dominical, Jornal do Brasil* (February 27, 1960), 4–5.

15. Ferreira Gullar, "Diálogo sobre o não-objeto," *Suplemento Dominical, Jornal do Brasil* (March 26, 1960): 4–5.

16. Victor Smirnoff, "La transaction fétichique," *Nouvelle revue de psychanalyse* 2 (Paris: Gallimard, 1970), 52. Maldonado had called precisely for a concrete art to satisfy the need for real things, not phantoms (Pérez-Barreiro, "The Negation of All Melancholy Arte Madí," 62). The "Manifiesto Invencionista" published in the *Revista Arte-Concreto-Invención* in Buenos Aires in 1946 stated: "the old phantasmagorias no longer satisfy the aesthetic demands of the new man, formed in a reality that has demanded of him his total presence, without reserve. So closes here the prehistory of the human spirit" (Maldonado, *Escritos Preulmianos*, 39).

17. Waldemar Cordeiro, "Problemática da arte contemporânea," in *Waldemar Cordeiro*, ed. Analívia Cordeiro (São Paulo: Caboverde Design Digital, Galeria Brito Cimino, 2001), CD-ROM.

18. Michael Fried's seminal "Art and Objecthood" essay attributes to 1960s U.S. minimalist (abstract) an "apparent hollowness . . . the quality of having an inside," which for Fried obliquely described "a fairly common type of American dream"—presumably a hollow one. Michael Fried, "Art and Objecthood," in *Art and Objecthood: Essays and Reviews* (Chicago: University of Chicago Press, 1998), 156.

19. Hal Foster, *The Return of the Real: The Avant-garde at the End of the Century* (Cambridge, MA: MIT Press, 1996), 24.

20. "Bôca" [mouth] also appears in several poems alongside "no â mago do ô mega" in the 1956 *Noigandres* 3, including Haroldo de Campos's "semi di zucca" and Augusto de Campos's "ovo novelho."

21. See, in particular, Jacques-Alain Miller's essay "Suture (Elements of the Logic of the Signifier)," *Screen* 18, no. 4 (1977/78): 24–34.

22. Haroldo de Campos, "entre par(edes)ênteses," *Noigandres* 3 (1956).

23. Wlademir Dias-Pino, "Sólida," author's edition, Rio de Janeiro, 1962.

24. Clemente Padin, "Poetry and Participation," trans. Paula Einoder-Boxer, http://xoomer.alice.it/kareninazoom/POETRY_AND_PARTICIPATION.htm.

25. Jacques Lacan, *La relation d'objet: Seminàire, 1956–1957* (France: s.n., 1980–89), 177.

26. Alexandre Kojève, *Introduction to the Reading of Hegel Lectures on the Phenomenology of Spirit*, assembled by Raymond Queneau, ed. Allan Bloom, trans. James. H. Nichols Jr. (Ithaca: Cornell University Press, 1980), 38.

27. Jacques Lacan, *La relación del objeto* (Buenos Aires: Ediciones Paidós, 1994), 238.

28. Severo Sarduy, *Barroco* (Buenos Aires: Sudamericana, 1974), 18.

29. Jacques Lacan, *The Ethics of Psychoanalysis, 1959–1960* (New York: Norton, 1992), 118; Sianne Ngai, *Ugly Feelings* (Cambridge, MA: Harvard University Press, 2005).

30. Ferreira Gullar, "Não," in *Tropicália: Uma revolução na cultura brasileira (1967–1972)* (São Paulo: Cosac Naify, 2007), 384.

31. Augusto de Campos, *Poesia, 1949–1979: VIVAVAIA* (São Paulo: Ateliê Editorial, 2000), 96. The concept of isomorphism was borrowed by the concretes from gestalt theory and denoted the correspondence of structures between dissimilar realities.

32. Rosalind Coward and John Ellis, *Language and Materialism: Developments in Semiology and the Theory of the Subject* (Boston: Routledge and Paul, 1977), 47.

33. In "Poetry as a Means for the Structuring of a Social Environment," Eugen Gomringer notes that alongside concrete poetry emerged "an emotional and realistic poetry," thus implicitly opposing concretism to "realism." Yet he quickly reverses the labels, noting that such "emotional" poetry was "not really a return to reality, nor is it realistic, unless one seeks realism in one's daily bread, in the world of the worker, in the trivia of everyday life. . . . [I]t is, in fact, significant to note how often these so-called realistic poems have as their foundation a model derived from Concrete Poetry." Eugen Gomringer, "Poetry as a Means for the Structuring of a Social Environment," trans. Mark Cory, *Visible Language* 10, no. 3 (Summer 1976): 234.

34. Haroldo de Campos, *Metalinguagem: Ensaios de teoria e crítica literária* (Petrópolis: Editora Vozes, 1970), 92–93.

35. Jean Starobinsky, *Words upon Words: The Anagrams of Ferdinand de Saussure*, trans. Olivia Emmet (New Haven: Yale University Press, 1979).

36. An odd coincidence: in the 1930s Cuban critic Juan Marinello was inspired by Pound's take on ideograms to argue: "Rereading [Pound] today I wonder whether the Chinese, that have in their grammars . . . empty words and half-charged words [*palabras vacías y palabras a medio cargar*], are not destined to be the great poets of the twenty-first century." Juan Marinello, *Poética: Ensayos en entusiasmo* (Madrid: Espasa-Calpe, 1933), 33–34.

37. Ferreira Gullar, *Cultura posta em questão* (Rio de Janeiro: Editora Civilização Brasileira, 1965); Gullar, *Vanguarda e subdesenvolvimento: Ensaios sobre arte* (Rio de Janeiro: Civilização Brasileira, 1969).

38. Rogério Camara has built a helpful online database of process/poems at www.poemaprocesso.com.

39. Neide Dias de Sá, personal communication with the author, July 2009.

40. "Pão poema-processo com 2m é comido por 5 mil pessoas na Feira de Arte de Recife," *Jornal do Brasil*, April 7, 1970, first section in *Processo: Linguagem e comunicação*, ed. Wlademir Dias-Pino (Petrópolis: Editora Vozes, 1971), n.p.

41. Wlademir Dias-Pino, "O poema/processo não acredita em LSD," *Jornal das Letras*, 1971, reproduced in *Wlademir Dias-Pino, Poesia/poema*, org. Rogério Camara and Priscilla Martins, 140, http://www.poemaprocesso.com/introducao.php.

42. Hélio Oiticica, *Aspiro ao grande labirinto* (Rio de Janeiro: Rocco, 1986), 18.

43. Celso Favoretto calls this a "passagem pelo objeto" [passing through the object]. Celso Favoretto, "Tropicália: A Explosão do Obvio," in *Tropicália: Uma revolução na cultura brasileira (1967–1972)*, 89. Lygia Clark would recall, "It is obvious that the issue of categories is finishing and only the question of the name 'non-object' would be the impasse. Mário Pedrosa thinks that in the plastic arts the name could be the trans-object because the transcendence comes from the object itself." Clark, *Lygia Clark: Fundació Antoni Tàpies, Barcelona, 21 octubre–21 dicimbre 1997, MAC, galeries contemporaines des Musées de Marseille, 16 enero–12 abril 1998, Fundação de Serralves, Oporto, 30 abril–28 junio 1998, Société des Expositions du Palais des Beaux-Arts, Bruselas, 24 julio–27 setiembre 1998* (Barcelona: Fundació Antonio Tàpies, 1998), 141.

44. "Proposition" would also be Joseph Kosuth's term to replace art "works." Benjamin Buchloch, "Conceptual Art, 1962–1969: From the Aesthetic of Administration to the Critique of Institutions," *October* 55 (Winter 1990): 108n3.

45. Hélio Oiticica, "Esquema geral da nova objetividade," in *Nova objetividade brasileira: Exposição, Museu de Arte Moderna* (Rio de Janeiro, 1967), reprinted in Oiticica, *Aspiro ao grande labirinto*, 84–98.

46. Maria Alice Milliet, *Lygia Clark: Obra-trajeto* (São Paulo: Edusp, 1992), 26; Maurice Merleau-Ponty, *Phenomenology of Perception*, trans. Colin Smith (New York: Routledge, 2002), xi–xii.

47. Hélio Oiticica, "Tropicália," *Folhetim, Folha de São Paulo*, January 8, in *Tropicália: Uma revolução na cultura brasileira (1967–1972)*, 240.

48. Lygia Clark, "Carta a Madame Karlikow," Associação Cultural "O Mundo de Lygia Clark" (unpublished manuscript, Rio de Janeiro), n.p. I am grateful to the Associação Cultural "O Mundo de Lygia Clark" for permission to consult and cite Clark's unpublished diaries.

49. Jacques Lacan, *Anxiety*, trans. Cormac Gallagher (London: Karnac Books, 2002), 114.

50. Monica Amor similarly discusses Clark's interest in fusing inside and outside, and notes that rather than salvage the subject from constructivist objectivism Clark "repositioned the subject of production and reception." Monica Amor, "From Work to Frame, in Between, and Beyond: Lygia Clark and Hélio Oiticica, 1959–1964," *Grey Room*, no. 38 (Winter 2010): 34.

51. Michael Hardt and Antonio Negri, *Empire* (Cambridge, MA: Harvard University Press, 2000), 187–88.

52. Lygia Clark, Diary, August 20, 1971, Associação Cultural "O Mundo de Lygia Clark," Rio de Janeiro, n.p.

53. Clark's relation to objects was of a piece with currents emerging in New York, Buenos Aires, and Europe in movements such as Spanish informalism and Italian Arte Povera. Argentine artist Rubén Santantonín's "art of things" was to be "predominantly sensorial": "Non-objects. Non-persons. Non-painting. Non-sculpture. Non-work of art." Andrea Giunta, *Avant-Garde, Internationalism, and Politics: Argentine Art in the Sixties*, trans.

Peter Kahn (Durham, NC: Duke University Press, 2007), 131. The list recalls what Benjamin Buchloch calls proto-conceptualist stances from opposite ends of the aesthetic spectrum: Cage wrote of Rauschenberg's White Paintings, "No subject, No image, No taste, No object," and of Reinhardt, "No lines or imaginings, no shapes or composings or representings . . . no accidents or ready-mades, no things, no ideas, no relations" (Buchloch, "Conceptual Art, 1962–1969," 112).

54. Lygia Clark, Diary, Paris 4, Associação Cultural "O Mundo de Lygia Clark," Rio de Janeiro, n.p.

55. Lygia Clark, "Carta a Raymundo Amado," Associação Cultural "O Mundo de Lygia Clark." Rio de Janeiro, n.p.; Ferreira Gullar, *Lygia Clark: Textos de Ferreira Gullar, Mário Pedrosa, Lygia Clark* (Rio de Janeiro: Edição FUNARTE, 1980), 25–27.

56. Brito, *Neoconcretismo*, 78; Ferreira Gullar, *Ferreira Gullar: In Conversation with Ariel Jiménez* (New York: Fundación Patricia Phelps Cisneros, 2012), 79.

57. Lygia Clark, Diary, March 17, 1969, and Diary, 1960, "Bichos," both in Associação Cultural "O Mundo de Lygia Clark," Rio de Janeiro, n.p.

58. See Lygia Clark, Diary, 1959, Associação Cultural "O Mundo de Lygia Clark," Rio de Janeiro, n.p.: "I am already beginning to feel the form's void. . . . The form only exists in absolute relation to this void. That reminds me that perhaps in real affective life it means that acceptance of the void of femininity and its importance with respect to the male organ. . . . Then, is the problem of life and art the same one?" [Já começo a sentir o vazio da forma. . . . A forma só existe em relação absoluta com este vazio. Isto me lembra que talvez na vida real afetiva significa que a aceitação do vazio da feminilidade e a sua importância com relação ao órgão masculino. . . . Então, o problema vida e arte é um só?]

59. Lygia Clark, Diary, Rio Volta de Paris, 1964, Associação Cultural "O Mundo de Lygia Clark," Rio de Janeiro, n.p.

60. Parts of this passage are also cited, in a slightly different translation, in Clark, *Lygia Clark: Fundació Antoni Tàpies*, 174–76.

61. See, for instance, Lygia Clark's diary entry from August 20, 1971, Associação Cultural "O Mundo de Lygia Clark," Rio de Janeiro, n.p.: "Agora sei a inversão dos valores A casa é o corpo, é ainda o útero onde eu estive e agora na gafe que chamei O corpo é a casa é o verdadeiro nascimento que se faz" [Now I know the inversion of the values (the artwork named) *A casa é o corpo* (The house is a body) is still the uterus where I was and now in a gaffe that I called *The body is the* the true birth occurs.] Lygia Clark, Diary, Paris 4, 1964, "Sonhei que estava fazendo amor," Associação Cultural "O Mundo de Lygia Clark," Rio de Janeiro, n.p.

62. Paulo Herkenhoff, "Lygia Clark," *Lygia Clark: Fundació Antoni Tàpies, Barcelona, 21 octubre–21 dicimbre 1997, MAC, galeries contemporaines des Musées de Marseille, 16 enero–12 abril 1998, Fundação de Serralves, Oporto, 30 abril–28 junio 1998, Société des Expositions du Palais des Beaux-Arts, Bruselas, 24 julio–27 setiembre 1998* (Barcelona: Fundació Antonio Tàpies, 1998), 53.

63. Roberto Pontual, "Lygia Clark: A fantasmática do corpo," *Jornal do Brasil*, September 21, 1974, n.p. I owe this reference to Herkenhoff, "Lygia Clark."

64. Lygia Clark, "Textos não publicados C VI B B 4 ABAHAM [*sic*] NICOLAS," Associação Cultural "O Mundo de Lygia Clark," Rio de Janeiro.

65. Lygia Clark, Diary, 1963–65, Associação Cultural "O Mundo de Lygia Clark," Rio de Janeiro, n.p.

EPILOGUE

1. Sarduy's lifelong partner, Francois Wahl, writes that while he seems to remember Sarduy mentioning Clark, "je ne crois pas qu'ils se soient rencontrés" [I don't believe they met] (email to the author, October 2, 2011). Yve-Alain Bois similarly has stated that he recollected no such meeting, and that, furthermore, Clark associated little with either other Latin American (non-Brazilian) artists or with the French intelligentsia of which Sarduy was a part (email to the author, February 15, 2013).

2. Sarduy had written about metaphor and movement in 1966 in relation to Góngora; here language becomes unhinged from its usual orbit, freed and unleashed to circle in new ways. Severo Sarduy, "Sobre Góngora: La metáfora al cuadrado," *Nuevo Mundo*, no. 6 (1966): 84–86.

3. Severo Sarduy, *Ensayos Generales Sobre el Barroco* (Buenos Aires: Fondo de Cultura Económica, 1987), 216.

4. Zuenir Ventura, *1968: O ano que não terminou* (São Paulo: Planeta, 2008), 54.

Works Cited

Abraham, Nicolas. "The Shell and the Kernel." Trans. Nicholas Rand. *Diacritics* 9, no. 1, The Tropology of Freud (Spring 1979): 15–28.

Abraham, Nicolas, and Maria Torok. *The Shell and the Kernal Renewals of Psychoanalysis*. Trans. Nicholas T. Rand. Chicago: University of Chicago Press, 1994.

Adams, Brooks. *America's Economic Supremacy*. London: Macmillan, 1900.

Adelman, Jeremy. *Sovereignty and Revolution in the Iberian Atlantic*. Princeton: Princeton University Press, 2006.

Adorno, Theodor. *Aesthetic Theory*. Trans. Robert Hullot-Kentor. Minneapolis: University of Minnesota Press, 1997.

———. *Notes to Literature, Volume I*. Trans. Sherry Weber Nicholson. New York: Columbia University Press, 1991.

Agamben, Giorgio. *Stanzas: Word and Phantom in Western Culture*. Trans. Ronald L. Martinez. Minneapolis: University of Minnesota Press, 1993.

Aguilar, Gonzalo. *Poesía concreta brasileña: Las vanguardias en la encrucijada modernista*. Rosario: Beatriz Viterbo, 2003.

Aguilar, José Antonio, and Rafael Rojas. *El Republicanismo en Hispanoamérica*. Mexico City: CIDE, 2002.

Aguilar, Luis. *Cuba 1933: Prologue to Revolution*. Ithaca: Cornell University Press, 1972.

Almanza Alonso, Rafael. *En torno al pensamiento económico de José Martí*. Havana: Editorial Ciencias Sociales, 1990.

Álvarez-Tabío Albo, Emma. *La invención de la Habana*. Barcelona: Editorial Casiopea, 2000.

Amor, Monica. "From Work to Frame, in Between, and Beyond: Lygia Clark and Hélio Oiticica, 1959–1964." *Grey Room*, no. 38 (Winter 2010): 20–37.

Andrade, Gênese. "Afinidades eletivas: Haroldo de Campos traduz os hispano-americanos." São Paulo: Caracol Revista do Programa de Pós-graduação em Língua Espanhola e Literaturas Espanhola e Hispano Americana Universidade de São Paulo. No. 1. 2010. http://www.revistas.usp.br/caracol/article/view/57637.

Anghie, Antony. *Imperialism, Sovereignty and the Making of International Law*. Cambridge: Cambridge University Press, 2005.

Araújo, Ricardo. *Poesia visual, vídeo poesia*. São Paulo: Editora Perspectiva, 1999.

Armas, Ramón de. "Año nuevo." *Revista telefónica cubana* (April–May 1926): 17–18.

Arrighi, Giovanni. *Adam Smith in Beijing: Lineages of the Twenty-First Century*. New York: Verso, 2007.

———. *The Long Twentieth Century: Money, Power and the Origins of Our Times*. New York: Verso, 1994.

Avelar, Idelber. "A Arqui-Textura de Sousândrade: Poética e Política." *Limites: Anais do 30 Congresso da Associação Brasileira de Literatura Comparada*, 685–90. São Paulo: Edusp, 1995.

"Bajo el signo de Martí." *Revista de avance* 5, no. 46 (May 15, 1930): 144.

Balakrishnan, Gopal. *The Enemy: An Intellectual Portrait of Carl Schmitt*. New York: Verso, 2000.

Balfour, Ian. *The Rhetoric of Romantic Prophecy*. Stanford, CA: Stanford University Press, 2002.

Ballentyne, Tony, and Antoinette Burton. "Empires and the Reach of the Global." In *A World Connecting, 1870–1945*, ed. Emily Rosenberg, 285–431. Cambridge, MA: Belknap, 2012.

Basualdo, Carlos, ed. *Tropicália: Uma revolução na cultura brasileira (1967–1972)*. São Paulo: Cosac Naify, 2007.

Batchen, Geoffrey. "Electricity Made Visible." In *New Media, Old Media: A History and Theory Reader*, ed. Wendy Chun and Thomas Keenan, 27–44. New York: Routledge, 2006.

Baucom, Ian. *Specters of the Atlantic: Slavery, Finance Capital and the Philosophy of History*. Durham, NC: Duke University Press, 2005.

Beckert, Sven. *The Monied Metropolis: New York City and the Consolidation of the American Bourgeoisie, 1850–1896*. Cambridge: Cambridge University Press, 2001.

Beckman, Ericka. *Capital Fictions: The Literature of Latin America's Export Age*. Minneapolis: University of Minnesota Press, 2013.

Beniger, James. *The Control Revolution: Technological and Economic Origins of the Information Society*. Cambridge, MA: Harvard University Press, 1986.

Benítez Rojo, Antonio. *The Repeating Island: The Caribbean and the Postmodern Perspective*. 2nd edition. Trans. James Maraniss. Durham, NC: Duke University Press, 1996.

Benjamin, Walter. *The Arcades Project*. Trans. Howard Eiland and Kevin McLaughlin. Cambridge, MA: Harvard University Press, 1999.

Bennett, Jane. *Vibrant Matter: A Political Ecology of Things*. Durham, NC: Duke University Press, 2009.

Benton, Lauren. *A Search for Sovereignty: Law and Geography in European Empires, 1400–1900*. New York: Cambridge University Press, 2009.

Berbel, Márcia, Rafael Marquese, and Tâmis Parron. *Escravidão e política Brasil e Cuba, c. 1790–1850*. São Paulo: FABESP, 2010.

Bilac, Olavo. *Vossa Insôlencia Crônicas*. Ed. Antonio Dimas. São Luis: Edições AML, 2002.

Birkenmaier, Anke. *Alejo Carpentier y la cultura del surrealismo en América Latina*. Madrid: Iberoamericana Vervuert, 2006.

Bogost, Ian. *Alien Phenomenology: Or What It's Like to Be a Thing*. Minneapolis: University of Minnesota Press, 2012.

Bosco Amores Carradeño, Juan. *Cuba y España, 1868–1898: El final de un sueño*. Pamplona: Astrolabio, 1998.

Brito, Ronaldo. *Neoconcretismo: Vértice e ruptura do projeto construtivo brasileiro*. 1985. Reprint. São Paulo: Cosac & Naify Edições, 1999.

Britt-Arredondo, Christopher. *Quixotism: The Imaginative Denial of Spain's Loss of Empire*. Albany: State University of New York Press, 2005.

Brown, Bill. *A Sense for Things: The Object Matter of American Literature*. Chicago: University of Chicago Press, 2004.

———, ed. *Things*. Chicago: University of Chicago Press, 2004.

Brown, Nicholas. *Utopian Generations: The Political Horizon of Twentieth-Century Literature*. Princeton: Princeton University Press, 2005.

Brull, Mariano. *Poemas en menguante*. Paris: Impr. Le Moil & Pascaly, 1928.

Bryant, Levi. *The Democracy of Objects*. Ann Arbor: Open Humanities Press, 2011.

Buarque de Hollanda, Heloisa. *Impressões de viagem: CPC, vanguarda e desbunde, 1960–1970*. São Paulo: Brasiliense, 1981.

Buchloch, Benjamin. "Allegorical Procedures: Appropriation and Montage in Contemporary Art." *Artforum* 47 (September 1982): 43–56.

———. "Conceptual Art, 1962–1969: From the Aesthetic of Administration to the Critique of Institutions." *October* 55 (Winter 1990): 105–43.

Buck-Morss, Susan. *Dreamworld and Catastrophe: The Passing of Mass Utopia in East and West*. Cambridge, MA: MIT Press, 2002.

———. "Hegel and Haiti." *Critical Inquiry* 26, no. 4 (Summer 2000): 821–65.

Bulmer-Thomas, Victor. *The Economic History of Latin America Since Independence*. 2nd ed. New York: Cambridge University Press, 1994.

Bulmer-Thomas, Victor, John Coatsworth, and Roberto Cortés Conde, eds. *The Cambridge Economic History of Latin America*. 1st ed. Vol. 2. Cambridge: Cambridge University Press, 2006. *Cambridge Histories Online*. March 17, 2014. http://dx.doi.org/10.1017/CHOL9780521812900.

Byrne, Bonifacio. "Los muebles." In *La poesía moderna en Cuba (1882–1925): Antología crítica*, ed. Felix Lizaso and José Antonio Fernandez de Castro, 127–30. Madrid: Casa Editorial Hernando S.A., 1926.

———. *Poesía y prosa*. Havana: Letras Cubanas, 1988.

Cabrera, Lydia. *Anaforuana: Ritual y símbolos de la iniciación en la sociedad secreta Abakuá.* Miami: Ediciones R, 1975.

———. *La sociedad secreta Abakuá.* Miami: Ediciones C. R., 1970.

Cadava, Eduardo. *Words of Light: Theses on the Photography of History.* Princeton: Princeton University Press, 1997.

Calasans, José. *Canudos na literatura de cordel.* São Paulo: Atica, 1984.

Camara, Rogério, and Priscilla Martins, coords. *Poema processo.* Brasilia: PPG Artes/UnB, 2011.

———, orgs. *Wlademir Dias-Pino, Poesia/poema.* http://www.poemaprocesso.com/introducao.php.

Camargo Moraes Figueiredo, Ana Cristina. *Liberdade é uma calça velha, azul e desbotada: Publicidade, cultura de consumo e comportamento político no Brasil (1954–1964).* São Paulo: Editora Hucitec, História Social USP, 1998.

Campos, Augusto de. "Informação e redundância na música popular." In *Balanço da bossa: Antología crítica da moderna música popular brasileira*, 179–89. São Paulo: Editora Perspectiva, 1968.

———. *Poesia, 1949–1979: VIVAVAIA.* São Paulo: Ateliê Editorial, 2000.

Campos, Augusto de, and Haroldo de Campos. *Os Sertões dos Campos: Duas vezes Euclides.* Rio de Janeiro: Editora 7Letras, 1997.

Campos, Augusto de, and Haroldo de Campos. *ReVisão de Sousândrade.* São Paulo: Edições Invenção, 1964.

Campos, Augusto de, Haroldo de Campos, and Décio Pignatari. "Plano-piloto para poesia concreta." *Noigandres* 4 (1958). Reprinted in *Teoria da poesia concreta: Textos críticos e manifestos, 1950–1960* (1965), ed. Augusto de Campos, Haroldo de Campos, and Décio Pignatari, 4th ed., 215–18. São Paulo: Ateliê, 2006.

———, eds. *Teoria da poesia concreta: Textos críticos e manifestos, 1950–1960* (1965). 4th ed. São Paulo: Ateliê, 2006.

Campos, Haroldo de. *O arco-íris branco: Ensaios de literatura e cultura.* Rio de Janeiro: Imago, 1997.

———. *A arte no horizonte do provável e outros ensaios.* São Paulo: Editora Perspectiva, 1969.

———. "entre par(edes)ênteses." *Noigandres* 3 (1956).

———. *Ideograma: Lógica, poesia, linguagem.* Trans. Heloysa de Lima Dantas. São Paulo: Editora Cultrix, 1977.

———. "Kurt Schwitters ou o Júbilo do objeto." In Haroldo de Campos, *A arte no horizonte do provável e outros ensaios*, 35–54. São Paulo: Editora Perspectiva, 1969.

———. *Metalinguagem: Ensaios de teoria e crítica literária.* Petrópolis: Editora Vozes, 1970.

———. "no â mago do ô mega." *Noigandres* 3 (1956).

———. "A obra de arte aberta." In *Teoria da poesia concreta: Textos críticos e manifestos, 1950–1960* (1965). Ed. Augusto de Campos, Haroldo de Campos, and Décio Pignatari, 4th ed., 49–53. São Paulo: Ateliê, 2006.

———. *Signantia quasi coelum = Signância quase céu*. São Paulo: Editora Perspectiva, 1979.

Campos Johnson, Adriana. *Sentencing Canudos: Subalternity in the Backlands of Brazil*. Pittsburgh: University of Pittsburgh Press, 2010.

Candlin, Fiona, and Raiford Guins, eds. *The Object Reader*. New York: Routledge, 2009.

Cañizares-Esguerra, Jorge. *Puritan Conquistadors: Iberianizing the Atlantic, 1550–1700*. Stanford, CA: Stanford University Press, 2006.

———. "Some Caveats About the 'Atlantic' Paradigm." *History Compass* 1 (2003) NA 004: 1–4.

Carpentier, Alejo. *Baroque Concerto*. Trans. Asa Zatz. London: A. Deutsch, 1991.

———. *Concierto barroco*. Mexico, D.F.: Siglo XXI, 1974.

———. *Cuentos*. Havana: Letras Cubanas, 1979.

———. *Écue-yamba-ó novela afrocubana*. Havana: Editorial Arte y Literatura, 1977.

Carrión, Miguel de. "El doctor Risco." In *La última voluntad y otros relatos*. Alexandria, VA: Alexander Street Press, 2007.

———. *Las impuras*. Havana: Editorial Letras Cubanas, 1984.

Carvalho, Helba. "Da poesia concreta ao poema-processo um passeio pelo fio da navalha." Master's thesis, University of São Paulo, 2002.

Casals Meseguer, Xavier. "Franco 'El Africano.'" *Journal of Spanish Cultural Studies* 7, no. 3 (2006): 207–24.

Castells, Manuel. *The Rise of the Network Society*. 2nd ed. Vol. 1 of *The Information Age: Economy, Society and Culture*. Malden, MA: Wiley Blackwell, 2000.

Castro-Klarén, Sara. "Santos and *Cangaceiros*: Inscription Without Discourse in *Os Sertões* and *La Guerra del fin del mundo*." *Modern Language Notes* 101, no. 2 (1986): 366–88.

Cheah, Pheng. *Spectral Nationality: Passages of Freedom from Kant to Postcolonial Literatures of Liberation*. New York: Columbia University Press, 2004.

Chiampi, Irlemar. *Barroco e modernidade: Ensaios sobre literatura latinoamericana*. Petrópolis: Editorial Perspectiva, 1998.

Cirne, Moacy. *Vanguarda: Um projeto semiológico*. Petrópolis: Editora Vozes, 1975.

Clark, Lygia. "Carta a Madame Karlikow." Associação Cultural "O Mundo de Lygia Clark." Rio de Janeiro.

———. "Carta a Raymundo Amado." Associação Cultural "O Mundo de Lygia Clark." Rio de Janeiro.

———. Diary, 3, 1955. Associação Cultural "O Mundo de Lygia Clark." Rio de Janeiro.

———. Diary, 1959. Associação Cultural "O Mundo de Lygia Clark." Rio de Janeiro.

———. Diary, 1960, "Bichos." Associação Cultural "O Mundo de Lygia Clark." Rio de Janeiro.

———. Diary, 1963–65. Associação Cultural "O Mundo de Lygia Clark." Rio de Janeiro.

———. Diary, Paris 4, 1964. "Sonhei que estava fazendo amor." Associação Cultural "O Mundo de Lygia Clark." Rio de Janeiro.

———. Diary, March 17, 1969. Associação Cultural "O Mundo de Lygia Clark." Rio de Janeiro.

———. Diary, August 20, 1971. Associação Cultural "O Mundo de Lygia Clark." Rio de Janeiro.

———. *Lygia Clark: Fundació Antoni Tàpies, Barcelona, 21 octubre–21 dicimbre 1997, MAC, galeries contemporaines des Musées de Marseille, 16 enero–12 abril 1998, Fundação de Serralves, Oporto, 30 abril–28 junio 1998, Société des Expositions du Palais des Beaux-Arts, Bruselas, 24 julio–27 setiembre 1998*. Barcelona: Fundació Antonio Tàpies, 1998.

———. "Textos não publicados C VI B B 4 ABAHAM [*sic*] NICOLAS." Associação Cultural "O Mundo de Lygia Clark." Rio de Janeiro.

Clayton, Michelle. *Poetry in Pieces: César Vallejo and Lyric Modernity*. Berkeley: University of California Press, 2012.

Coelho, Frederico. *Livro ou livro-me os escritos babilônicos de Hélio Oiticica (1971–1978)*. Rio de Janeiro: EdUERJ, 2010.

Coelho, Maria Teresa Pinto. *Apocalipse e regeneração: O ultimatum e a mitologia da pátria na literatura finissecular*. Lisbon: Edições Cosmos, 1996.

Conselheiro, Antônio. *Breviario de Antônio Conselheiro*. Ed. Walnice Nogueira Galvão and Fernando da Rocha Peres. Salvador: Universidade Federal da Bahia, Centro de Estudos Baianos Odebrecht, 2002.

Cordeiro, Waldemar. "A física da arte." In *Waldemar Cordeiro*, ed. Analívia Cordeiro. São Paulo: Caboverde Design Digital, Galeria Brito Cimino, 2001. CD-ROM.

———. "O neo-plasticismo e a construtivismo, do ponto-da-vista de pura visualidade." In *Waldemar Cordeiro*, ed. Analívia Cordeiro. São Paulo: Caboverde Design Digital, Galeria Brito Cimino, 2001. CD-ROM.

———. "O Objeto." *Ad-Arquitetura*, no. 20 (1956). In *Waldemar Cordeiro: Uma Aventura da Razão*, ed. Aracy Amaral. São Paulo: Museu de Arte Contemporânea da Universidade de São Paulo, 1986.

———. "Problemática da arte contemporânea." In *Waldemar Cordeiro*, ed. Analívia Cordeiro. São Paulo: Caboverde Design Digital, Galeria Brito Cimino, 2001. CD-ROM.

———. *Waldemar Cordeiro: Uma aventura da Razão*. Ed. Aracy Amaral. São Paulo: Museu de Arte Contemporânea da Universidade de São Paulo, 1986.

Costa, Emília Viotti da. "Brazil: The Age of Reform, 1870–1889." In *The Cambridge History of Latin America*, vol. 6, *ca. 1870 to 1930*, ed. Leslie Bethell, 488–98. New York: Cambridge University Press, 1989.

Costa Lima, Luiz. "O campo visual de uma experiência antecipadora: Sousândrade." In *ReVisão de Sousândrade*, 2nd ed., ed. Augusto de Campos and Haroldo de Campos, 395–424. São Paulo: Edições Invenção, 1982.

———. *Terra Ignota: A construção de Os Sertões*. Rio de Janeiro: Civilização Brasileira, 1997.

Coward, Rosalind, and John Ellis. *Language and Materialism: Developments in Semiology and the Theory of the Subject*. Boston: Routledge and Paul, 1977.

Cunha, Euclides da. *Obra completa*. Ed. Afrânio Coutinho. 2nd ed. Vols. 1–2. Rio de Janeiro: Editora Nova Aguilar, 1995.

———. *Rebellion in the Backlands*. Trans. Samuel Putnam. Chicago: University of Chicago Press, 1944.

Darío, Rubén. "Amar hasta fracasar." *Mundial Magazine* 5, no. 27 (July 1913): 284–85. Reprinted in *Rubén Darío Cuentos Completos*, ed. Ernesto Mejía Sánchez, 432–36. Managua: Nueva Nicaragua, 1993.

———. "Los Anglosajones." In *Peregrinaciones*. http://www.cervantesvirtual.com/obra-visor/peregrinaciones—0/html/ff0811ae-82b1–11df-acc7–002185ce6064_1.htm#9.

Daston, Lorraine, and Peter Galison, eds. *Objectivity*. Boston: Zone Books, 2007.

de Guzmán, María. *Spain's Long Shadow: The Black Legend, Off-Whiteness and Anglo-American Empire*. Minneapolis: University of Minnesota Press, 2005.

de la Fuente, Alejandro. *A Nation for All: Race, Inequality and Politics in Twentieth-Century Cuba*. Chapel Hill: University of North Carolina Press, 2001.

———. "Slave Law and Claims-Making in Cuba: The Tannenbaum Debate Revisited." *Law and History Review* 22, no. 2 (2004): 339–69.

de Onís, Federico. "Martí y el modernismo." In *Antología crítica de José Martí*, ed. Manuel Pedro González, 155–66. Mexico City: Publicaciones de la Editorial Cultura, 1960.

Deleuze, Gilles. *Difference and Repetition*. Trans. Paul Patton. New York: Columbia University Press, 1994.

———. "Postscript on the Societies of Control." *October* 59 (Winter 1992): 3–7.

De Man, Paul. *The Resistance to Theory*. Minneapolis: University of Minnesota Press, 1986.

Derrida, Jacques. *Specters of Marx: The State of Debt, the Work of Mourning and the New International*. Trans. Peggy Kamuf. New York: Routledge, 1994.

Dias-Pino, Wlademir. "O poema/processo não acredita em LSD." *Jornal das Letras*, 1971. In *Wlademir Dias-Pino, Poesia/poema*, org. Rogério Camara and Priscilla Martins, 140. http://www.poemaprocesso.com/introducao.php.

———. *Processo: Linguagem e comunicação*. Petrópolis: Editora Vozes, 1971.

———. "Sólida." Author's edition. Rio de Janeiro, 1962.

Díaz, Duanel. "Hasta sus últimas consecuencias: Dialécticas de la Revolución Cubana." Ph.D. diss., Princeton University, 2012.

Díaz-Quiñones, Arcadio. *El arte de bregar: Ensayos*. San Juan: Ediciones Callejón, 2000.

Dolar, Mladen. *The Voice and Nothing More*. Cambridge, MA: MIT Press, 2006.

Elliot, John. *Empires of the Atlantic World: British and Spanish in America, 1492–1830*. New Haven: Yale University Press, 2006.

Espadas Burgos, Manuel. "Las lecturas históricas del 98." In *La nación soñada: Cuba, Puerto Rico y Filipinas ante el 98*, ed. Consuelo Naranjo Orovio, Miguel Angel Puig-Samper, and Luis Miguel García Mora Aranjuez, 697–712. Madrid: Doce Calles, 1996.

Evelyn, Ashley. "The Formation of Transnational Black Identity Among African-Descendants in Early Twentieth Century Cuba." Senior thesis, Princeton University, 2013.

Fabra, Nilo María. *Presente y futuro: Nuevos cuentos*. Barcelona: Gili, 1897.

Fabris, Annateresa. "Waldemar Cordeiro: Computer Art Pioneer," *Leonardo On-line* 30, no. 1 (February 1997). http://www.leonardo.info/isast/spec.projects/fabris.html.

Favoretto, Celso. "Tropicália: A Explosão do Obvio." In *Tropicália: Uma revolução na cultura brasileira (1967–1972)*, ed. Carlos Basualdo, 81–96. São Paulo: Cosac Naify, 2007.

Fédida, Pierre. "La relique et le travail du deuil." *Nouvelle revue de psychanalyse 2 (objets du fetichisme)*, no. 2 (1970): 249–54.

Ferguson, Robert. *The Short Sharp Life of T. E. Hulme*. London: Allen Lane, 2002.

Fernández, Susan. *Encumbered Cuba: Capital Markets and Revolt, 1878–1895*. Gainesville: University of Florida Press, 2002.

Fernandez Elías, D. Clemente. *Novísimo tratado completo de filosofía del derecho o derecho natural con arreglo á los adelantos y estado actual de esta ciencia exponiendo las doctrinas de Ahrens, Taparelli, Krause, Kant, Hegel, Savigni, Almetyer y otros notables autores con su estudio histórico sobre el desenvolvimiento de la ciencia del derecho*. Madrid: Leocadio López, 1874.

Ferrer, Ada. *Insurgent Cuba: Race, Nation and Revolution, 1868–1898*. Chapel Hill: University of North Carolina Press, 1999.

Ferris Thompson, Robert. *Flash of the Spirit: African and Afro-American Art and Philosophy*. New York: Vintage, 1984.

Festa, Lynn Mary. *Sentimental Figures of Empire in Eighteenth-Century Britain and France*. Baltimore: Johns Hopkins University Press, 2006.

Fioretos, Aris. *The Solid Letter: Readings of Friedrich Hölderlin*. Stanford, CA: Stanford University Press, 1999.

Fischer, Sibylle. *Modernity Disavowed: Haiti and the Cultures of Slavery in the Atlantic*. Durham, NC: Duke University Press, 2004.

Flynn, Dennis O., and Arturo Giráldez. *China and the Birth of Globalization in the 16th Century*. Burlington: Ashgate, 2010.

Foster, Hal. *The Return of the Real: The Avant-garde at the End of the Century*. Cambridge, MA: MIT Press, 1996.

Fox, E. Inman. Introduction to *La guerra del Transvaal y los misterios de la Banca de Londres*. Ed. E. Inman Fox, 9–20. Madrid: Taurus, 1974.

Freedgood, Elaine. *The Ideas in Things: Fugitive Meaning in the Victorian Novel. Chicago: University of Chicago Press, 2006.*

French, Jennifer. *Nature, Neo-colonialism, and the Spanish American Regional Writers.* Hanover, NH: University Press of New England, 2005.

Fried, Michael. "Art and Objecthood." In *Art and Objecthood: Essays and Reviews.* Chicago: University of Chicago Press, 1998.

Gallagher, John, and Ronald Robinson. "The Imperialism of Free Trade." *Economic History Review*, 2nd ser., 6, no. 1 (1953): 1–15.

Gallo, Rubén. "Severo Sarduy, Jacques Lacan y el psicoanálisis: Entrevista con François Wahl." *Revista Hispánica Moderna*, nos. 1–2 (June–December 2006): 51–60.

Ganivet, Ángel. *Los trabajos del infatigable creador Pío Cid.* Madrid: V. Suárez, 1911.

García Marruz, Fina. *El amor como energía revolucionaria en José Martí.* Havana: Centro de Estudios Martianos, 2003.

———. "El tiempo en la crónica norteamericana de Martí." In *En torno a José Martí: Coloquio Internacional.* Bordeaux: Biere, 1974.

García Rodríguez, Gloria. *La esclavitud desde la esclavitud: La visión de los siervos.* Mexico City: Centro de Investigacíon Científica "Ing. Jorge L Tamayo," 1996.

Gato de Jesús, Matheus. "'Tempo e melancholia': República, modernidade e cidadania negra nos contos de Astolfo Marques (1876–1918)." *Lua Nova* 85 (2012): 133–85.

Gilroy, Paul. *The Black Atlantic: Modernity and Double Consciousness.* Cambridge, MA: Harvard University Press, 1993.

Giunta, Andrea. *Avant-Garde, Internationalism, and Politics: Argentine Art in the Sixties.* Trans. Peter Kahn. Durham, NC: Duke University Press, 2007.

Glade, William. "Latin America and the International Economy." In *The Cambridge History of Latin America*, vol. 4, *1870 to 1930*, ed. Leslie Bethell, 1–56. New York: Cambridge University Press, 1986.

Glissant, Édouard. *Caribbean Discourse.* Trans. Michael Dash. Charlottesville: University of Virginia Press, 1999.

Gómez de la Serna, Ramón. *Mi tía Carolina Coronado.* Buenos Aires: Emecé, 1942.

Gomringer, Eugen. "Poetry as a Means for the Structuring of a Social Environment." Trans. Mark Cory. *Visible Language* 10, no. 3 (Summer 1976): 227–41.

Gonçalves, João Felipe. "The 'Apostle' in Stone: Nationalism and Monuments in Honor of José Martí." In *The Cuban Republic and José Martí: Reception and Use of a Symbol*, ed. Mauricio Font and Alfonso Quiroz, 18–33. Lanham, MD: Lexington Books, 2006.

González Cuevas, Pedro Carlos. *Maeztu: Biografía de un nacionalista español.* Madrid: Marcial Pons, 2003.

González Echevarría, Roberto. *Alejo Carpentier: The Pilgrim at Home.* Ithaca: Cornell University Press, 1977.

———. "Guillén as Baroque: Meaning in *Motivos de Son.*" Reproduced in *Las vanguardias en el Caribe: Cuba, Puerto Rico y República Dominicana*, ed. William Luis, 459–76. Orlando, FL: Iberoamericana Vervuert, 2010.

———. "Modernidad, modernismo y nueva narrativa: El recurso del método." *Revista Interamericana de Bibliografía* 30 (1980): 157–63.

———. *La ruta de Severo Sarduy*. Hanover: Ediciones del norte, 1987.

———. "Son de la Habana: La ruta de Severo Sarduy." *Revista Iberoamericana* 37, no. 76–77 (July–December 1971): 725–40.

González-Stephan, Beatriz. "Invenciones tecnológicas. Mirada postcolonial y nuevas pedagogías: José Martí en las exposiciones universales." In *Galerías del progreso: Museos, exposiciones, y cultura visual en América Latina*, ed. Jens Andermann and Beatriz González-Stephan, 221–53. Rosario: Beatriz Viterbo, 2006.

Gough, Maria. *The Artist as Producer: Russian Constructivism in Revolution*. Berkeley: University of California Press, 2005.

Grazia, Victoria de. *Irresistible Empire: America's Advance Through Twentieth Century Europe*. Cambridge, MA: Harvard University Press, 2005.

Guerra, Lillian. *The Myth of José Martí: Conflicting Nationalisms in Early Twentieth-Century Cuba*. Chapel Hill: University of North Carolina Press, 2005.

———. *Visions of Power in Cuba: Revolution, Redemption, and Resistance, 1959–1971*. Chapel Hill: University of North Carolina Press, 2012.

Guillén, Nicolás. *Obra Poética Tomo I, 1922–1958*, ed. Ángel Augier. Havana: Letras Cubanas, 2004.

———. *West-Indies, Ltd*. Havana: Imp. Ucar, García y cía, 1934.

Guillory, John. *Cultural Capital: The Problem of Literary Canon Formation*. Chicago: University of Chicago Press, 1993.

Gullar, Ferreira. *Cultura posta em questão*. Rio de Janeiro: Editora Civilização Brasileira, 1965.

———. "Diálogo sobre o não-objeto." *Suplemento Dominical, Jornal do Brasil* (March 26, 1960): 4–5.

———. *Etapas da arte contemporânea: Do cubismo ao neoconcretismo*. São Paulo: Livraria Nobel, 1985.

———. *Experiência neoconcreta: Momento-limite da arte*. São Paulo: Cosac Naify, 2007.

———. *Ferreira Gullar: In Conversation with Ariel Jiménez*. New York: Fundación Patricia Phelps Cisneros, 2012.

———. *Lygia Clark: Textos de Ferreira Gullar, Mário Pedrosa, Lygia Clark*. Rio de Janeiro: Edição FUNARTE, 1980.

———. "Teoria do não-objeto." *Suplemento Dominical, Jornal do Brasil* (December 19–20, 1959): n.p.

———. *Vanguarda e subdesenvolvimento; ensaios sobre arte*. Rio de Janeiro: Civilização Brasileira, 1969.

Gunder Frank, Andre. *ReOrient: Global Economy in the Asian Age*. Berkeley: University of California Press, 1998.

Hamacher, Werner. "*Lingua Amissa*: The Messianism of Commodity Language and Derrida's *Specters of Marx*." In *Ghostly Demarcations: A*

Symposium on Jacques Derrida's "Specters of Marx," ed. Michael Spinker, 168–212. London: Verso, 1999.

Hardt, Michael, and Antonio Negri. *Empire.* Cambridge, MA: Harvard University Press, 2000.

Harman, Graham. "The Third Table." *Documenta Notebook* 85 (2012): 1–31.

———. *Tool-Being: Heidegger and the Metaphysics of Objects.* Chicago: Open Court, 2002.

Henríquez Ureña, Pedro. *Ensayos críticos.* Havana: Imprenta de Esteban Fernández, 1905.

Hennessy, Alistair. "Ramiro de Maeztu: *Hispanidad* and the Search for a Surrogate Imperialism." In *Spain's 1898 Crisis: Regenerationism, Modernism, Post-colonialism,* ed. Joseph Harrison and Alan Hoyle, 105–17. New York: Manchester University Press, 2000.

Herkenhoff, Paulo. "Lygia Clark." *Lygia Clark: Fundació Antoni Tàpies, Barcelona, 21 octubre–21 dicimbre 1997, MAC, galeries contemporaines des Musées de Marseille, 16 enero–12 abril 1998, Fundação de Serralves, Oporto, 30 abril–28 junio 1998, Société des Expositions du Palais des Beaux-Arts, Bruselas, 24 julio–27 setiembre 1998,* 36–53. Barcelona: Fundació Antonio Tàpies, 1998.

Hernández Catá, Alfonso. *Alfonso Hernández Catá: Sus mejores cuentos.* Ed. Eduardo Barrios. Santiago: Nascimento, 1936.

———. *Manicomio.* Madrid: Compañia Ibero-Americana de Publicaciones, 1931.

Hölderlin, Friedrich. *Friedrich Hölderlin: Essays and Letters on Theory.* Trans. Thomas Pfau. Albany: State University of New York Press, 1988.

Huidobro, Vicente. *Finis Britannia: Une redoutable société secrète s'est dressée contre l'imperialisme anglais.* Paris: J Budry & cie, 1923.

Hulme, Thomas Ernest, and Karen Csengeri. *The Collected Writings of T. E. Hulme.* Oxford: Clarendon Press, 1994.

Iarroci, Michael. *Properties of Modernity: Romantic Spain, Modern Europe, and the Legacies of Empire.* Nashville: Vanderbilt University Press, 2006.

Ibarra, Jorge. *Prologue to Revolution.* Trans. Marjorie Moore. Boulder, CO: Lynne Rienner, 1998.

Ichaso, Francisco. "Las 'Jitanjáforas' o el Cheer Lírico." *Excélsior-El País* (October 3, 1929). In Alfonso Reyes, *El libro de las jitanjáforas y otros papeles seguidos de retruécanos, sonetórpidos y porras deportivas.* Madrid: Iberoamericana Verveurt, 2011.

Iglesias Utset, Marial. *Las metáforas del cambio en la vida cotidiana: Cuba, 1898–1902.* Havana: Ediciones UNIÓN, 2003.

James, C.L.R. *The Black Jacobins.* New York: Vintage, 1963.

Jameson, Frederic. *Marxism and Form.* Princeton: Princeton University Press, 1974.

———. "Periodizing the 60s." *Social Text,* no. 9/10, The 60's Without Apology (Spring–Summer 1984): 178–209.

———. *Representing Capital: A Reading of Volume I.* New York: Verso, 2011.

———. "Time and the Concept of Modernity." In *Anytime*, ed. Cynthia Davidson, 208–17. Cambridge, MA: MIT Press, 1999.

———. *Valences of the Dialectic*. New York: Verso, 2009.

Jitrik, Noé. *Las contradicciones del modernismo: Productividad poética y situación sociológica*. Mexico City: Colegio de México, 1978.

Jover, José María. *1898: Teoría y práctica de la redistribución colonial*. Madrid: Fundación Universitaria Española, 1979.

Kac, Eduardo. *Telepresence and Bio Art: Networking Humans, Rabbits and Robots*. Ann Arbor: University of Michigan Press, 2005.

Kadir, Djelal. *Columbus and the Ends of the Earth: Europe's Prophetic Rhetoric as Conquering Ideology*. Berkeley: University of California Press, 1992.

Kiaer, Christina. *Imagine No Possessions: The Socialist Objects of Russian Constructivism*. Cambridge, MA: MIT Press, 2005.

Kirkpatrick, Gwen. *The Dissonant Legacy of Modernismo: Lugones, Herrera y Reissig, and the Voices of Modern Spanish American Poetry*. Berkeley: University of California Press, 1989.

Kittler, Friedrich. *Discourse Networks, 1800/1900*. Trans. Michael Metteer with Chris Cullens. Stanford, CA: Stanford University Press, 1990.

———. *Gramophone, Film, Typewriter*. Trans. Geoffrey Winthrop-Young and Michael Wutz. Stanford, CA: Stanford University Press, 1999.

———. *Literature Media Information Systems*. Ed. John Johnson. Amsterdam: G & B Arts International, 1995.

Klaic, Dragan. *The Plot of the Future: Utopia and Dystopia in Modern Drama*. Ann Arbor: University of Michigan Press, 1991.

Kojève, Alexandre. *Introduction to the Reading of Hegel Lectures on the Phenomenology of Spirit*. Assembled by Raymond Queneau, ed. Allan Bloom, trans. James. H. Nichols Jr. Ithaca: Cornell University Press, 1980.

Kosik, Karel. *Dialectics of the Concrete: A Study on Problems of Man and World*. Trans. Karel Kovanda with James Schmidt. Boston: D. Riedel, 1976.

Kotz, Liz. *Words to Be Looked at: Language in 1960s Art*. Cambridge, MA: MIT Press, 2010.

Kraniauskas, John. "Difference Against Development: Spiritual Accumulation and the Politics of Freedom." *Boundary* 2 32 (Summer 2005): 53–80.

Lacan, Jacques. *Anxiety*. Trans. Cormac Gallagher. London: Karnac Books, 2002.

———. *The Ego in Freud's Theory and in the Technique of Psychoanalysis, 1954–1955*. Trans. Sylvana Tomaselli. New York: Norton, 1978.

———. *The Ethics of Psychoanalysis, 1959–1960*. New York: Norton, 1992.

———. *La relación del objeto*. Buenos Aires: Ediciones Paidós, 1994.

———. *La relation d'objet 1956–1957*. Paris: Editions du Seuil, 1994.

Landeira, Ricardo. *Ramiro de Maeztu*. Boston: Twayne, 1978.

Larraga, Ricardo. *Mariano Brull y la poesía pura en Cuba*. Miami: Ediciones Universales, 1994.

Latour, Bruno. *Reassembling the Social: An Introduction to Actor-Network-Theory.* New York: Oxford University Press, 2005.

Le Goff, Jacques. *Medieval Civilization, 400–1500.* Trans. Julia Barrow. Cambridge, MA: Basil Blackwell, 1990.

Lee, Daniel. "Civil Law and Civil Sovereignty: Popular Sovereignty, Roman Law and the Civilian Foundations of the Constitutional State in Early Modern Political Thought." Ph.D. diss., Princeton University, 2010.

Lenin, Vladimir Il'ich. *Imperialism, the Highest Stage of Capitalism.* Moscow: Foreign Languages Publishing House, 1947.

Leroi-Gourhan, Andre. *Gesture and Speech.* Trans. Anna Bostock Berger. Cambridge, MA: MIT Press, 1993.

Levenson, Michael. *A Genealogy of Modernism: A Study of English Literary Doctrine, 1908–1922.* New York: Cambridge University Press, 1984.

Levine, Robert. *The History of Brazil.* Westport, CT: Greenwood Press, 1999.

———. *Vale of Tears: Revisiting the Canudos Massacre in Northeastern Brazil, 1893–1897.* Berkeley: University of California Press, 1992.

Lezama Lima, José. *La expresión americana.* Havana: Editorial Letras Cubanas, 2010.

Lezama Lima, José, and Cintio Vitier. *Martí en Lezama.* Havana: Centro de Estudios Martianos, 2000.

Librandi Rocha, Marília. *Maranhão-Manhattan.* Rio de Janeiro: 7Letras, 2009.

Lima Mendonça, Antônio Sérgio. *Poesia de vanguarda no Brasil de Oswald de Andrade ao poema visual.* Petrópolis: Editora Voces, 1970.

Lippard, Lucy. *Six Years: The Dematerialization of the Art Object from 1966 to 1972.* 1973. Reprint, Berkeley: University of Calfornia Press, 1997.

Lissitzky, Lazar Markovich. "THE BOOK: Topology of Typography." Merz, no. 4, Hanover, July 1923. In *El Lissitzky: Life, Letters, Texts*, ed. Sophie Lissitzky-Küppers. Greenwich, CT: New York Graphic Society, 1967.

———. "The Film of El's Life." In *El Lissitzky: Life, Letters, Texts*, ed. Sophie Lissitzky-Küppers. Greenwich, CT: New York Graphic Society, 1967.

———. "Our Book." In *El Lissitzky: Life, Letters, Texts*, ed. Sophie Lissitzky-Küppers. Greenwich, CT: New York Graphic Society, 1967.

Lissitzky-Küppers, Sophie, ed. *El Lissitzky: Life, Letters, Texts.* Greenwich, CT: New York Graphic Society, 1967.

Lizaso, Félix, and José Antonio Fernandez de Castro, eds. *La poesía moderna en Cuba (1882–1925): Antología crítica.* Madrid: Casa Editorial Hernando S.A., 1926.

Lobo, Luiza. *Épica e modernidade em Sousândrade.* Rio de Janeiro: Presença, 1986.

———. *Tradição e ruptura: "O Guesa" de Sousândrade.* São Luis: Edições Sioge, 1979.

López, Alfred. *José Martí and the Future of Cuban Nationalisms.* Gainesville: University of Florida Press, 2006.

Luis, William, ed. *Las vanguardias en el Caribe: Cuba, Puerto Rico y República Dominicana.* Orlando, FL: Iberoamericana Vervuert, 2010.

Lukács, George. *History and Class Consciousness: Studies in Marxist Dialectics*. Trans. Rodney Livingstone. Cambridge, MA: MIT Press, 1968.

Maddison, Angus. *Contours of the World Economy*. New York: New York University Press, 2007.

Maeztu, Ramiro de. *Authority, Liberty and Function in the Light of the War; A Critique of Authority and Liberty as the Foundations of the Modern State and an Attempt to Base Societies on the Principle of Function*. London: G. Allen & Unwin, 1916.

———. *Autobiografía*. Madrid: Editora Nacional, 1962.

———. *Con el directorio militar*. Madrid: Editora Nacional, 1957.

———. *Defensa de la hispanidad*. Madrid: Rialp, 1998.

———. *Don Quijote, Don Juan y la Celestina Ensayos en simpatía*. Madrid: Visor Libros, 2004.

———. "The End of Romanticism." *The New Age* 17, no. 22 (September 30, 1915): 521–22.

———. *La guerra del Transvaal y los misterios de la Banca de Londres*. Ed. E. Inman Fox. Madrid: Taurus, 1974.

———. *Hacia otra España*. Bilbao: Cardenal, 1899.

———. *Un ideal sindicalista*. Madrid: Editorial Nacional, 1960.

———. Letter to Mr. Warner Fite. Madrid, January 9, 1927. Warner Fite collection, 1906–1928. Rare Books: Manuscripts Collection (MSS). Princeton University. Princeton Serrano 112, sides 1 and 2.

———. "On the Primacy of Things." *The New Age* 18, no. 22 (March 30, 1916): 515–16.

———. "On the Primacy of Things." *The New Age* 17, no. 26 (October 28, 1915): 617–19.

———. *El sentido reverencial del dinero*. Madrid: Editora Nacional, 1957.

Magubane, Zine. *Bringing the Empire Home: Race, Class, and Gender in Britain and Colonial South Africa*. Chicago: University of Chicago Press, 2004.

Maier, Charles. "Leviathan 2.0: Inventing Modern Statehood." In *A World Connecting, 1870–1945*, ed. Emily Rosenberg, 29–196. Cambridge, MA: Belknap, 2012.

Mainer, José-Carlos. *La doma de la quimera: Ensayos sobre nacionalismo y cultura en España*. Madrid: Iberoamericana, 2004.

Maldonado, Tomás. *Escritos Preulmianos*. Ed. Carlos A. Méndez Mosquera y Nelly Perazzo. Buenos Aires: Ediciones Infinito, 1997.

Mañach, Jorge. *El espíritu de Martí: Curso de 1951*. Havana: Cooperativa estudiantil E. J. Varona, 1952.

"Manifesto neoconcreto." *Suplemento Dominical, Jornal do Brasil* (March 22, 1959): 4–5.

Mao, Douglas. *Solid Objects: Modernism and the Test of Production*. Princeton: Princeton University Press, 1998.

Marinello, Juan. *Obras martianas*. Caracas: Fundación Biblioteca Ayacucho, 1987.

———. *Poética: Ensayos en entusiasmo*. Madrid: Espasa-Calpe, 1933.

Márquez Villanueva, Francisco. Introduction to *Aita Tettauen*, by Benito Pérez Galdós, 7–21. Madrid: Ediciones AKAL, 2004.

Marrero, Vicente. *Maeztu*. Madrid: Rialp, 1955.

Martí, José. *José Martí: Selected Writings*. Trans. Esther Allen, ed. Roberto González Echevarría. New York: Penguin Books, 2002.

———. *Obras completas*. Vols. 1–22. 2nd ed. Havana: Editorial de Ciencias Sociales, 1975.

———. *Obras completas: Edición crítica*. Vols. 1–15. Havana: Centro de Estudios Martianos, 2000.

———. *Poesía completa, edición crítica*. Mexico City: Universidad Nacional Autónoma de México, 1998.

———, comp. *Los poetas de la guerra*. New York: "América" Editorial, S. Figueroa, 1893.

Martin-Márquez, Susan. *Disorientations: Spanish Colonialism in Africa and the Performance of Identity*. New Haven: Yale University Press, 2008.

Martínez Carmenate, Urbano. *Bonifacio Byrne*. Havana: Editora Política, 1999.

Marx, Karl. *The Grundrisse*. Ed. and trans. David McLellan. New York: Harper and Row, 1971.

Marx, Karl, and Friedrich Engels. *Das Kapital: A Critique of Political Economy*. Ed. Serge Levitsky. Chicago: H. Regnery, 1959.

Masiello, Francine. "Rethinking Neocolonial Esthetics: Literature, Politics, and Intellectual Community in Cuba's Revista de Avance." *Latin American Research Review* 28, no. 2 (1993): 3–31.

Masotta, Oscar. *Conciencia y estructura*. Buenos Aires: Editorial Jorge Álvarez, 1968.

Maturana, Humberto, and Francisco Varela. *Autopoesis and Cognition: The Realization of the Living*. Boston: D. Reidel, 1980.

McLuhan, Marshall. *Understanding Media*. New York: McGraw-Hill, 1964.

Medeiros, Givaldo. *Artepaisagem a partir de Waldemar Cordeiro*. São Paulo: Fauusp, 2004.

Mejías-López, Alejandro. *The Inverted Conquest: The Myth of Modernity and the Transatlantic Onset of Modernism*. Nashville: Vanderbilt University Press, 2009.

Merleau-Ponty, Maurice. *Phenomenology of Perception*. Trans. Colin Smith. New York: Routledge, 2002.

Michalski, Sergiusz. "Neue Sachlichkeit: A Style and a Name." Trans. Michael Claridge. *New Objectivity: Painting, Graphic Art and Photography in Weimar Germany, 1919–1933*. Los Angeles: Taschen, 2003.

Miller, Jacques-Alain. "Suture (Elements of the Logic of the Signifier)." *Screen* 18, no. 4 (1977/78): 24–34.

Miller, Paul. *Elusive Origins: The Enlightenment in the Modern Caribbean Historical Imagination*. Charlottesville: University of Virginia Press, 2010.

Milliet, Maria Alice. *Lygia Clark: Obra-trajeto*. São Paulo: Edusp, 1992.

Mitchell, W.J.T. "Romanticism and the Life of Things: Fossils, Totems, and

Images." In *Things*, ed. Bill Brown, 227–44. Chicago: University of Chicago Press, 2004.

Moreira Duarte, Sebastião. *A épica e a época de Sousândrade: Pequena introdução à leitura d'O Guesa*. São Luis: Edições AML, 2002.

Moreno Fraginals, Manuel. *El ingenio*. Vol. 3. Havana: Editorial Ciencias Sociales, 1978.

———. "Plantation Economies and Societies in the Spanish Caribbean, 1860–1930." In *The Cambridge History of the Latin America*, vol. 4, ed. Leslie Bethell, 187–232. New York: Cambridge University Press, 1986.

Moten, Fred. *In the Break: The Aesthetics of the Black Radical Tradition*. Minneapolis: University of Minnesota Press, 2003.

Mott, Luiz. *Escravidão, homossexualidade e demonologia*. São Paulo: Ícone, 1988.

Mullen, Harryette. "African Signs and Spirit Writing." *Callaloo* 19, no. 3 (1996): 670–89.

Nerín, Gustau. *La guerra que vino de África*. Barcelona: Crítica, 2005.

Ngai, Sianne. "A Foul Lump Started Making Promises in My Voice: Race, Affect, and the Animated Subject." *American Literature* 74, no. 3 (2002): 571–601.

———. *Ugly Feelings*. Cambridge, MA: Harvard University Press, 2005.

Nogueira Galvão, Walnice. *No calor da hora: A Guerra de Canudos nos jornais, 4. Expedição*. São Paulo: Atica, 1974.

Ochoa, Todd Ramón. *Society of the Dead Quita Manaquita and Palo Praise in Cuba*. Berkeley: University of California Press, 2010.

Oiticica, Hélio. *Aspiro ao grande labirinto*. Rio de Janeiro: Rocco, 1986.

Ollé, Manel. *La empresa de China: De la Armada Invencible al Galeón de Manila*. Barcelona: Acantilado, 2002.

Olson, Theodore. *Millennialism, Utopianism, and Progress*. Toronto: University of Toronto Press, 1982.

Ong, Walter. *Orality and Literacy: The Technologizing of the Word*. New York: Methuen, 1982.

Ortiz, Fernando. "Más acerca de la poesía mulata: Escorzos para su estudio." *Revista Bimestre Cubana* 37, no. 1 (January–June 1936): 23.

———. *Los Negros Esclavos*. Havana: Editorial de Ciencias Sociales, 1975.

———. "Los últimos versos mulatos." *Revista Bimestre Cubana* 35, no. 3 (1935): 321–36. Reprinted in *Las vanguardias en el Caribe: Cuba, Puerto Rico y República Dominicana*, ed. William Luis, 545–57. Orlando, FL: Iberoamericana Vervuert, 2010.

Pabón, Jesús. "El 98, acontecimiento internacional." In *Madrid, Ministerio de Asuntos Exteriores, 1952*. Reprinted in *Días de Ayer*, 139–95. Barcelona: Alpha, 1963.

Padin, Clemente. "Poetry and Participation." Trans. Paula Einoder-Boxer. http://xoomer.alice.it/kareninazoom/POETRY_AND_PARTICIPATION.htm.

Palmié, Stephan. *Wizards and Scientists: Explorations in Afro-Cuban Modernity and Tradition*. Durham, NC: Duke University Press, 2002.

Pan-Montojo, Juan. "El atraso económico y la regeneración." In *Más se perdió en Cuba: España, 1898 y la crisis de fin de siglo*, 261–334. Ed. Juan Pan-Montojo. Madrid: Alianza Editorial, 1998.

———."Introducción: ¿98 o fin de siglo?" In *Más se perdió en Cuba: España, 1898 y la crisis de fin de siglo*, 9–30. Ed. Juan Pan-Montojo. Madrid: Alianza Editorial, 1998.

———, ed. *Más se perdió en Cuba: España, 1898 y la crisis de fin de siglo.* Madrid: Alianza Editorial, 1998.

"Pão poema-processo com 2m é comido por 5 mil pessoas na Feira de Arte de Recife." *Jornal do Brasil*, April 1970, first section. In *Processo: Linguagem e comunicação*, ed. Wlademir Dias-Pino, n.p. Petrópolis: Editora Vozes, 1971.

Pappademos, Melina. *Black Political Activism and the Cuban Republic.* Chapel Hill: University of North Carolina Press, 2011.

Paz, Octavio, and Haroldo de Campos. *Transblanco: Em torno a Blanco de Octavio Paz.* 2nd ed. São Paulo: Editora Siciliano, 1994.

Pedroso, Regino. *Regino Pedroso.* Ed. Osvaldo Navarro. Havana: UNEAC, 1975.

Pérez Jr., Louis. *Cuba Between Empires, 1878–1902.* Pittsburgh: University of Pittsburgh Press, 1982.

———. "Cuba c. 1939–1950." In *The Cambridge History of Latin America*, vol. 7, ed. Leslie Bethell, 417–56. New York: Cambridge University Press, 1990.

———. *On Becoming Cuban: Identity, Nationality and Culture.* Chapel Hill: University of North Carolina Press, 1999.

Pérez-Barreiro, Gabriel. "The Negation of All Melancholy Arte Madí/Concreto-Invencion, 1944–1950." In *Art from Argentina, 1920–1944*, ed. David Elliott. Oxford: Museum of Modern Art Oxford, 1994.

Pérez Galdós, Benito. *Aita Tettauen.* Madrid: Ediciones AKAL, 2004.

Pérez Nápoles, Rubén. *José Martí: El poeta armado.* Madrid: Algaba Ediciones, 2004.

Perrone, Charles. "The Imperative of Invention: Brazilian Concrete Poetry and Intersemiotic Creation." http://www.ubu.com/papers/perrone.html#foot19.

———. *Seven Faces: Brazilian Poetry Since Modernism.* Durham, NC: Duke University Press, 1995.

Pignatari, Décio. "Vanguarda como antiliteratura." *Revista Convivium* 4, no. 4/6 (July/August/September 1965). Reprinted in *Contracomunicação*, 121–26. Cotia: Ateliê editorial, 2004.

Piqueras, José. *Cuba, emporio y colonia: La disputa de un mercado interferido (1878–1895).* Madrid: Fondo de Cultura Económica de España, 2003.

Polanyi, Karl. *The Great Transformation: The Political and Economic Origins of Our Time.* Boston: Beacon Press, 1944.

Pomeranz, Kenneth. *The Great Divergence: China, Europe and the Making of the World Economy.* Princeton: Princeton University Press, 2000.

Pontual, Roberto. "Lygia Clark: A fantasmática do corpo." *Jornal do Brasil*, September 21, 1974.

Poovey, Mary. *Genres of the Credit Economy: Mediating Value in Eighteenth- and Nineteenth-Century Britain*. Chicago: University of Chicago Press, 2008.

"Por el mundo de las '*jitanjáforas*' Mariano Brull, gran poeta cubano, sugirió al escritor mexicano Alfonso Reyes sus curiosas teorías recientes." *Excélsior-El País* (October 1, 1929). In Alfonso Reyes, *El libro de las jitanjáforas y otros papeles seguidos de retruécanos, sonetórpidos y porras deportivas*, ed. Adolfo Castañón, 137–44. Madrid: Iberoamericana Verveurt, 2011.

Portuondo, Jose Antonio. "El pragmatismo y las purezas de la realidad." In José Antonio Ramos, *Coaybay*, 361–85. Havana: Editorial Arte y Literatura, 1975.

Portuondo, Jose Antonio, and Cira Romer, coords. *Historia de la literatura cubana*. Vol. 2. Havana: Editorial Letras Cubanas, 2002.

Price, Rachel. "Early Brazilian Digital Culture; or, The Woman Who Was Not B.B." *Grey Room*, no. 47 (Spring 2012): 60–79.

Pro Ruiz, Juan. "La política en tiempos del Desastre." In *Más se perdió en Cuba: España, 1898 y la crisis de fin de siglo*, ed. Juan Pan-Montojo, 151–260. Madrid: Alianza Editorial, 1998.

"Protesta contra la 'negrificacion' de Cuba al importarse negros de Haití y Jamaica por compañías azucareras que quieran pagar jornales bajos." *Revista de avance* 4, no. 39 (October 15, 1929): 287.

Quint, David. *Epic and Empire: Politics and Generic Form from Virgil to Milton*. Princeton: Princeton University Press, 1993.

Ramos, José Antonio. *Coaybay*. Havana: Impr. "El siglo XX," 1926.

———. "Cubanidad y mestizaje." *Estudios afrocubanos* 1 (1937): 92–113.

———. Letter signed by José Antonio Ramos to José de la Luz León en Ginebra, Barcelona y la Habana. Archivo Nacional de Cuba, Donativos y remisiones, 1931–37, Legajo 524, número de orden 55.

———. *El traídor, La Leyenda de las Estrellas y La Recurva*. Havana: La Verónica, 1941.

Ramos, Julio. *Desencuentros de la modernidad: Literatura y Política en el Siglo XIX*. Mexico City: Fondo Económico de la Cultura, 1989.

———. *Divergent Modernities: Culture and Politics in 19th Century Latin America*. Trans. John Blanco. Durham, NC: Duke University Press, 2001.

Rancière, Jacques. "The Aesthetic Revolution and Its Outcomes: Emplotments of Autonomy and Heteronomy." *New Left Review* 14 (March/April 2002): 133–51.

———. "The Politics of Literature." *SubStance: A Review of Theory and Literary Criticism* 33, no. 1 (2004): 10–24.

Redfield, Marc. "Imagi-Nation: The Imagined Community and the Aesthetics of Mourning." In *Grounds for Comparison: Around the Work of Benedict Anderson*, ed. Pheng Cheah and Jonathan Culler, 75–105. New York: Routledge, 2003.

Reinert, Sophus. *Translating Empire: Emulation and the Origins of Political Economy*. Cambridge, MA: Harvard University Press, 2011.

Reyes, Alfonso. "Alcance a las jitanjáforas." *Revista de avance* 4, no. 46 (May 1930): 133–40.

———. "Las jitanjáforas." In *La experiencia literaria*, 178–218. Buenos Aires: Editorial Losada, 1942.

———. "Las jitanjáforas." *Libra* (Buenos Aires, Winter 1929). In *El libro de las jitanjáforas y otros papeles seguidos de retruécanos, sonetórpidos y porras deportivas*, ed. Adolfo Castañón, 21–59. Madrid: Iberoamericana Verveurt, 2011.

———. *El libro de las jitanjáforas y otros papeles seguidos de retruécanos, sonetórpidos y porras deportivas*. Ed. Adolfo Castañón. Madrid: Iberoamericana Verveurt, 2011.

Ripoll, Carlos. *Índice de la "Revista de avance," 1927–1930*. New York: Las Américas Pub., 1969.

Riverand, Julio de. "El historicismo martiano en la idea del equilibrio del mundo." *Anuario del Centro de Estudios Martianos* 2 (1979): 111–34.

Roa, Raul. "Martí poeta nuevo." *Revista de avance* 1, no. 10 (August 30, 1927): 254.

Roh, Franz. *German Art in the Twentieth Century*. Trans. Catherine Hutter. Greenwich, CT: New York Graphic Society, 1968.

Rojas, Rafael. *José Martí: La invención de Cuba*. Madrid: Editorial Colibrí, 2000.

———. *Tumbas sin sosiego*. Barcelona: Anagrama, 2006.

Roldán de Montaud, Inés. *La restauración en Cuba el fracaso de un proceso reformista*. Madrid: Consejo Superior de Investigaciones Científicas Centro de Humanidades Instituto de Historia, 2000.

Rosen, Margit, ed. *A Little-Known Story About a Movement, a Magazine, and the Computer's Arrival in Art: New Tendencies and Bit International, 1961–1973*. Cambridge, MA: MIT Press, 2011.

Rosenberg, Emily. *Financial Missionaries to the World: The Politics and Culture of Dollar Diplomacy, 1900–1930*. Cambridge, MA: Harvard University Press, 1999.

Saldaña-Portillo, María Josefina. *The Revolutionary Imagination in the Americas and the Age of Development*. Durham, NC: Duke University Press, 2003.

"La saleta o 'Living Room.'" *Social* (May 1922): 45.

Sant'Anna, Affonso Romano de. "Empire State Building." *Revista Civilização Brasileira* 17 (January/February 1968): 117–19.

Santamaría García, Antonio, and Alejandro García Álvarez. *Economía y colonia: La economía cubana y la relación con España, 1765–1902*. Madrid: Consejo Superior de Investigaciones Científicas Instituto de Historia, 2004.

Santí, Enrico Mario. "Textual Politics: Severo Sarduy." *Latin American Literary Review* 8, no. 16, Hispanic Caribbean Literature (Spring 1980): 152–60.

———. "Thinking Through Martí." In *Re-Reading José Martí (1853–1895):*

One Hundred Years Later, ed. Julio Rodríguez-Luís. Albany: State University of New York Press, 1999.

Sarduy, Severo. "Anamorphoses." *Quinzaine litteraire*, no. 50 (May 1, 1968): 5.

———. *Anamorphosis*. Caracas: Monte Ávila, 1982.

———. *Barroco*. Buenos Aires: Sudamericana, 1974.

———. "Barroco Americano." In *Antología*, ed. Gustavo Guerrero, 174–81. Mexico City: Fondo de Cultura Económica, 2000.

———. *Ensayos Generales Sobre el Barroco*. Buenos Aires: Fondo de Cultura Económica, 1987.

———. "Exiliado de si mismo." *El País* (April 4, 1992): 9. In Severo Sarduy, *Antología*, ed. Gustavo Guerrero, 55–58. Mexico City: Fondo de Cultura Económica, 2000.

———. "Hacia la concretud." *Blanco* (Fall 1979): 12–19.

———. *Obra completa*. Ed. Gustavo Guerrero and Francois Wahl. Vols. 1–2. Paris: Colección Archivos, 1999.

———. "Rumo à concretude." In Haroldo de Campos, *Signantia Quasi Coelum = Signancia quase céu*, 117–25. São Paulo: Editorial Perspectiva, 1979.

———. "Sabe Usted lo que es 'concretud'?" In *Antología*, ed. Gustavo Guerrero, 240–42. Mexico City: Fondo de Cultura Económica, 2000.

———. "Sobre Góngora: La metáfora al cuadrado." *Nuevo Mundo*, no. 6 (1966): 84–86.

———. "Towards Concreteness." Trans. Amelia Simpson. *Latin American Literary Review* 14, no. 27, Brazilian Literature (January–June 1986): 61–69.

———. "Vers la concretude." *Barcelona: América Latina, Cahiers Confrontations*, no. 5 (1981): 53–60.

Sassen, Saskia. *Territory, Authority, Rights from Medieval to Global Assemblages*. Princeton: Princeton University Press, 2006.

Schmitt, Carl. "Grossraum Versus Universalism: The International Legal Struggle over the Monroe Doctrine." Trans. Matthew Hannah. In *Spatiality, Sovereignty and Carl Schmitt: Geographies of the Nomos*, ed. Stephen Legg, 46–54. New York: Routledge, 2011.

———. *The Nomos of the Earth in the International Law of the Jus Publicum Europaeum*. Trans. G. L. Ulmen. New York: Telos Press, 2003.

———. *Political Theology: Four Chapters on the Concept of Sovereignty*. Trans. George Schwab. Chicago: University of Chicago Press, 2006.

Schulman, Ivan. "Historia colectiva e individual en la obra de José Martí." In *En torno a José Martí: Coloquio Internacional*, 95–117. Bordeaux: Biere, 1974.

Schwarz, Roberto. "Cultura e política, 1964–1969: Alguns esquemas." In *O Pai de Família e outros estudos*, 61–92. Rio de Janeiro: Paz e Terra, 1978.

Sevcenko, Nicolau. *Literatura como missão: Tensões sociais e criação cultural na Primeira República*. São Paulo: Brasiliense, 1983.

Simon, Iumna Maria, and Vinicius Dantas. *Poesia Concreta: Seleção estudos biográfico, histórico e crítico e exercícios*. São Paulo: Abril Educação, 1982.

Simondon, Gilbert. *Du mode d'existence des objets techniques*. Paris: Éditions Montaigne, 1958.

Sio, Arnold. "Interpretations of Slavery: The Slave Status in the Americas." *Comparative Studies in Society and History* 7, no. 3 (April 1965): 289–308.

Sloterdijk, Peter. *Esferas II (Globos)*. Trans. Isidoro Reguera. Madrid: Ediciones Siruela, 2004.

Smirnoff, Victor. "La transaction fétichique." *Nouvelle revue de psychanalyse* 2 (1970): 41–64.

Soares, Carlos Eugênio, and Flávio Gomes. "Sedições, Haitianismo e conexões no Brasil escravista: Outras margens do Atlântico negro." *Novos estudos*, CEBRAP, no. 63 (July 2002): 131–44.

Sousandrade, Joaquim de. *O Guesa errante*. Ed. Luiza Lobo. São Luis: Academia Maranhense de Letras, 2012.

Sousândrade, Joaquim de. "From O Guesa Errante: The Wall Street Inferno." Trans. Robert Brown. *Poems for the Millennium: The University of California Press Book of Romantic & Postromantic Poetry*, vol. 3, ed. Jerome Rothenberg and Jeffrey C. Robinson, 665–62. Berkeley: University of California Press, 2009.

———. *O Guesa errante*. London: Cooke and Halsted, the Moorfields Press, 1884[?].

———. *Harpa de Ouro, 1889–1899*. Ed. Jomar Moraes. São Luis: Edições Sioge, 1969.

———. *Sousândrade: Inéditos*. Ed. Frederick G. Williams and Jomar Moraes. São Luis: Departmento de Cultura do Estado, 1970.

———. *Sousândrade, Prosa*. Ed. Frederick G. Williams and Jomar Moraes. São Luis: Ediçoes SIOFE, 1978.

———. *Poesia e prosa reunidas de Sousândrade*. São Luis: Edições AML, 2003.

———. *Sousândrade: O terremoto clandestino*. Ed. Augusto and Haroldo de Campos. Rio de Janeiro: Ministério da Educação e Cultura, Instituto Nacional do Livro, 1964.

Starobinsky, Jean. *Words upon Words: The Anagrams of Ferdinand de Saussure*. Trans. Olivia Emmet. New Haven: Yale University Press, 1979.

Stevens, Jacqueline. *Reproducing the State*. Princeton: Princeton University Press, 1999.

Stewart, Susan. *Poetry and the Fate of the Senses*. Chicago: University of Chicago Press, 2001.

Stiegler, Bernard. *Technics and Time, I: The Fault of Epimetheus*. Trans. Stephen Barker. Stanford, CA: Stanford University Press, 1998.

———. *Technics and Time, II: Disorientation*. Trans. Stephen Barker. Stanford, CA: Stanford University Press, 2009.

Süssekind, Flora. *Cinematograph of Words: Literature, Technique and Modernization in Brazil*. Trans. Paulo Henriques Britto. Stanford, CA: Stanford University Press, 1997.

Tamayo, Frank. "Universalismo español." *Revista de avance* 1, no. 3 (April 15, 1927): 46.
Tannenbaum, Frank. *Slave and Citizen*. 1946. Boston: Beacon Press, 1992.
Taunay, Alfredo d'Escragnolle. *O encilhamento: Scenas contemporâneas da bôlsa em 1890, 1891 e 1892*. Rio de Janeiro: Domingos de Magalhães, 1894–95.
Teja, Ada María. *La poesía de José Martí entre naturaleza e historia: Estudios sobre la antítesis y la síntesis*. Cosenza: Marra, 1990.
Thacker, Andrew. "A Language of Concrete Things." In *T. E. Hulme and the Question of Modernism*, ed. Edward P. Comentale and Andrzej Gasiorek, 39–55. Abingdon: Ashgate, 2006.
Topik, Steven C., and Allen Wells. "Commodity Chains in a Global Economy." In *A World Connecting, 1870–1945*, ed. Emily Rosenberg, 593–813. Cambridge, MA: Belknap Press, 2012.
"Uprising in Cuba." *Philadelphia Tribune*, May 25, 1912, p. 4.
Vallejo, César. "XLIX." In *Trilce*. Ed. Julio Ortega. Madrid: Cátedra, 1991.
Ventura, Zuenir. *1968: O ano que não terminou*. São Paulo: Planeta, 2008.
Villacañas, José Luís. *Ramiro de Maeztu y el ideal de la burguesía en España*. Madrid: Espasa-Calpe, 2000.
Wahl, François. "Severo de la rue Jacob." In *Obra completa*, vol. 2, ed. Gustavo Guerrero and Francois Wahl, 1447–1547. Paris: Colección Archivos, 1999.
Wallerstein, Immanuel. "States? Sovereignty? The Dilemmas of Capitalists in an Age of Transition." In *States and Sovereignty in the Global Economy*, ed. David A. Smith, Dorothy J. Solinger, and Steven C. Topik, 20–33. New York: Routledge, 1999.
Walzer, Michael. *Exodus and Revolution*. New York: Basic Books, 1985.
Weiss, Rachel. *To and From Utopia in the New Cuban Art*. Minneapolis: University of Minnesota Press, 2011.
Wey Gómez, Nicolás. *Tropics of Empire: Why Columbus Sailed South to the Indies*. Cambridge, MA: MIT Press, 2008.
Williams, Frederick. "Sousândrade: A Study of His Life and Works." Ph.D. diss., University of Wisconsin, 1971.
———. *Sousândrade: Vida e obra*. São Luis: Edições Sioge, 1976.
Williams, Gareth. "Imagined Secularization: The Nomos of the Earth and the Challenge of the Western Hemispheric Interstate System." *South Atlantic Quarterly* 104, no. 2 (2005): 329–36.
Woolf, Virginia. "Objetos sólidos." Trans. José Rodríguez Feo. *Orígenes* 6, no. 23 (1949): 6–10.
Zakai, Avihu. *Exile and Kingdom: History and Apocalypse in the Puritan Migration to America*. New York: Cambridge University Press, 1992.
Zanetti, Oscar. *La República: Notas sobre economía y sociedad*. Havana: Editorial de Ciencias Sociales, 2006.
Žižek, Slavoj. *Enjoy Your Symptom*. 1992. New York: Routledge, 2008.
———. *The Parallax View*. Cambridge, MA: MIT Press, 2006.

Index

Page numbers in *italics* indicate figures.

FLASHPOINTS

1. *On Pain of Speech: Fantasies of the First Order and the Literary Rant,* Dina Al-Kassim
2. *Moses and Multiculturalism,* Barbara Johnson, with a foreword by Barbara Rietveld
3. *The Cosmic Time of Empire: Modern Britain and World Literature,* Adam Barrows
4. *Poetry in Pieces: César Vallejo and Lyric Modernity,* Michelle Clayton
5. *Disarming Words: Empire and the Seductions of Translation in Egypt,* Shaden M. Tageldin
6. *Wings for Our Courage: Gender, Erudition, and Republican Thought,* Stephanie H. Jed
7. *The Cultural Return,* Susan Hegeman
8. *English Heart, Hindi Heartland: The Political Life of Literature in India,* Rashmi Sadana
9. *The Cylinder: Kinematics of the Nineteenth Century,* Helmut Müller-Sievers
10. *Polymorphous Domesticities: Pets, Bodies, and Desire in Four Modern Writers,* Juliana Schiesari
11. *Flesh and Fish Blood: Postcolonialism, Translation, and the Vernacular,* S. Shankar
12. *The Fear of French Negroes: Transcolonial Collaboration in the Revolutionary Americas,* Sara E. Johnson
13. *Figurative Inquisitions: Conversion, Torture, and Truth in the Luso-Hispanic Atlantic,* Erin Graff Zivin
14. *Cosmopolitan Desires: Global Modernity and World Literature in Latin America,* Mariano Siskind
15. *Fiction Beyond Secularism,* Justin Neuman
16. *Periodizing Jameson: Dialectics, the University, and the Desire for Narrative,* Phillip E. Wegner
17. *The Practical Past,* Hayden White
18. *The Powers of the False: Reading, Writing, Thinking Beyond Truth and Fiction,* Doro Wiese
19. *The Object of the Atlantic: Concrete Aesthetics in Cuba, Brazil, and Spain, 1868–1968,* Rachel Price